Media Ethics and Justice in the Age of Globalization

Media Ethics and Justice in the Age of Globalization

Edited by

Shakuntala Rao
State University of New York, USA

Herman Wasserman
University of Cape Town, South Africa

palgrave
macmillan

First published 2015 by
PALGRAVE MACMILLAN

Palgrave Macmillan in the UK is an imprint of Macmillan Publishers Limited, registered in England, company number 785998, of Houndmills, Basingstoke, Hampshire RG21 6XS.

Palgrave Macmillan in the US is a division of St Martin's Press LLC, 175 Fifth Avenue, New York, NY 10010.

Palgrave Macmillan is the global academic imprint of the above companies and has companies and representatives throughout the world.

Palgrave® and Macmillan® are registered trademarks in the United States, the United Kingdom, Europe and other countries.

ISBN 978–1–137–49825–0

This book is printed on paper suitable for recycling and made from fully managed and sustained forest sources. Logging, pulping and manufacturing processes are expected to conform to the environmental regulations of the country of origin.

A catalogue record for this book is available from the British Library.

A catalog record for this book is available from the Library of Congress.

Contents

Foreword

This book is published at a time when three major new horizons for research and public culture across the world are opening up. The first is the changing nature of the media environment on a global scale. The second is the growth among media researchers, and also among general citizens across the world, about the ethics and morality of media as well as media's role in public and private culture. This new urgency to normative debate about media will not be satisfied by a replaying of an older media 'ethics lite' that replays the journalistic rule book, as Shakuntala Rao and Herman Wasserman make clear in their Introduction. It is a question instead of challenging the principles and limits of that old rule book and insisting that citizens, not just professional journalists, have both rights and responsibilities in relation to the media environment that all of us, potentially, are now involved in shaping.

A third and more specific horizon is the new debate about injustice, that is, about the legal, political, and philosophical frameworks through which we can think about justice and injustice in relation to media processes and media resources. This debate has been opened up and inspired by Amartya Sen's recent work on injustice and his challenging of the dominance of John Rawls' maximalist model for working out what a just society is that, through its excessive complexity and elaboration, had come to block new work in applied areas such as the justice or injustice in media.

This book is important because it addresses all three intersecting horizons. In doing so, it gathers a new readership of activists, citizens, and media and communications researchers and points us all in the direction of a sustained and theoretically informed debate about whether media institutions can be different, and specifically more just, and how we can build campaigns to that end most effectively.

I am delighted to have been asked to provide a foreword to this important book.

Nick Couldry
London School of Economics

Contributors

Muhammad I. Ayish received his PhD from the University of Minnesota, USA, and is Professor of Mass Communication at the American University of Sharjah, UAE. He was previously Dean of Communication at the University of Sharjah (2002–2008). He has over 75 articles and book chapters published internationally in addition to four books, the most recent being *Explorations in Global Media Ethics* (co-edited with Shakuntala Rao, 2012). His research interests include media ethics, Arab media, media convergence, and media and cultural identity.

Bharat Bhushan is a senior academic consultant with the Indian Council of Social Science Research, New Delhi, India. He has been a journalist for over 25 years and was the founding editor of *Mail Today*. Earlier, he was the executive editor of the *Hindustan Times*, editor of *The Telegraph*, editor of the *Express News Service*, Washington correspondent of *The Indian Express*, and assistant editor with *The Times of India*. He was educated at Imperial College London, UK; Centre for Development Studies, Trivandrum; and the Birla Institute of Technology and Science, Pilani, India. He has written for *The Straits Times* (Singapore), *The Daily Times* (Pakistan), *The Kathmandu Post* (Nepal), *Outlook* magazine, Index on Censorship, and *The BRICS Post*. He is a columnist for *The Asian Age* and *Business Standard* newspapers besides hosting a weekly television program on foreign affairs, titled 'India's World'.

Clifford G. Christians is Research Professor of Communications, Professor of Media Studies, and Professor of Journalism Emeritus, Institute of Communications Research, University of Illinois at Urbana-Champaign, USA. He is the author/co-author of *Ethics for Public Communication; Good News: Social Ethics and the Press; Normative Theories of the Media; Media Ethics: Cases and Moral Reasoning* (9th edition); *Moral Engagement in Public Life: Theories for Contemporary Ethics; Communication Ethics and Universal Values*; and *Key Concepts in Critical Cultural Studies*.

Nick Couldry is Professor of Media, Communications, and Social Theory in the Department of Media and Communications at the London School of Economics, UK. His books include *Media Rituals: A Critical*

Approach (2003), *Why Voice Matters: Culture and Politics after Neoliberalism* (2010), and *Media Society World: Social Theory and Digital Media Practice* (2012). He has held the Chair of International Communication Association and Vice-Chair of the Mediatization Temporary Working Group of the European Communication Research and Education Association. He has held visiting positions at the University of Pennsylvania, University of Stockholm, RMIT Melbourne, Roskilde University, Södertorn University at Stockholm, University of Technology Sydney, and University of Toulouse. He has given invited lectures and seminars in Brazil, Chile, Holland (Utrecht, Gronigen), Portugal, Sweden, and the United States.

Vipul Mudgal has worked as Reporter and Senior Editor for the *Hindustan Times*, *India Today*, BBC, and *Asia Times* in India, the United Kingdom, and Thailand for over 20 years. He has a PhD in Media Studies from Leicester University, UK, and is a recipient of the Nehru Centenary British Fellowship and the Jefferson Fellowship at the East-West Centre, Hawaii. He currently heads the Publics and Policies Programme and the Inclusive Media Project at the Centre for the Study of Developing Societies (CSDS) in Delhi, India.

Shahan Mufti is Assistant Professor of Journalism at the University of Richmond in Virginia, USA. His work has been published in *Harper's Magazine*, *The Atlantic Monthly*, *The New York Times Magazine*, *Boston Sunday Globe*, *The Nation*, *Bloomberg Businessweek*, *Columbia Journalism Review*, and other publications. He was based in Pakistan between 2007 and 2009 as a correspondent for *The Christian Science Monitor*. A graduate of Middlebury College at Vermont and the graduate journalism program at New York University, he is a former Fulbright Scholar to India. His non-fiction book *The Faithful Scribe: A Story of Islam, Pakistan, Family and War* was published in 2013.

Shakuntala Rao is a Professor and Chair at the Department of Communication Studies, State University of New York, USA. She received her PhD in Communication from the University of Massachusetts, USA. Her teaching and research interests are in global media ethics, journalism practices, and popular culture. She has published influentially and extensively in both communication and interdisciplinary journals such as the *Journal of Communication*, *Journalism Studies*, *Journal of Mass Media Ethics*, and *Journal of Broadcasting and Electronic Media*. She is the co-editor (with Muhammad Ayish) of the anthology *Explorations in Global Media Ethics*.

Prasun Sonwalkar is a former journalist and has covered several key events and issues in India and the United Kingdom, including insurgencies in Northeast India and the rise of Hindutva politics, for *The Times of India, Free Press Journal, Business Standard, Press Trust of India,* and *Indo-Asian News Service,* among other news organizations. A Commonwealth Scholar, his research has been published in edited collections and journals such as *Media, Culture & Society; Journalism: Theory, Practice and Criticism; International Communication Gazette; Contemporary South Asia;* and *Modern Asian Studies.*

Stephen J. A. Ward is an internationally recognized media ethicist, educator, consultant, keynote speaker, and award-winning author. He is an ethics columnist for the PBS website MediaShift, for the Canadian portal www.j-source.ca, and for the Canadian magazine *Media.* He is Founding Chair of the Ethics Committee of the Canadian Association of Journalists (CAJ) and a co-author of the CAJ's two codes of ethics. He has been director of the Turnbull Center at the University of Oregon's School of Journalism in Portland and founder of the Center for Journalism Ethics at the School of Journalism, University of Wisconsin-Madison, USA. He is also former director of the Graduate School of Journalism at the University of British Columbia in Vancouver. He was a reporter, war correspondent, and newsroom manager for 14 years. He covered conflicts in Yugoslavia, Bosnia, and Northern Ireland. He is the author of the award-winning book *The Invention of Journalism Ethics: The Path to Objectivity and Beyond* and many other books and articles. His new book *Radical Media Ethics* will be published in early 2015. He has a PhD in Philosophy from the University of Waterloo, Ontario.

Herman Wasserman is Professor of Media Studies at the University of Cape Town, South Africa. He holds a doctorate from the University of Stellenbosch, South Africa, and has worked as a newspaper journalist before starting his academic career. He has published widely on media in post-apartheid South Africa. His books include *Tabloid Journalism in South Africa* (2010; winner of the Rhodes Vice-Chancellor's Book Award) and the edited collections *Press Freedom in Africa: Comparative Perspectives* (2013), *Popular Media, Democracy and Development in Africa* (2011), and *Media Ethics Beyond Borders* (with Stephen J. A. Ward, 2010).

Lee Wilkins is a Professor and Chair of the Department of Communication at Wayne State University, Michigan, USA. Her research focuses on media ethics, media coverage of the environment, and hazards and risks. She is a co-author of one of the best-selling college media ethics texts, *Media Ethics: Issues and Cases*, now in its fifth edition. She is the associate editor of the *Journal of Mass Media Ethics*. She has taught ethics as a visiting faculty member at the Poynter Institute in St Petersburg, Florida, and has a joint appointment in the Harry S. Truman School of Public Affairs at the University of Missouri, Columbia, where she teaches about communicating risk to the public.

1
Introduction

Shakuntala Rao and Herman Wasserman

For the past two decades, 'globalization' has been the buzz word within and beyond media and journalism studies. Globalization has decisively unmade the coherence that the modernist project of the 19th- and 20th-century nation-states promised to deliver – the neat marriage between territory, language, culture, and identity. As Geertz noted, 'All modern nations – even Norway, even Japan – contradict themselves: They contain multitudes' (Geertz 1973, p. 122). Scholars have generally acknowledged the multiple trajectories to and dimensions of globalization, as reflected in its various histories, processes, and forms of interconnectedness. The multidimensionality of media globalization was exemplified, for example, in the way in which mobile phone video footage of the execution of Saddam Hussein rapidly circulated around the world within hours of the event via a combination of mobile phone cameras, Internet access, and transnational media organizations. Audiences as far afield as Australia, Bangladesh, and Chile awoke to grainy images of the noose around Hussein's neck as he argued with his executioners. Each media culture, however, reserved the right to disseminate the information as it saw fit: media in the United States largely shied away from showing any of the gory footage; meanwhile, media in India and *Al Jazeera*, broadcasting throughout the Middle East, ran the majority of the video. Other examples of globalized media content can be noted from recent years, ranging from the serious, as with the rapid spread of and widespread outcries over the 'Muhammad Cartoons', first published by the Danish newspaper *Jyllands Posten*, to the absurd, as with the misplaced melodrama of the 'Kony 2012' campaign, to the silliness of the light-hearted 'Harlem Shake' and 'Happy' viral videos. This book recognizes that journalism and media practice do not stand *outside* of such globalizing processes and, in the same vein, that processes

1

of globalization are not immune to – in fact, are shaped by – particular journalistic and media practices. In exploring media globalization, it is important to recognize that there are multiple forms of global interconnectedness; that is, the relationship between media and globalization is reflexive and dialectical. The need to employ a contextualizing approach to the understanding of media globalization and ethics forms the basis of this book.

Global communication has been aided by a number of technological advances – in particular, fax machines, mobile phones, text messages, and the Internet – which, taken in combination, have made it easier to communicate the world over. The rapid and massive expansion of the amount of information available on the Internet has enabled unprecedented and instantaneous access and has resulted in the increased international exchange of cultural and political data. The further individualization of media reception has transformed the way people seek and process news and entertainment. In particular, young people increasingly look to sources other than the traditional mainstream media to get their news. Audiences can no longer be expected to simply read newspapers or to watch television as a one-way process in which they are and remain passive. In India, for instance, a staggering 900 million people – approximately 75% of the population – have access to mobile technology; as such, most major news outlets in the country expect high levels of interaction with their consumers. In Africa, the uptake of mobile telephones has been similarly phenomenal, with implications for the ways in which news is consumed, how people interact online, and how everyday practices such as banking and shopping are conducted. In South Africa, for instance, more people access the Internet via mobile phones than via fixed-line Internet access. The extent to which social media and mobile phones can facilitate political mobilization has been much debated, especially after the 'Arab Spring' uprisings of recent years in the Middle East and North Africa. In China, a GlobeScan survey found that 71% of Internet users rely on social media to access information that would otherwise not be available to them, such as information critical of the ruling Communist Party as well as information on the environmental responsibility records of private companies. In response to central authorities having banned global social media sites such as Twitter, Facebook, and YouTube, Chinese Internet users have developed their own widely used platforms for social networking and microblogging. According to this survey, China has more than double the number of Internet users than the United States and more than 300 million Chinese consumers make frequent use of some form of social media.

China's case has shown that websites, Internet message and bulletin boards, chat rooms, instant messaging services, and blogs each make a contribution to the creation of a new public sphere for debate while also providing a forum in which ordinary citizens are able to express their views – a forum that the government has found difficult to control. New social movements and interest groups use old and new media alike to foster the development of electronic and transnational communities, with such communities also often acting as democratic forums. New technologies have helped to revive flagging democratic processes by providing additional avenues for people to participate in a democratic public sphere. In India, such participation was demonstrated in the case of organized mass protests against the corruption of the judiciary and government inaction in the face of gender-based crimes. The social media zeitgeist was captured in the reporting of the case of 19-year-old Sambhavi Saxena, who was arrested during one such protest. On her journey to and during her time at the police station, the 19-year-old tweeted to India and the world, highlighting her plight. Her tweet – 'Illegally being held here at Parliament St Police Station Delhi w/15 other women. Terrified, pls RT' – led more than 1,700 people to re-tweet her original message. According to Favstar, the social media analytics site, her tweets reached over 200,000 people within hours. This had the effect of galvanizing civil society, as lawyers and activists quickly arrived at the police station to offer help and advice.

Globalization, and its relationship with media, should not be viewed uncritically or celebrated as a wholly benign force. Globalization theorists such as Castells have hinted at the unevenness of globalization or the 'imperfect globalization of the network society', where not everyone is connected to a network (Castells 1996). Scholars like Norris (2001) have focused on the global digital divide and the question of 'information poverty' in the Global South, while McChesney, a political economist, argued in his most recent book, *Digital Disconnect* (2013), that even in media-saturated countries such as the United States the capitalist underpinnings of digital media have exerted detrimental effects on public debates and democratic life. Despite the at-times contentious debates about the impact and value of new media, even the most skeptical of scholars have had to acknowledge the reality that network societies, linked together via media, can no longer be ignored.

Often absent from debates on media globalization and from the scholarly literature that interprets contemporary media, connectivity has been a sustained discussion of ethics. While there have been discussions of the global digital divide and the fact that such a divide has led to 'information haves and information have-nots' (Norris 2001, p. 12), as well as examinations of the ethical dilemmas surrounding issues such as privacy, copyright, and pornography in online media (Ess 2009), discussions that connect media globalization to concerns of ethics and justice have remained marginal. We concur with those theorists who have suggested that all global interactions between peoples, nations, states, and cultures must be understood in ethical terms (Der Derian 2009). Global actors are generally concerned with acting ethically and take pains to point out, first, the ethical flaws in the actions of others and, second, their own ethical superiority. Global communication is not only about struggles of and for power, as political scientists and classical realists often argue, or the structural forces that enter into play in the domain of international interactions, as political economists assert, but it is also about the ethical element of such communication. Moreover, taking 'the ethical turn' also helps us achieve a more nuanced understanding of the interplay of politics and power between global communications actors, states, and cultures (Garber, Hanssen, and Walkolitz 2000, p. xii). One argument that will be put forth in this book is that the very act of analyzing media and journalism practice is itself an action that is open to ethical evaluation.

Global media ethics: Thick or thin?

In any situation in which audiences and producers participate in media, ethical considerations inform all phases of production, dissemination, and reception. This is apparent in the way in which we characterize global media, the global circumstances in which we find ourselves, reflections on how and why events have transpired as they have, and what lines of action are open to us given the circumstances. Both audiences and journalists, for instance, vigorously debated whether Libyan dictator Muammar Gaddafi's final moments, which had been recorded using mobile phone cameras, ought to have been televised. Social media around the world lit up with questions such as 'What constitutes privacy for the dead?'; 'What the audiences are "authorized" to see?'; 'What is considered gratuitous?'; and 'Are media outlets editorially justified in showing the mutilating of his body?'

What is puzzling, however, is that despite the fact that in everyday engagement we often frame the context and our interactions with media in ethical terms, it is a common assumption that the ethical dimensions of media and journalism are, in some general sense, 'thin'. Despite the ubiquitous use of ethical language, many persist in holding the position that ethical concerns are of minor importance in the practicing of global media and journalism, at least as compared to the pragmatic concerns of attracting an audience in a fragmented media market or the utilitarian goals of impacting political reality or facilitating social change. There is, furthermore, a widespread perception that the ethics of the media are far less important than the ethics of other actors operating in the field – such as the ethics of Gaddafi's executioners or the ethics of the Libyan provisionary government, which could neither halt nor contain the violence. There are, too, good reasons for retaining the view that the ethical language and commitments of the global media are 'thin'.

Many consider the following reasons to be self-evident. First, it is often said that the media merely 'hold up a mirror' to the reality 'out there', and it is a mirror of the practices and values of individual societies and states – a mirror that reflects the struggle of and for power within societies rather than the sharing of common ethical goals. Second, we often understand media in a global context, as an agent of 'them' whose ethical commitments are radically different from 'ours', rather than as a bridge between 'us' *and* 'them'. In this view, we are, so to speak, trapped in our own ethical community with no overarching cosmopolitan ethicality to provide us with a shared framework. Media cannot, we believe, provide a forum in which we will be able to seek out, develop, and express a language of commonality. Another version of this argument can be found among those who portray the existing world order as constituting a 'clash of civilizations' or as a domain of cultural conflict. People formulate their ideas about their relationships with others in ethical terms, but between us and those who are ethically different there exists no mechanism that allows for the resolution of differences concerning what constitutes justice, a just society, or a good life. Third, and a factor that seems to point to the limited salience of ethics in media, is the limited time and effort that individuals, governments, media organizations, and states reserve for serious and sustained discussions of media ethics. Whereas time and money are expended on journalistic training and the acquisition of relevant skills, comparatively few resources are committed to media and journalistic ethics. When media ethics reach the public domain – as, for instance, in the crisis that erupted in the United Kingdom in the aftermath of the phone-hacking scandal that led to the Leveson inquiry – the answer seems to be to push for the implementation of procedural changes such as state-mandated laws, regulations, or legislation in lieu of drilling more deeply into the substantive values of the media's role in a democratic society. Fourth and finally, a factor that supports the

'thin' view of media ethics is found in the notion that individual ethical commitments are a matter of individual choice and that, therefore,
it is wrong to suppose that rational inquiry will reveal what the true
ethical stance ought to be for all parties. This belief therefore bars people from considering, at any level of detail, arguments for and against
rival ethical positions. If one's ethical stance is personal, then there is no
point in looking for a single overarching ethical belief system applicable to all parties, everywhere, for all time – because, by definition, there
are many different individual ethical creeds. All one can and must do is
select that which is most relevant to one's self. When one applies this
belief to media, almost all parochial practices take on a certain level of
cultural legitimacy, as journalism is viewed as defined by self-contained
professional practices that cannot extend beyond the society's borders.
In a globalized, mediated society marked by increasing cosmopolitanism
and geopolitical interrelationships, such a relativist position cannot be
defended.

Global media ethics are a response to the dilemmas of globalization
and the need to address injustices that span national jurisdictions and
spheres of influence. Globalization has created global dilemmas that
require global solutions – dilemmas that *cannot* be addressed within
individual nation-states or single jurisdictions. Environmental concerns,
for instance, connect with concerns over development and economics,
which in turn impact political concerns such as migration and citizenship. The water crisis in India, for example, has led to massive migration
by the rural poor to cities and mass suicides by farmers, the melting of
the Himalayan glaciers has led to a rise of sea levels, and drinking water
scarcity caused by the worst drought in centuries is creating havoc in
the impacted farming communities; as a result, India has experienced
some of the worst food inflation in the world. Scientists believe that a
combination and the interaction of population pressure, rapid industrial
growth, and climate change are to blame for the scarcity of freshwater
resources. It is important to adopt the globe as the proper frame of reference for all ethical considerations; one must remain fundamentally
interdisciplinary and committed to combining theory with policy and
practice.

We must reject the notion that media and journalistic ethics in a
global context should be considered 'ethics lite'. The scholars contributing to this book assume that the search for a global media ethics is
fundamentally linked to the most basic of ethical principles, namely
the acknowledgment that human life is sacred, that human beings

have inherent dignity, and that human relations should be based on truth-telling and non-malfeasance. Christians and Nordenstreng (2004, p. 4) have referred to these assumptions as universal 'protonorms'. The authors and editors of this book start from the assumption that key actors – media owners, journalists, media scholars, and educators – arrive at an ethical dilemma or consideration familiar with specific practices and with their own internal ethical structures and that these constitutive practices are themselves underpinned by rather thick sets of ethical values that constrain in many complex ways the potential actions of all actors. To make global media ethics 'thick' would require an understanding of local media and journalistic practices, their short-comings and strengths, and their applicability in larger, global, media contexts.

Bertrand (2000), architect of the activist-motivated model of media accountability, made a passionate plea to turn what has become the usual approach to media ethics upside down, in which he reminded the reader that 'the most important person for a newspaper is not the advertiser, the newsmaker or the shareholder: it has always been the reader' (p. 43). In his critique of media, he asked two questions: 'What's wrong with media?' and 'What's wrong with journalists?' (p. 44). In his response, he asserted that commercialization, the concentration of own-ership, the decline in the quality of news reporting, and incompetence, in combination with those factors described earlier in this Introduction, contributed to a general disregard for the audience. Bertrand acknowl-edged that 'media ethics globally have greatly improved', as journalists today are better educated, more diverse, and more aware of the mission of journalism; he noted, however, that breaches of journalistic ethics seem frequent. He offered a glimpse of the possible 'thickening' of the language of media ethics and proposed the following:

> Journalists must acquire general culture, specialized knowledge, and a sense of priorities. They should be aware of the obligations of news people to the population, of the rights of readers/listeners/viewers. They must distinguish between entertainment and information, between real events and fabricated events, between interesting and important events... They must cultivate openness to, a curiosity for, new ideas, unexplored fields, foreign cultures, non-famous, non-powerful folk... Journalists must cultivate confidence and humility so as to be capable of accountability.
>
> (Bertrand 2000, p. 230)

Like Bertrand, Ward attempted to develop a 'thick' language for global media ethics, writing that '[h]istorically, journalism ethics has been parochial with its standards applying to particular groups. Little is said about whether or not journalists have a responsibility to citizens beyond their town or country, ... Journalism ethics, it seems, stops at the border' (Ward 2010, p. 158). Cosmopolitan values should inform a discourse of journalism ethics which, for Ward, meant the 'flourishing of humanity at large' (p. 160) and the advocating for 'common needs and aspirations that [journalists] share with other humans', such as aspirations to 'life, liberty and justice'. Ward rejected the definition of cosmopolitanism as a form of privilege, instead offering his readers a general outline as to what the cosmopolitan journalist could consider as part of his or her ethical system: she or he should promote the rational and moral dignity, investigate inequality, aid in improving the quality of social life, report on diversity and representation, assist with the developing of media literacy and the evaluation of media, and make use of global comparisons. Ward's cosmopolitan journalist was 'non-parochial' and rejected 'anti-cosmopolitan nationalism' in order to achieve some semblance of international justice (see Ward's chapter in this book).

Such cosmopolitan ethics, however, remain problematic if they are unable to account for, or allowed to remain ignorant of, power imbalances and social, political, and historical differences within and between cultures. Ayish (in this book), Berenger and Taha (2013), and Rao and Wasserman (2007) have pointed to the significance of including power and history in the language of global media ethics. For Rao and Wasserman, the history of oppression and colonialism in Africa and South Asia, and the suppression of indigenous knowledge systems in particular, has allowed the West 'to go on with their work in relative ignorance of non-Western histories', which has not seemed to have affected the quality of their work; they write, 'This is a gesture, however, that "we" cannot return' (p. 33). Referring to this imbalance as the 'inequality of ignorance' (p. 33), Rao and Wasserman problematized Western ethical theories that embrace the entirety of humanity without paying attention to the historical, cultural, and political varieties of that humanity. The search, they argued, is not for 'endangered authenticities (the pure native and/or the pre-colonial state to which one can return)' but for a means of producing a discourse that is 'free from colonial reminiscing or, more important, developing an indigenous economic and political model that is able to address local concerns' (p. 34). Ayish, in his chapter in this book, invokes the Arab-Islamic idea of justice, with its dual elements of fairness and responsibility, as being of significance for global media institutions. Berenger and Taha, also writing about the Middle East, alluded to 'contextual ethics', which encourage media practitioners to 'acknowledge that other ethical frameworks might exist elsewhere – and some aspects might even be worth imitating, such as conduct codes and abstractions of media free from government interventions – but they are pragmatic in their application, tempered and hardened by years of oppression, punishment, and intimation by government authorities that have created impermeable political cultures that include mass media behavior' (2013, p. 90). Such authors – those who look back at history as they search for comparative regional, linguistic, and philosophical frameworks within which they can better understand ethics and media – are not issuing a call for moral relativism, but rather they are making an attempt to reprise the language, ethics, and traditions that were suppressed in the long and torturous processes of imperialism and colonialism. It is a further acknowledgment that ethics take shape in specific contexts and situations, and ethical concepts and principles remain vague until they are interpreted within everyday practices and experiences.

Justice in global media ethics: Sen's approach

Scholars of global media ethics consider questions such as 'What is justice?'; 'Can the duties of justice be global?'; and 'How can we practically move towards a more just world?' An increased emphasis on justice in recent decades in the social sciences and humanities can be traced to John Rawls' influential 1971 work *A Theory of Justice*. Although at that time a revival of applied ethics was already well under way, Rawls' work ensured that justice received increased attention in fields such as philosophy and ethics; the level of attention such matters receive has continued to increase at a phenomenal rate in recent decades, and in all areas of applied ethics – including bioethics, climate ethics, healthcare ethics, and business ethics. This development has resulted in discussions, some of which dissolve the traditional divide between ethics and justice while also succeeding at connecting individual duties with institutional responsibilities. The result has been a renewed interest in global ethics and global justice.

In this book, we advocate for 'thickening' the language and practices of global media ethics. This book is a follow up of two global media ethics roundtables, one held in Stellenbosch, South Africa, the other in Dubai, United Arab Emirates. The paper from the previous two roundtables were anthologized as two books, *Media Ethics Beyond Borders* (2010) and *Explorations in Global Media Ethics* (2012), and focused on Africa and the Middle East. This anthology focuses on media and journalism practices in South Asia and is influenced by questions of justice and injustice as posed in *The Idea of Justice* (2009), the most recent work of Indian economist, philosopher, and Nobel Laureate Amartya Sen. While acknowledging that Sen had written little about media and journalism practices, the authors are nevertheless conscious of Sen's expression 'against injustice' (2009, p. 21), the concept being seen as inseparable from discourses of media regulations, journalistic practices, and media and civil society. It is difficult to identify any single aspect of Sen's work that media and journalism scholars can wholly integrate into the development of universals as well as his idea of justice. Justice as an ethical concept resonates with the substantive protonorms of truth, nonviolence, and human dignity and carries with it implications for the procedural notions of media regulation and accountability.

Sen's groundbreaking work on famine and poverty, for which he garnered much international acclaim, is inherently connected to his later scholarship on justice. He theorized that deprivations and injustices such as famine resulted from a lack of freedom and choice. Famines, he argued, could occur without any significant decline in food production in a given country or region (1987). The phenomenon of famine was better understood, he wrote, as one of entitlement. For reasons having to do with income and relative prices, a group of people may be unable to secure an adequate amount of food to ensure their survival, even if enough food is available where they live. He discovered that famines have never occurred in democracies, no matter how poor the populace or illiberal the democracy. The explanation he gave was that democratic pressures on government led to the implementation of measures designed to prevent famines. Levels of income are often used to measure poverty – understandable, for many reasons, such as the relatively widespread availability of data about income. Although some have described poverty as a lack of money, according to Sen, the concentration solely on income is inadequate in many contexts. Income is instrumentally significant but other factors may merit more attention than they have up until now received – for example, age, gender, health, and location. Information about income may not tell the full story about the deprivations that many suffer. A focus solely on income also may obscure the avenues of research and policy most likely to lead to effective solutions. Sen has argued that we ought to concentrate our attention on ensuring the substantive freedoms of all peoples. In contrast to the influential utilitarian tradition of ethics, which considers measures of well-being, and in contrast to the proposals put forth by other theorists such as Rawls, Sen wrote that we should be concerned with the opportunities people have to pursue their objectives. This means that the concept of 'functionings' in a capability set – what a person can do or be – is central to analyses of poverty, deprivation, and injustice. A person's 'capability set' is the different combinations of functionings that are feasible for him or her to achieve (Sen 1999, p. 79). Sen wrote, 'Capability is thus a kind of freedom: the substantive freedom to achieve alternative functioning combinations (or, less formally put, the freedom to achieve various lifestyles)' (1999, p. 75). A frequent example of Sen's contrasts two people who are not eating enough. One is starving because she is destitute, the other fasting while affluent. The two are equally hungry but have different capability sets or substantive freedoms. Capabilities are a kind of freedom – the substantive freedom 'to choose a life one has reason to value' (1999, p. 285). Sen understood the expansion of freedoms to be the primary end and means of development: 'Development consists of the removal of various types of unfreedoms that leave people with little choice and little opportunity of exercising their reasoned agency' (1999, p. 88). Development, he argued, 'requires the removal of major sources of unfreedom: poverty as well as tyranny, poor economic opportunities as well as systematic social depravation, neglect of public facilities as well as intolerance, or overactivity of repressive states' (1999, p. 3).

Embracing Sen's thesis, this book focuses on ethics and injustice. Why, asked Sen, do most philosophers refuse to think about injustice as deeply or as subtly as they do about justice? He wrote of the importance of actual behavior – inter alia, combining the operation of the principles of justice with the actual behavior of people – and of grounding assessments of injustice by combining social behavior with social institutions. 'What really happens to people', wrote Sen, 'cannot but be a central concern of a theory of justice' (2009, p. 200). He recognized that the realization of justice is 'not just a matter of judging institutions and rules, but of judging the societies themselves' (2009, p. 20). Arguing for a 'realization-focused perspective on justice', Sen advocated in favor of a global citizenry that was not merely about trying to achieve, or dreaming about achieving, some perfectly just society or social arrangement but 'about preventing manifestly severe injustices' (2009, p. 21). He wrote, 'When people across the world agitate to get more global justice ... they are not clamoring for some kind of "minimal humanitarianism". Nor are they agitating for a "perfectly just" world society, but for the elimination of some outrageously unjust arrangements' (2009,

p. 26). For Sen, the focus on justice had to shift from the realization of just institutions to the manifest discourse against injustice.

Recognizing democracy's intrinsic value in redressing injustices, Sen provided a normative definition of democracy:

> What exactly is democracy? We must not identify democracy with majority rule. Democracy has complex demands, which certainly include voting and respect for election results, but it also requires the protection of liberties and freedoms, respect for legal entitlements, and the guaranteeing of free discussion and uncensored distribution of news and fair comment. Even elections cannot be deeply defective if they occur without the different sides getting an adequate opportunity to present their respective cases, or without the electorate enjoying the freedom to obtain news and to consider the views of the competing protagonists. Democracy is a demanding system, and not just a mechanical condition (like majority rule) taken in isolation.
>
> (2003, p. 6)

The definition of democracy is normative in the sense that Sen recognized the ideals of democracy were to be found not in its institutions but in its practice. He advocated not just the presence of a minimal democracy but a *deepening* of democracy. In shallow democracies, citizens do little more than vote – if they vote at all. Deeper democracies require modes of participation in addition to balloting and majority rule – for example, the opportunity for free discussion, the obtaining of news, and reasoned deliberation. It is the central argument of this book that media can play an important role in the deepening of democratic processes when it reflects on the ethical dimension of its practices within specific communities and, more broadly, within the global information society. Sen contended that 'the struggle for democracy around the world … is the most profound challenge of our times' (2003, p. 7) but also that the conception of democracy is often excessively narrow. His strong endorsement of democratic 'practice', and his distinguishing it from democratic ideals and institutions, has meant that democratic citizens must 'make democracy work' (2003, p. 6) by committing themselves to and engaging in the practice of democracy. In an ideal arrangement, the media would be able to provide a space in which citizens could practice democracy in their everyday lives. Such practices would include striving to broaden and qualitatively deepen human well-being and would extend agency and political dignity to the socially marginalized. Ethical media can insist on procedural fairness and equality before the law and provide space for inclusive deliberation.

In the context of reasoned deliberation, in particular, and its significance to making democracy work and achieving justice, Sen located the importance of an 'unrestrained and healthy media' (2009, p. 254). The absence of a free media, wrote Sen, and the suppression of the people's ability to communicate with each other have the effect of directly reducing the quality of human life even if an authoritarian state happens to be rich in terms of gross national product. Without media's ability to disseminate information, it would be difficult to engage in public reasoning and deliberation, and therefore difficult to achieve justice. A free and unrestrained media can directly contribute to free speech, allow for the dissemination of knowledge and critical scrutiny, and provide a protective function by giving voice to the neglected and disadvantaged. If democracy is a history of people's participation in public reasoning, it is in a well-functioning media that one finds the most important space of and for public reasoning. In rejecting 'discussionless justice' (2009, p. 255), Sen asserted that it is a free, energetic, and efficient media that would be best positioned to facilitate the needed discursive process about democracy. 'Media is important', wrote Sen, 'not only for democracy but for the pursuit of justice in general' (2009, p. 254). A free press, for Sen, was not by mere definition a press that promoted justice or spoke out against injustice. In his critique of the Indian media, Sen wrote of the class bias inherent in Indian news coverage and how the media had deepened the division between 'a fortunate fifth of the population who are doing just fine on the basis of the economic progress that is taking place in India, and the rest who are being left firmly behind' (2012, p. 11). Yet even with a level of durable ambiguity surrounding – or, at times, the failure of – a democratic media's role in reasoned deliberation, Sen asserted that journalism can give us space to voice demands of and for equality, freedom, and development and from unjust violations of liberty.

A criticism of Sen's approach both to justice in global, national, regional, and local public policies and for democratic governance is that it leaves too many evaluative issues unresolved (Gotoh and Dumouchel 2011). What are the possibilities of Sen's theory of justice for the functioning of global media? Is there room to assess justice, injustice, and social justice within the context of media practices and, subsequent to that, within the practicing of democracy? How can Sen's position 'against injustice' be articulated as intrinsic to the project of global media ethics? We assume that the discursive nature of Sen's alternative theory of justice adds 'thickness' to the language of global media ethics. While it may be difficult to resolve the overall balance of the comparative claims of equity considerations that lie in the heterogenous literature on ethics and justice – for instance, the writings of authors such as Rawls, Dworkin, and Habermas, as well as the literatures surrounding related topics, such as utilitarianism or social welfare function approaches – Sen's approach has given concrete meaning to the ethical practicing of journalism and how such practices can strengthen legal and civil societies. Journalism, although deeply connected to the practices and practicing of democracy, has frequently been seen as a skill-oriented task of writing, reading, and editing, and not often enough as about reflecting, changing, or creating. The transmittal role of media has superseded – even in the strongest of democracies – its role as a transformative and ethical agent. Sen wanted to theorize the media's role of public reasoning as the opportunity for citizens to participate in political discussions and thus to put themselves in a position to influence public choice. Democracy, he wrote, has demands that transcend the ballot box; media and journalism must articulate those demands.

Global media and journalism face critical scrutiny like never before as their potential to reach millions of diverse audiences around the globe continues to increase. The advent of digital technologies has been accompanied by celebratory discourses on their democratic potential. Because these technologies have put the means of media production in the hands of every citizen with Internet access, a camera, or a mobile phone, the opportunities for citizen participation in making media have never been greater; with the proliferation of technology, however, has also come criticism of the depth of the contribution that journalism can make to democratic discourse. The general criticism has been well articulated by Ian Hargreaves (2005, p. 23), a former journalist, who wrote:

> Journalism stands accused of sacrificing accuracy for speed, purposeful investigation for cheap intrusion, and reliability for entertainment. Dumbed down news media are charged with privileging sensation over significance and celebrity over achievement.

There is no doubt that new media technologies continue to offer fresh means of engendering anxiety and are an extension of these concerns, but hopes must be balanced against fears. Sen's approach to justice reinvigorated the deepening of democracy via public reasoning and public deliberation, and old and new media alike have the ability to disseminate such discussions.

It is ethics that bind individuals. Individuals are free to choose, but there is no randomness of ends because the diversity of choice is constrained by ethical considerations. In other words, the socially destructive potential that lurks in the randomness of ends – which is amplified considerably by the availability of social media – is restrained in modern times by ethics. Ethics, according to this definition, is integrative because it is underpinned by the recognition of the 'Other' as being, first and foremost, an unmarked, anonymous individual, analogous to the 'Self'. If that is the recognition, if one were to invoke Charles Taylor, individual goals as well as the modalities by which these goals can be attained are kept in check by the ethical self. No longer do certain classes or communities – in the case of India, caste; in South Africa, race; in China, religion – enjoy the sole right to a given profession or lifestyle, nor is it permissible that justice can be differentially delivered. An ethical media would strive to develop the capabilities of all people, without privilege or exclusion. The historical imposition of relations of aspiration and primordial ties had been upheld at all levels because of what Gellner (1994, p. 8) called the 'tyranny of cousins' – a system that separates people into mutually suspicious strata and sects in the name of promoting identity. Complementing this tyranny of dense, interactive, primordial ties is the tight grip on vertical mobility. Once the monopoly on knowledge has been taken away from the upper reaches of priests and patriarchs, and that knowledge has begun to be disseminated, we are no longer willing to suspend our judgment simply because it comes from a pre-designated and authorized hallowed quarter over which we have no control. This includes the functioning of media. The opening up of the means of media production to citizens has eroded the claims of an elite class of journalists and media producers to knowledge and truth. Global media now have the imperative to become more transparent and adopt a set of 'open ethics' (Ward and Wasserman, 2010), which envisions a greater role for citizens in the co-production of meaning and truth. The exclusion of voices on the basis of identity, belonging, caste, or ethnicity is no longer tenable by an ethical media in the era of media globalization. The shift of the primordial self to the ethical self is referred to by Gupta as a move 'from Nation-State to Knowledge-State' (2009, p. 224). Media are the foundation of a Knowledge-State, where the old fascination with 'blood and memory' loses its grip and draws its 'emotive power and symbolic energy from devising alternative routes to universal fraternity'. The erosion of these boundaries by means of media globalization notwithstanding, the global public sphere continues to be marked by exclusions, hierarchies, and silences. For global media theorists, developing a 'thick' language of ethics, a fair and just global media that can develop the capabilities of people from diverse geographical, social, political, and cultural backgrounds so that those people may gain membership in a global Knowledge-State is and remains the challenge.

Themes of the book

This book brings together a range of perspectives from around the globe to address questions of media ethics both in local contexts and in a transnational, global environment. One might ask if it is possible to draw from the multiple trajectories of the chapters in this book to discern a general argumentative pattern of media ethics and justice. Is there a common denominator running through such seemingly disparate investigations of theories and practices of media ethics and justice in democracies as diverse as India, the United Arab Emirates South Africa, Pakistan, and the United States? These questions pertain not only to the challenge of organizing the different contributions into a coherent book but also to the question of how the specific relates to the global – precisely the question that lies at the heart of scholarly debates of global media ethics. In such debates, there is general acknowledgment that similarities between ethical systems and ethical universals have to emerge through local specificities, rather than the other way around – to impose 'global norms' uniformly on localities can lead to new forms of cultural imperialism (Wasserman 2011). The chapters included in this book focus on this process of organic emergence. Although there are certain recurring themes and frequent overlapping arguments – especially in the chapters written by working journalists and editors – the answer, it seems fair to conclude, is that no single gestalt presents itself, no matter the altitude of our bird's-eye view. Rather, in the presentation of case studies, contextualized debates, and specific examples, the central concept of justice in media ethics is illuminated from various angles. A common theme in these chapters is the acknowledgment that ethics and justice are central to the evolution and deepening of a democratic public sphere saturated with media images and narratives.

The chapters collectively advance a discussion of media ethics, justice, and globalization, and all have building the theoretical foundations required of a global media ethics as their aim. While they draw on contexts as diverse as Indian (Rao and Bhushan's chapters), South African (Wasserman's chapter), and Arab-Islamist traditions (Ayish's chapter), the aim of this here is to provide non-Western contexts with the same sense of legitimacy and prominence as theories about universalism drawn from Western traditions, which are also included here (in Christians', Ward's, and Wilkins' chapters). Too often in global media ethics literature, non-Western perspectives on theories of universal values are relegated to the margins if included at all, presented as case studies and not engaged on a theoretical level. Too often theories of social responsibility, democracy, and justice derived from non-Western and multiple global contexts are omitted from the discussion. The juxtaposition of various theoretical frameworks in this section is an attempt to signal that theory, too, is culturally and contextually specific. Sen asserted that democracy, like reason, is not the exclusive and benevolent product of Western Enlightenment but, as in India, democracy, justice, and reason have long histories of practice. Such an assertion appealed to us in our effort to develop a rigorous and inclusive rubric for global media ethics.

In Ayish's chapter, he has provided a glimpse of how significant justice is to Arab-Islamic traditions. He argues that no value apart from belief in God is as central to Islamic philosophy and politics as is the notion of justice. While he recognizes that the value of justice has been placed at the center of a comprehensive physical and moral system, the Arab-Islamic world has also been the site of varied injustices. Ayish notes that justice is explicitly stated as a goal in many of the Arab media codes of ethics and media charters, but he maintains that it is difficult to ascertain how such ethical ideals affect day-to-day media practice.

Rao's chapter applies Sen's theory of *nyaya* (justice) to journalism and media practices in the newly globalized, commercialized, and liberalized media in India, and to its possible theoretical relevance in developing a workable framework for global media ethics. She argues that Sen's analysis and use of *nyaya* can illuminate our understanding of justice, such that it has the potential to play a hugely constructive role in the development of a theory of justice. *Nyaya* cannot be confined to a project dedicated to justice and injustice (*anyaya*) in nations that are already free and the distribution of wealth in those that are already prosperous. Understanding the nature and source of deprivation and inequity is central to the removing of *anyaya*. If one identifies reducing the deprivation of resources or poverty as a guiding principle of global media ethics and juxtaposes that with nonviolence and the sacredness of human lives, reasoned deliberation among members of the media would be required as they make a concerted effort to become and remain cognizant of their role in providing a space for discussions of not only class inequity based on income inequality but also the deprivation of the capability or potential to live a flourishing and fulfilling life.

In his chapter, Wasserman uses examples from South Africa and India as a point of departure to discuss the ethical role of the media in democratic societies marked by significant internal inequalities. For Wasserman, social justice as a global ethical concept has to take account of the different ways in which media relate to respective societies. He warns against forms of universalism that are based on assumptions that citizens can access media to participate in reasoned deliberation in similar ways in different localities. Although Wasserman agrees that justice as a central ethical concept – rooted in the protonorm of human dignity – possesses universal resonance, his analysis of the South African example emphasizes that global norms and values must be sited within a concrete local context.

Christians argues that a new orientation toward justice is needed – one that can form the basis for an alternative rationale and mission for media. For Christians, justice as an ethical concept is rooted in the protonorm of human dignity. If we acknowledge that the idea of justice is inherent to all humans, civil society becomes the space in which restorative justice is developed. Although such restorative justice is experienced most deeply in local contexts, Christians points to transnational collaborations by civil society movements working for social justice as an illustration of the possibilities of global activism emerging from specific locales. Justice as a protonorm that transcends geographic and cultural boundaries then becomes the guiding principle for an ethical media.

Ward argues for a global media ethics that would be appropriate for a globally interconnected world. Justice, for him, is rooted in the notion of a common humanity. Ward sees globalism, however, as ethically prior – but not ethically exclusive – to parochial values. When we think about justice, Ward argues, we should think globally, not locally. In arguing for a cosmopolitan approach to justice as a global ethical value, he rejects localism but cautions that universalism does not imply universal consent on ethical values. Universal principles are normative rather than empirical, and they are proposed as normative arguments. Local conceptions of ethical values such as justice may be tolerated as long as they do not violate 'basic universal principles'.

Wilkins' chapter focuses on collaboration in journalistic work. The changing news media environment requires journalists and media organizations to think more creatively about collaboration with others while retaining independence and autonomy as ethical cornerstones. When understood ethically, this type of collaboration requires a reflection on justice as an ethical value that is rooted in the principles of reciprocity and capability. Wilkins draws on examples from different international contexts to show how the reciprocity and capabilities approaches can promote justice. Understood this way, justice – through the lens of reciprocity and capabilities – can provide an ethically informed but practically oriented foundation for collaborative agreements in global media.

Sonwalkar gives readers a historical account of how ethics and justice came to be an integral part of Indian media starting with the activist journalism of Raja Rammohun Roy in the mid-19th century. His chapter provides a reference point against which the development of journalism ethics in India and in the global context can be framed. At a time when spurious journalistic practices were narrowing the range of facts and opinions available to citizens for use in making informed choices, Sonwalkar's analysis focused on a historical moment marked by significant highs. A close examination of Roy's intervention in early Indian journalism, Sonwalkar suggests, reveals that Roy placed great emphasis on an ethics of no harm, justice, and public good and that it is important to recall Roy's contribution in times when global journalism and democratic practices face a crisis of accountability.

Vipul Mudgal's chapter critiques the insidious practice of 'paid news' and draws attention to how it has weakened the previous consolidation of India's democratic public sphere and civil society. Mudgal problematizes 'paid news' in the context of political communication, where, on the one hand, a market-driven media shun even basic notions of professional ethics while, on the other hand, an incremental mediation of politics tends to render democratic processes vulnerable to ill-motivated distortions. He argues that despite elemental flaws in India's commercial media systems, the practice can be tackled by a strong judicial system, the strengthening of citizen oversight, a reinforcing of professional ethics among journalists, and the fostering of a watchful civil society.

Mufti's chapter provides a vivid account of how the television media in Pakistan reshape the role of judiciary and legislative practices. Mufti argues that the intense competition among private television channels in Pakistan ensures that the free flow of information – however faulty and tainted – will continue. The news channels, and the news media writ large, eventually will need to define for themselves their own role in society. As Pakistan resets its institutions following a tumultuous few years that have seen the rise of the judiciary as a political force, TV news channels will need to define for themselves how they will use their newfound power and influence to create an open, just, and democratic society.

In his chapter, Bharat Bhushan describes the various changes that are taking place in the Indian media to show how such changes have made it difficult to practice ethical journalism in the country. The author highlights that practices such as paid news, the declining role of editors, and the merging of advertising and news divisions are disastrous for the consolidation and strengthening of Indian democracy. As the dominance of a single party, the Congress party, has declined and the polity has gotten fractured, the role of providing the alternative voice was thrust upon the media. In the era of coalition politics, where parties and politicians change sides often, and in completely unpredictable ways, the media's role has become diffused. The author argues that if a large section of the media remains as compromised and at the mercy of politicians and business houses as it is today, their ability to be irreverent is to that extent subdued.

There is significant interplay between these chapters. We have a welter of competing theories, interpretations, and experiences of what is to be considered as global media ethics; if such ethics or universals are possible given the diversity of cultural and geopolitical contexts; what was the intended meaning of justice and how media are to interpret justice and injustice; and whether global media ethics, however understood, can be applied with equal assurance to journalists and media practitioners working in countries as diverse as the United Arab Emirates, South Africa, Pakistan, and India. Some authors saw the dominance of commercialization and the privatization model in media as counterproductive to a justice-based model. Rao's chapter on *nyaya* as an ethical foundation for global media is linked to Mudgal's and Bhushan's chapters – who, in analyzing issues created by the rise of paid news, its increased emphasis on commercialization, and the diminished role of investigative reporting, speak of how difficult it is to write about justice and injustice in a media environment solely focused on profits and advertising revenues. Christians' insistence on universal protonorms suggests that any critique of a democratic media must not take us too far from ethical universals of the sacredness of human life or human dignity. If we are to accept justice as an ethical universal then these chapters give us reasons as to why universals are desirable and necessary, albeit difficult to achieve.

The conclusions of these chapters are not uniform; instead, they point to the complexity of ethical challenges journalists and media professionals face in emerging democracies, the breadth and depth of injustices, and the inadequacy of the judicial system and civil society in those places to create the conditions necessary for public reasoning and liberty. Several chapters allude to the difficulties of practicing journalism and media ethically in an environment in which media are increasingly privatized and commercialized, and where changing patterns of media ownership are having an adverse impact on media content and practices. Read together, these chapters allude to deliberative democracy in South Asia as evolving, and historically viable, but the development – or recognition – of media as a platform of public reason, one able to act as or provide a voice 'against injustice', continues to be halting.

To borrow a metaphor from another context, what we hear in reading these diverse and stimulating pieces is the sound of ground being cleared for what might be a new paradigm, but it is too early to tell what the shape of that paradigm will be and whether or not it will be coherent and unified. Such a conclusion should not dissuade us from pursuing the heterotopic space of global media ethics, even if there do not appear to be any single, totalizing vantage point from which to speak.

References

Berenger, R. D. and M. Taha 2013. 'Contextual Ethics and Arab Mass Media', in Stephen J. A. Ward (ed.), *Global Media Ethics*, pp. 89–109. New York: Wiley-Blackwell.

Bertrand, Claude J. 2000. *Media Ethics and Accountability Systems*. New Brunswick: Transaction Publishers.

Castells, Manuel. 1996. *The Rise of the Network Society*. Malden: Blackwell.

Christians, C. and K. Nordenstreng. 2004. 'Social Responsibility Worldwide', *Journal of Mass Media Ethics*, 19(1): 3–28.

Der Derian, James. 2009. *Virtuous War: Mapping the Military-Industrial-Media-Entertainment Network*. New York: Routledge.

Ess, Charles. 2009. *Digital Media Ethics*. Cambridge: Polity Press.

Garber, M., B. Hanssen, and R. Walkowitz. 2000. 'Introduction: The Turn to Ethics', in M. Garber, B. Hanssen, and R. Walkowitz (eds.), *The Turn to Ethics*, pp. vii–xii. New York: Routledge.

Geertz, Clifford. 1972. *The Interpretation of Cultures*. New York: Basic Books.

Gellner, Ernest. 1994. *Conditions of Liberty: Civil Society and Its Rivals*. London: Penguin.

Gotoh, R., and P. Dumouchel. 2011. 'Introduction', in R. Gotoh and P. Dumouchel (eds.), *Against Injustice: The New Economics of Amartya Sen*, pp. 1–33. Cambridge: Cambridge University Press.

Gupta, Dipankar. 2009. *The Caged Phoenix: Can India Fly?* Washington, DC: Woodrow Wilson Center Press.

Hargreaves, Ian. 2005. *Journalism: A Very Short Introduction*. New York: Oxford University Press.

McChesney, Robert W. 2013. *Digital Disconnect: How Capitalism Is Turning the Internet against Democracy*. New York: The New Press.

Norris, Pippa. 2001. *Digital Divide: Civic Engagement, Information Poverty, and the Internet Worldwide*. Cambridge: Cambridge University Press.

Rao, S. and H. Wasserman. 2007. 'Global Media Ethics Revisited: A Postcolonial Critique', *Global Media and Communication*, 3(1): 29–50.

Sen, Amartya. 1987. *On Ethics and Economics*. New York: Blackwell.

——. 1999. *Development as Freedom*. New York: Knopf Press.

——. 2003. 'Democracy and Its Global Roots: Why Democratization Is Not the Same as Westernization', *The New Republic*, October 6, pp. 28–35.

——. 2009. *The Idea of Justice*. Cambridge: Harvard University Press.

——. 2012. 'The Glory and the Blemishes of the Indian News Media', *The Hindu*, January 7, p. 12.

Ward, Stephen J. A. 2010. *Global Journalism Ethics*. Montreal: McGill-Queen's University Press.

Ward, S. J. A. and H. Wasserman 2010. 'Towards an Open Ethics: Implications of New Media Platforms for Global Ethics Discourse', *Journal of Mass Media Ethics*, 25(4): 275–292.

Wasserman, H. 2011. 'Towards a Global Journalism Ethics via Local Narratives: Southern African Perspectives', *Journalism Studies*, 12(6): 791–803.

2
The Moral Priority of Globalism in a Media-Saturated World

Stephen J. A. Ward

The greatest task of moral theory today is to transform itself into a global ethics that challenges dominant forms of parochial ethics, from ethnocentricity to nationalism and political realism. We should be radical in the ways of moral invention, envisaging a global ethics and a global media ethics for our interconnected world.

The chapter advances a moral globalism that places greater ethical weight on global values than on parochial values. When we consider global issues, love of human rights and human flourishing and love of international justice outweigh love of family, ethnicity, or nation.

My thesis is that moral globalism, such as cosmopolitanism, should be ethically prior but not ethically exclusive. Global ethics should not exclude considerations of parochial values from ethical reasoning *tout court*. Instead, globalists should deploy a strategy of incorporation, restraint, and demotion of parochial values. We need to 'think' of the parochial and the global at the same time, ranking parochial values by importance and evaluating their ethical weight in specific situations.

The tension between globalism and parochialism affects our notions of justice. We need to think globally, not locally, about justice. We need to challenge a parochial view of justice as sets of norms and institutional arrangements that differ from culture to culture, with no possibility of overarching global principles. Parochialism toward justice prevents the development and implementation of much-needed global principles of justice based on our fundamental humanity. As I will argue below, even a recent attempt to formulate a minimalist approach to global justice – put forward as a new and more defensible form of parochialism – is flawed and inconsistent. After sketching the tenants of cosmopolitanism and anti-cosmopolitanism, I argue indirectly for the priority of globalism and cosmopolitanism. I show how cosmopolitanism can respond satisfactorily to objections from parochial critics, how the criticisms are not persuasive, and how the critics' positions have internal problems. My aim is modest. I do not 'prove' globalism's priority. I seek only to establish the plausibility of cosmopolitanism and its priority thesis, and the implausibility of parochial alternatives.[1]

The construction of global ethics is important because our globalized world throws up new and difficult issues that our old parochial systems were never meant to adjudicate. The establishment of globalism's priority is an essential part of that construction. If globalism cannot show why it is prior, then its approach to ethics and its support for types of global ethics, such as global media ethics, are in question.

The debate between globalism and localism has important implications for media ethics, and such key issues as global justice. As I will argue, a parochial (or local) understanding of media ethics is no longer sufficient. It can lead to narrow, biased coverage and public misunderstandings about global issues and events. Localism, as an approach to ethics, blocks (or discourages) the necessary and important reconstruction of media ethics as a global media ethics. The ethics for today's global media needs to be based on a commitment to globalism in general, and to the invention of global ethical principles for media practice.

My focus in this chapter is not on media ethics per se. My focus is broader. I seek to undermine a philosophical approach to ethics called 'localism' so as to encourage, indirectly, the development of all forms of global ethics. A full and adequate account of global media ethics is beyond the scope of this chapter.[2] However, I hope my comments on news media toward the end of this chapter indicate how globalism would re-shape media ethics.

Parochialism and globalism

In the past, it was not difficult for many of us to keep local and global values in separate 'boxes' and ignore the tension between the two sets of values. We embraced *both* the values of family and nation and the 'brotherhood of man'. Since we lived in a non-global world, the problems of the 'Other' did not call for regular (and complex) ethical discussions. Our parochialism was supported by the ethics of our news media. For most of its history, the basis of journalism ethics (Ward 2005) has been the promotion of the interests of parochial publics, from religious and political groups to the nation at large.

Today, in a global world, the tensions between domestic and global values are increasingly prominent and difficult to resolve. Many of us continue to practice a parochial ethics bound by cultural and national borders. When we in the North see people starving in Africa, we may think that someone should do something; yet, we may say (Shapcott 2010, p. 3): 'We owe more to our own kind and less to outsiders, and then only after our domestic duties have been dispatched.' The assumption is that the parochial has moral priority over the global.

Normative parochialism and globalism

'Parochial' (from the latin *parochia*) originally referred to what belonged to the parish. A person was parochial if they took a great interest in parochial affairs, as opposed to non-parochial affairs. To be non-parochial was to take a great interest in what happened beyond the parish. 'Parochialism' came to designate this preference for the parochial, the near, and the dear.

Today, the language of the 'parish' has been replaced with the language of the 'local' in its many forms – one's community, region, cultural group, or nation. The non-parochial has become almost synonymous with what is 'global' – peoples and nations beyond my borders.

When is parochialism or globalism an ethic? It is when we assert that it is morally *correct* to prefer the parochial over the global, or the global over the parochial. Here we choose to embrace what I call 'normative parochialism' or 'normative globalism'.

Normative forms of parochialism and globalism are defined by their priority theses: All forms of normative parochialism assert the greater value of the parochial than the non-parochial. Where they conflict, parochial values should trump (or should usually trump) non-parochial values. Normative globalism contends the opposite: Global values have greater value than parochial values. Global values should trump (or should usually trump) parochial duties.[3]

Parochialism is a theoretical and practical problem for global ethics. Theoretically, how can globalism both assert global values and recognize local duties? Practically, globalists worry that parochial attitudes may induce officials and the public to follow narrow policies in global affairs, where wider, more generous, ethical responses are needed.

Globalization raises thorny ethical questions:

1. *Universalism:* Are there universals that can guide global policy? If so, what are the universal civil rights? What are the universal principles of justice?
2. *What kind of international system?* How should the international system be structured so as to respond to global problems? Should

nation-states be supplemented by supra-national institutions or a world government?
3. *Issues of response:* When should countries intervene in the affairs of other countries? Who is responsible for ending poverty in the world's poorest nations? How much foreign aid should nations contribute? Should nations reduce trade tariffs even if it increases unemployment?

Each question starts a debate between globalism and parochialism. At the bottom of the debate stands the fundamental question: How should members of bounded communities, primarily nation-states, treat outsiders (Shapcott 2010, p. 2)? Or, What is the ethical significance of national interests and boundaries?

Cosmopolitanism and anti-cosmopolitanism

The parochial–global debate in political science, ethics, and international affairs circles around two opposing lines of thought: cosmopolitanism and anti-cosmopolitanism. Cosmopolitans are globalists who believe international issues should be evaluated by a commitment to the equal dignity of humans everywhere. Cosmopolitans call for substantive aid for distressed strangers and firm protection of human rights even if it comes at a cost to nations. The anti-cosmopolitan camp, which includes political realists and nationalists, is united in opposition to cosmopolitanism. They believe cosmopolitans ask for too much, overriding valid parochial concerns and duties.

Cosmopolitanism

Cosmopolitanism is an ethical theory with ancient roots. It is a theory about what we owe to others, especially foreigners. Cosmopolitanism began in ancient Greece and Rome, with Dionysus the Cynic, Cicero, and the Stoics. Enlightenment cosmopolitan thinkers include Voltaire, Bentham, and, most importantly, Kant. Modern cosmopolitans include Pogge (1994), Beitz (1994), Nussbaum (1996), Wiredu (1996), and Singer (1972). Also, Derrida (2000, 2001) espoused a cosmopolitan ethic of hospitality.

The basic moral principles are as follows:

1. *Equal moral concern:* All humans have equal value and dignity as members of humanity. Our concern for others is not parochial but universal.

2. *Universal inclusion:* (1) entails that the nationality, ethnicity, or gender of a person is morally irrelevant to whether someone comes under the protection of cosmopolitan principles. It rules out social arrangements that discriminate on the basis of caste, gender, race, or nationality.
3. *Ethics as universal:* (1) entails that ethics should be based on universal values that guide interactions among members of a borderless humanity.
4. *Individualistic moral concern:* The ultimate concern is for the individual, not states or societies, which are valued for promoting the welfare of individuals.
5. *Duties to foreigners:* We have moral duties to foreigners, not only charity.
6. *Global approach to issues:* We use (1)–(5) as our primary guide to global issues. Cosmopolitanism is prior than parochialism.

Cosmopolitan principles guide four types of global relations: (1) impact on the rest of the world, for example, how nations affect climate change; (2) impact on specific regions, for example, the impact of foreign mining on a developing country's environment; (3) responses to other people's impact on others, for example, foreign intervention to stop rights abuses;[4] (4) relations of assistance, for example, duties to a country devastated by famine. Given these relations, it is not surprising that global ethics is dominated by deontological discussions about what we owe others and how much we owe.

The duties claimed by cosmopolitans vary in strength and specificity. A 'weak' cosmopolitanism affirms some extra-national obligations such as negative duties to stop some specific action, for example, violating rights. Strong cosmopolitanism affirms many far-reaching obligations, including positive duties to do good, for example, to solve the problem of AIDS (Acquired Immune Deficiency Syndrome). Some thinkers are called 'institutional' cosmopolitans because they focus on the institutional reasons for global problems and they propose institutional reforms.[5] Cosmopolitanism is supported by different moral approaches. Cosmopolitans Caney (2006) and Pogge (1994) advance liberal cosmopolitanism. Caney, for example, formulates cosmopolitan principles of justice that are extensions of a liberal emphasis on social justice and rights. For example, Caney (2006) puts forward a number of principles for distributing the wealth of developed nations to less developed nations.

But not all liberals are cosmopolitans or global liberalists. Liberal John Rawls (2002) is an anti-cosmopolitan on international justice. As I discuss later, Rawls develops a theory of international justice that does not apply to all societies but only to liberal and 'decent' non-liberal societies. Some cosmopolitans are utilitarians like Singer (1972). The basic cosmopolitan principle is to increase the utility and well-being of every sentient creature. Others, like Shue (1996), are deontologists in spirit. Shue, for example, bases his theory of global justice not on utility but on the global importance of a number of basic rights.

Cosmopolitans' 'ethical identity' is defined by the common needs and aspirations that they share with other humans. Our parochial attachments have a prima facie right to be recognized but may be trumped by broader concerns. By making cosmopolitan principles primary, we show respect for humanity's rational and moral capacities wherever and however they are manifest. Cosmopolitanism acknowledges the stoic view that we live simultaneously in two communities: the local community of our birth and a community of humanity. In negotiating our way between these two communities, we should not allow local attachments to override fundamental human rights and duties. When there is no conflict with global values, we can live parochially.

Anti-cosmopolitanism and nationalism

Anti-cosmopolitans deny, doubt, or minimize cosmopolitan arguments that place strong international duties on nations and call for far-reaching reform of the global arena.

Recent normative theorists of nationalism, such as David Miller (2007) and Yael Tamir (1993), provide nuanced arguments that challenge cosmopolitanism in the areas of global justice and global political theory. Normative nationalism asserts the moral importance of nations, national autonomy, and national development. The parochial values associated with membership in a nation are ethically serious and, in many cases, primary to cosmopolitan values.

The values of nationality can be expressed as a number of duties: (a) duties of national government to its citizens and the national interest; (b) duties of citizens to fellow citizens; and (c) duties of citizens to their country. An example of (a) would be a government obligation to promote the well-being of citizens; of (b) would be my duty to come to the aid of fellow citizens, for example, how Americans helped the citizens of New Orleans after Hurricane Katrina; and of (c) is the duty of citizens to defend their nation in war. In sum, membership in a national community entails rights and duties for citizens and institutions. The nationalist priority thesis is that 'compatriots take first priority': we owe some things first and foremost to our country and fellow citizens, and sometimes to the exclusion of outsiders. Charity and duty start at home.

Criticisms and rebuttals

I have contrasted the perspectives of cosmopolitanism and anti-cosmopolitanism. I now examine several anti-cosmopolitan claims and provide cosmopolitan rejoinders.[6]

Universalism and 'local' ethics

One criticism of cosmopolitanism is its commitment to ethical universalism. This is the view that there are some moral principles, such as the right not to be tortured, that are valid for all people and provide a foundation for ethics. If, as a Canadian, I think that torturing Canadians is wrong but it is not wrong if the person is from Ghana, I violate universalism. My belief violates the universal principle of equal moral concern.

The principles of universalism are sometimes called principles of 'the common morality' (Gert 2004) – a morality whose principles apply to all people. These principles include injunctions to avoid harm, for example, prohibitions against murder, rape, and abhorrent cruelty. Other principles are positive injunctions to do good, such as being kind to all. Ethical universalism is opposed to all forms of parochialism that make non-universal principles the primary values, such as egoism, moral relativism, and nationalism.

Nationalism and moral relativism use a battery of arguments against universalism.

One argument is empirical. It asserts that, if we look around the world, we do not discover universals – principles accepted by all people. Instead, we find great variety among, and conflict between, ethical beliefs and systems. For example, some cultures stress individualism; others stress social solidarity and fitting into social schemes. Moreover, there are no universal criteria to impartially adjudicate the differences, for example, show that one system is superior to another.

Nationalists and other parochialists have an explanation for ethical differences and the attraction of parochial values: ethics is local, or localism. The principles of any ethical system are the product of local culture and do not extend beyond their origin. Localism is a modern expression of older contextual and relativist views of ethics. It is expressed at the start of Plato's *Republic*. It re-surfaces in romantic thought, such as in Herder's view of the cultural origins of individuality, in Hegel's statism, and in modern anthropology (see Shapcott 2010, pp. 52–53).

Localism presumes a sociology of ethics that begins with the fact that we learn moral values through social inculcation and education. By living in a culture, I absorb its ethical values. These values are parochial, not universal. I appreciate these values because they are part of the valued practices of my society. I am motivated to support them. Enforcement of these values is effective because non-compliant citizens come under pressure to comply from friends, the law, news media, and other institutions in my ethical ecology.

Localism amounts to three claims:

An existence claim: Ethics requires strong local support to exist and to have moral force.

A 'Justification is local' claim: Justification of principles is local or contextual, never universal and absolute.

A tolerance claim: In a plural world, we should tolerate different ethical systems.

Empirically, localism mistakenly believes that universalism depends on universal consent. Universal consent is too demanding as a criterion for any normative principle. Not even parochial values, such as love of one's country, obtain universal consent within a nation. Universalism is a normative theory about what values people should have, not an empirical theory about what values people do have. It maintains that certain universal principles are so important and based on common human needs that the principles *should* be adopted as the basis for morality. Universal principles are *proposed* as values that reasonable people cannot reject (see Scanlon 1998).[7] Support for such proposals are normative arguments about what principles best suit our ethical purposes.

Anti-cosmopolitans tend to exaggerate the amount of ethical difference in the world, and minimize our use of universals. For example, studies (Christians and Traber 1997, Hanitzsch, Plaisance, and Skewes 2013) have found a significant number of shared values across cultures and media cultures. Our ethical systems are redolent with universal values in three ways: We frequently appeal to universals; universals justify parochial values; and, often, parochial beliefs are local applications of universals. Within cultures, people follow Christianity and its universal principle of love; humanitarians quote Kant's categorical imperative to never treat others as only a means to an end; the golden rule is expressed in universal terms. Public moral reasoning has a universal component. When people argue against the mistreatment of animals or against the bullying of abusive husbands, they use universal principles such as the evil of inflicting pain on sentient creatures and the need for human dignity. Appeals to keep one's promises to colleagues and to not mislead friends are parochial applications of universal principles to keep promises and to tell the truth. It is more plausible to hold that ethical systems contain local *and* universal principles than to maintain that all ethics is local.

The argument against universalism confuses consent with rational justification. People's consent may be based on limited facts, propaganda, or bad logic. Nations can act immorally with the consent of a majority of citizens. Ethics does not rest rationally on consent and conformity. It rests on good moral reasons and informed consent. The objective of universalism is not the unrealistic goal of obtaining the consent of everyone on the planet, no matter how obtained. The goal is to obtain the rational agreement of as many ethically minded people as possible to common principles.

Furthermore, the 'justification is local' claim is questionable. There is no plausible local theory of rational justification. It makes no sense to say: 'Principle A is rationally justified because it fits my way of thinking, but maybe not yours.' Good moral reasons are good reasons to any rational person. The standards of reasoning are universal.

Therefore, localism struggles to formulate itself. It denies universals, but it appears to presume universal principles of reasoning, universal facts about ethics (e.g., it is local), and universal moral principles, such as tolerance for different cultures. If so, what happens to the claim that universals do not exist or have little force? An anti-universalism that presumes universals concedes important points to cosmopolitanism.

The 'global minimum' strategy

Some anti-cosmopolitans make room for moral universals by adopting a 'global minimum' strategy. Minimalists argue that nations owe a minimum of duties of justice to other nations. Anything else is a matter of charity or humanitarianism. A minimalist strategy continues to emphasize parochial values, while allowing for some global duties. Global minimum theories are hybrids of the national and the cosmopolitan, with a heavy weighting on national duties.

Miller is a global minimum theorist. He (Miller 2007, pp. 124–125) distinguishes between nations and states. He defines a nation, culturally, as an intrinsically valuable association of people linked to a particular territory with a distinct public culture of shared values. To be a member of a nation is to have certain rights and duties, as specified earlier.

Miller developed a theory of global justice that recognizes some cosmopolitan principles. He agrees that people everywhere are entitled to 'basic (human) rights' (Shue 1996), such as the right to liberty, security, and subsistence. He (2007, pp. 20–21) then imposes restrictions on what nations are morally required to do to protect these values. He rejects the idea that the goal of global justice is a world where all citizens enjoy the same level of prosperity, resources, or opportunities. He denies that all nations have an equal duty to achieve this goal. For Miller, the duty to ensure basic rights falls, first and foremost, on nations. The international community's role is to 'create the conditions' under which this responsibility can be discharged.

A global minimum strategy may appear to be a happy compromise between strong nationalism and strong cosmopolitanism. However, its attempt to limit rights and duties mainly to the national sphere, and to prioritize national duties, has serious problems.

Recall what was said above. Universals populate our ethical systems, ground many moral beliefs, and are instantiated as parochial moral statements. So we can anticipate problems in drawing a firm conceptual line between local and global values. We can now ask whether basic national values are easily divided from global values. Take, for example, the national duty of coming to the aid of distressed compatriots. This is a parochial expression of the universal duty to aid people in need. The basis for this duty is not (or, not only) a common nationality but a common humanity. Nations, to be consistent, should recognize a global duty to assist distressed foreigners, since the basis for assistance – a common humanity – is the same.

The same 'division' problem arises when we consider fundamental civil and political values, such as the rights and freedoms stated in national constitutions. Surely, in these bedrock national documents, we should find values that are clearly independent of global values. In many cases, we don't. Consider the US Declaration of Independence, a seminal national document if there ever was one. We read Jefferson's high-minded language on the Laws of Nature, God, and the 'self-evident' truth that 'all men are created equal, that they are endowed by their Creator with certain unalienable Rights, that among these are Life, Liberty and the pursuit of Happiness'.[8] This is Enlightenment universalism employed to resist tyranny and to justify rights and freedoms. Given this universalism, it would be inconsistent to say that the rights guaranteed in the US Constitution apply, in principle, only to Americans. Are they not rights that hold for all 'men' created equal?

Consider also the anti-cosmopolitanism of John Rawls.[9] Rawls put forward liberal egalitarian principles of justice in *A Theory of Justice* (1992) and other works. The primary principle is that each person has an equal claim to a fully adequate scheme of basic rights and liberties so long as that scheme is compatible with the same for others. The second 'difference' principle states that inequalities are only justified if they help the least advantaged (Rawls 2003, pp. 291–309). His global minimalism and anti-cosmopolitanism emerge when he discusses international justice in *The Law of Peoples* (1999). He denies that these principles are universal. We should not propose them as principles for all societies. The principles apply to only two kinds of societies (or 'peoples'): liberal democratic societies and decent, non-liberal societies that honor a modicum of rights. The principles do not apply to 'outlaw' states, despotisms, and societies burdened by economic and other problems. Why do they not apply? Rawls says that liberals would intolerantly impose their principles on others if they sought to extend them to quite different societies. It appears that a questionable localism is at work here – ethics is local and justification is contextual. Justice can be liberal, non-liberal, or otherwise. Tolerance is required.[10]

Rawls appears to be inconsistent in limiting his principles to two societies. He does *not* use parochial facts such as a citizen's ethnicity, position in society, or nationality to justify his principles. Quite the reverse. Contracting parties to the principles of justice for society are placed behind a 'veil of ignorance' to screen out parochial facts which could bias reasoning on matters of principle. Rawls identifies principles based on human psychology, human primary goods, and other nonparochial considerations. He says that a liberal conception of justice is based on the development of people's 'moral powers' to form a conception of the good and the just (Rawls 2003, pp. 18–21). But moral powers belong to people as human beings, not as citizens of a certain society. So how can Rawls, consistently and non-arbitrarily, draw a firm line between the local and global suitability of these principles? Shouldn't all humans be able to claim these rights and freedoms, at least in principle? Practically, it may be difficult to see how such principles could be accepted by some societies at this time. But a practical limit does not warrant a theoretical limit, especially if one proposes principles of *international* justice.

Saying that liberal principles of basic justice do not 'apply' to some societies comes perilously close to saying that people in those latter societies do not *have* such rights and duties. It makes rights a continent matter, depending on where someone is born. As Caney (2006, p. 82) writes, one cannot apply 'universalist arguments for citizens and not apply them to foreigners' when the very terms of the arguments (fundamental rights, the moral powers) do not allow a domestic/international split.

A second problem of the minimizing strategy is its treatment of human rights. Minimalists limit substantially the list of human rights. Rawls, for example, provides a relatively short list that includes a right to life (subsistence and security); liberty from slavery, serfdom, and forced occupation; sufficient liberty of conscience, and so on (Rawls 1999, p. 65).

This strategy is theoretically puzzling and practically worrisome. Theoretically, many of these human rights seem to be entailed by the aforementioned principles of justice. Why are these rights universal but not the principles? Also, how can Rawls be so confident that the list can stop with his last named right? Many of the rights he doesn't include appear to be worthy candidates, such as the right to democracy; voting rights for women or blacks; the right to protest low and unjust pay due to ethnicity. Practically, a minimal strategy is worrisome to those who advance human rights. Cosmopolitans (Caney 2006, p. 83) have worried that Rawls' limited list of international rights concedes too much to non-liberal societies and, by appealing to tolerance, it must tolerate the intolerable. These criticisms of Rawls may be too harsh. But the worry about 'missing' rights in minimalist theories is real.

The minimum strategy fails to recognize the close linkages among rights. Some rights entail or are causally linked with other rights. It is difficult to recognize the right to free expression and free association without also recognizing the right to democracy. The general right to subsistence appears to be inseparable from a more specific right to own property. We can debate these linkages, but the idea that rights form a holistic group of values is correct. Global ethics needs a comprehensive, non-minimal package of liberties and rights.

Therefore, our political ethics, especially in a global world, cannot be easily contained within borders. We have reason to be skeptical of attempts to firmly divide local and global values and to recognize only a *few* global principles.

The disanalogy arguments

Many anti-cosmopolitans, minimalist or not, consider the differences between the social and the political structure of the national and global domains to be so significant that they modify or block attempts to apply global ethics to nations. For example, these differences question the extension of existing domestic principles (e.g. of justice) to the global realm. The arguments have the same form: there exists a social or political property in the domestic realm. The property doesn't exist, or does not exist to the required degree, on the global level. There is a morally significant disanalogy between the local and the global. Therefore, parochial ethics (of some variety) is a valid and independent domain of ethics. Some of these arguments are similar to the reasons given for the existence claim of localism.

Anti-cosmopolitans stress three disanalogies: the global level lacks political enforcement, moral cohesiveness, and adequate recognition of special duties to a nation.

On enforcement, anti-cosmopolitans note that coercive governments exist at the national level to enforce ethical and legal principles. No such government exists at the global level. For example, no world government exists, playing a role analogous to national government.

This argument mistakenly assumes that global governance requires a world government. It underestimates the possibilities for global cooperation and presumes that existing trends could not lead eventually to effective international governance of global issues.

To the contrary, at least some level of international governance of global issues has been achieved and can be achieved. The development of an international governance system began some time ago with the creation of the Red Cross, the World Bank, the United Nations, the World Health Organization, and the International Atomic Energy Agency. More recently, the dominance of the all-powerful autonomous nation-state has been challenged by a 'global bazaar' (Malloch-Brown 2011, p. 10) of other political actors. Aside from supra-national political associations, such as the European Community, there are new non-state agents for global reform and cross-border surveillance of global wrongdoing. For example, a world-wide 'development community' of NGOs and other groups, often promoted by celebrities, is now a significant force in global affairs. There are human rights groups, global networks of social movements, and global media development organizations. If these trends continue, the result will be a multi-level system of interlocking agencies committed to the implementation of global goals, such as that described by the United Nation's Millennium Development goals.[11]

The cohesion argument claims that the disanalogy property is moral cohesiveness. The global arena consists of competing nations that do not have a common identity or moral code, unlike the common identity and shared values of citizens in nation-states and cultures. Miller (2007, pp. 12, 17–18), for example, says that national principles of social justice – the distribution of rights, opportunities, and resources among the members of large societies – cannot be extended to the global sphere because the latter lacks common values. What counts as distributive justice (and therefore, social justice) varies from country to country.

The cohesive argument too often portrays nations as unified, ideal moral agents when, in fact, many nations are corrupt and repressive. Also, in a global public sphere, there are forms of social cohesion and political identity other than national identity (Mason 1995, pp. 243–252). Nationalists overstate the dominance of national cohesiveness. For example, in developing countries such as Guatemala, a commitment to the national interest may not be as strong among traditional groups as a commitment to family and ethnic traditions. Public life in many nations is in a constant state of tension between groups with values. Moreover, a strong nationalism ignores the possibility that people can affirm both national and cosmopolitan principles and that they are capable of changing the nature and intensity of their attachments. People can become motivated to work for new principles and new global structures.

Finally, there is the special duties argument: cosmopolitanism can find no adequate place for special (parochial) duties like duties to one's nation (see Caney 2006, pp. 133–135).

Special duties are duties that some people owe to others due to the special nature of their relationship. For example, parents and doctors owe special duties of care to their children and patients, respectively. The special duty idea is used to critique cosmopolitanism. Nationalists claim that national duties are special duties that cannot be overridden by global duties. Borders matter, morally.

The cosmopolitan reply is that nationalists prematurely conclude that there cannot be a globalist evaluative approach that takes national values into account. One plausible approach, which I support, is to acknowledge that national special duties have prima facie ethical weight but that such claims must be carefully qualified, assessed, and restrained by cosmopolitan values. Evaluation is necessary because love of country can be abused by demagogues.

As for qualifications, the first qualification is that citizens only have special duties to their nation if they belong to ethical nations. We are not under a moral duty to serve morally suspect groups, from the mafia to neo-Nazi cells. Citizens have few or no special duties to corrupt nations whose leaders maintain unjust institutions and exploit the weak.

The second qualification is that nationalist or patriotic claims on citizens are best evaluated from a broader, ethical perspective – a globalist perspective. Parochial principles are too local and culture-bound to provide an adequate ethical position from which to judge such claims. For example, we should assess patriotic claims to support our country's intent to go to war by consulting cosmopolitan principles concerning, for example, the moral conditions for just war and a cosmopolitan prohibition on pursuing any form of colonialism.

In sum, the disanalogy arguments are not persuasive as arguments against the possibility of global ethics, or the priority thesis. However, the arguments do remind cosmopolitans that developing a global ethics is going to be more difficult than simply denying parochial values, or dismissing the differences between the domestic and global domains. A global ethics will have to bring the local and global together. Universal principles and governance structures must show tolerance and respect for cultural differences.

The tolerance arguments

Can cosmopolitanism show tolerance and respect? The answer is yes: So long as the ethical beliefs and practices in question do not violate basic universal principles, however we conceive of them. Tolerance and respect must be rationally supported; *earned,* not assumed. Wherever possible, cosmopolitans should show respect for different views, but they must not tolerate the intolerable where the facts of the case are clear.

The superiority of the cosmopolitan approach to tolerance becomes clear when we consider the problems that localism has with ethical variety at home and abroad.

At home, the problem is that localism is usually formulated as if there were only *one* set of ethical beliefs in a culture, or one clearly dominant ethical system. The validity of any principle or ethical system is conformity to this set of values. But what if there are several and conflicting ethical traditions, especially where sub-groups challenge dominant values, such as the inferiority of females. If conformity to a dominant value system defines ethical validity then, by definition, other value systems and attempts at reform within a culture are invalid. They are non-conforming. If the localist attempts to solve this problem by calling for tolerance for all ethical beliefs within a culture, then she undermines her argument for the ethical cohesion of cultures, in contrast to the global arena.

Similarly, localism's tolerance claim for foreign ethical systems is unsatisfactory. The claim is too accommodating if all it says is 'be tolerant of differing practices and norms'. How can we tolerate the subjection of females, the slavery of children, the ethnic cleansing of minorities, or the persecution of religions wherever they occur? We need to ask *who* is demanding respect for their values. Are they tyrants seeking to stay in power? We need to ask *what* beliefs or practices are demanding respect. To decide whether a controversial practice deserves respect requires close evaluation. As with claims of patriotism, a proper evaluation of practices across borders should use a global perspective and global principles.

Even if localists wish to critique some ethical beliefs outside their culture, their theory, as stated here, lacks the conceptual resources to do so. They have no basis for criticism. If ethical beliefs are valid within contexts and cultures, then every ethical system is as valid as every other. It seems that localists, to be consistent, must tolerate the intolerable.

Globalism and media

What has this debate between globalism and localism to do with news media?

First, the tension between globalism and localism exists in news media and media ethics. The debate is to what extent journalists should feel compelled to transcend their original and predominant commitment to localism in media ethics. Historically, journalism has been a parochial practice. Since the origin of modern journalism, journalists and newsrooms have written stories not for a global community but for much smaller groups of readers, from the populace of a city to the citizens of a nation. The entire economic and editorial basis for journalism has been the construction and sale of news to parochial audiences, often from the perspective of these audiences. Journalists were supposed to promote the national interests of their country, cover international events from their national perspective, and to support wars that involved their country. Journalism prioritized the local over the global.

The ethical justification for the priority of the local in journalism was, and remains, similar to the justification for prioritizing the local in ethics in general. Since the interests and values of the local community are considered concrete and 'real', journalists are ethically justified in promoting these interests. The idea of journalists serving humanity at large seems abstract and secondary. For this reason, the first explicit codes of ethics for journalism in the late 1800s and early 1900s were parochial codes. The meaning of serving the public was that of serving the local public.[12]

What is the general counter-argument for prioritizing the global in journalism ethics?

The argument can be summarized in one short sentence: Global power entails global responsibilities. It is therefore appropriate to ask about the ethics of global media, and to what extent it differs from the previous ethics of a non-global media rooted in individual nations and regions of the world. Of primary importance is the fact that our media-connected world brings together a plurality of different religions, traditions, ethnic groups, values, and organizations with varying political agendas, social ideals, and conceptions of the good. Media content deemed offensive by certain groups can spark not just domestic unrest but global tension. As happened with the publication of the cartoons of Mohammed by a Danish newspaper in 2005, news media (and other media) can spark cultural tensions and violence that ripples across borders. In such a climate, the role of media, and its ethics, must be re-examined.

A globally minded media are of great value because a biased and parochial media can wreak havoc in a tightly linked global world. Unless reported properly, North American readers may fail to understand the causes of violence in the Middle East or of a drought in Africa. Jingoistic reports can portray the inhabitants of other regions of the world as a threat. Reports may incite ethnic groups to attack each other. In times of insecurity, a narrow-minded, patriotic news media can amplify the views of leaders who stampede populations into war or the removal of civil rights for minorities. We need a cosmopolitan media that report issues in a way that reflects this global plurality of views and helps groups understand each other better. We need globally responsible media to help citizens understand the daunting global problems of poverty, environmental degradation, and political instability.

Therefore, globalization of media implies the development of a global media ethics. Global media ethics seeks to articulate and critique the responsibilities of a news media that is now global in content, reach, and impact. It is the project of developing aims, principles, and norms of practice specifically formulated for a global, media-linked world.

The prioritizing of global values in news media does not eliminate the consideration of local values. The issue is one of prioritizing human rights and other cosmopolitan values where they conflict with local interests. If a developed country's war against a developing country is to gain economic control over the latter's oil resources while violating the human rights of its citizens, then globalism obligates all journalists to report this violation of global values – including journalists from the developed country. If a country develops a mining project that contributes substantially to pollution worldwide, local media have an obligation, according to globalism, to critique the project from this wider perspective and not simply report on the project's local benefits such as new jobs. If the world gathers to create a new agreement to address climate change, globalism implies that journalists will not simply report the meeting and the proposed agreement in local terms – the benefits or costs of the agreement for the citizens of their country. They will, if they are globalists, transcend their parochial conception of journalism and report on the meeting from varying perspectives. They will not dismiss the positions of other countries that are critical of their own country's position. In the area of transnational issues, globalism is an especially important approach for journalism.

What globalism means for media ethics is being worked out by scholars and ethicists in a growing number of publications. In Ward (2013), for example, over 20 authors put forward concrete suggestions on what it would mean if journalists adopted a global attitude in their work. The authors called for, among other things, a new 'cosmopolitan empathy' among the press in covering disasters. Also, foreign reporters covering conflict should adopt a stance of responsible engagement in a global world that leaves behind an older commitment to 'straight' objective reporting.

Therefore, a global media ethics is being constructed according to the globalism defended in this chapter, a globalism that seeks to incorporate local values into a globally minded journalism.

Conclusion

In this chapter, I provided philosophical support for the moral priority of global and cosmopolitan approaches to ethics. I help to clear a path for global ethics by challenging unwarranted skepticism and identifying flawed objections.

Securing the priority thesis is only one part of global ethics. We need to do much more, such as creating models for reasoning about parochial claims and exploring the implications of this research for global media ethics.

I have put forward models for incorporating the parochial values of patriotism in ethics and in journalism ethics. I have argued (Ward 2010) for a universalism that takes account of patriotic claims if such claims are moderate, open to public scrutiny, and consistent with cosmopolitan principles. This approach could be part of a method for incorporating other parochial values into global ethics.

Also, I have argued that the philosophical quarrel between globalism and localism is an important debate within media ethics, and that the future construct of a more viable media ethic depends on prioritizing the global in our ethical reflections and principles.

The development of these ideas is an important future work for global scholars and ethicists. Global ethics, and global media ethics, is a work in progress. Much rests on our species' ability to construct and follow a global ethics in general and in media practice.

Notes

1. In Ward (2010), I argued directly and positively for cosmopolitanism in general, and for cosmopolitan media ethics.
2. For a full account, see Ward (2010).
3. I add the qualifier 'usually trump' to acknowledge that normative forms of parochialism and non-parochialism can allow exceptions to the primacy of their values in special situations.
4. On intervention issues, see Stewart and Knaus (2011).
5. On this distinction, see Beitz (1994, pp. 124–125) and Pogge (1994, p. 90).
6. For discussions of these claims, see Caney (2006) and Shapcott (2010).
7. See also Ward (2010, pp. 173–180), where I describe basic principles as proposals.
8. See the Declaration at http://www.archives.gov/exhibits/charters/declaration_transcript.html
9. For a good discussion of Rawls' minimalism, see Caney (2006, pp. 78–85).
10. There may be other reasons such as Rawls' political liberalism, which seeks a theory of justice that is not dependent on substantive principles of what is good or right.
11. See http://www.un.org/millenniumgoals
12. On the history of journalism codes and their parochial basis, see Ward (2005).

References

Beitz, Charles. 1994. 'Cosmopolitan Liberalism and the States System', in Chris Brown (ed.), *Political Restructuring in Europe: Ethical Perspectives*, pp. 124–125. London, UK: Routledge.

Caney, Simon. 2006. *Justice Beyond Borders: A Global Political Theory*. Oxford, UK: Oxford University Press.

Christians, Clifford and Michael, Traber. 1997. *Communication Ethics and Universal Values*. Thousand Oaks, CA: Sage.

Christians, Clifford G. and Stephen J. A. Ward. 2013. 'Anthropological Realism for Global Media Ethics', in Nick Couldry and Amit Pinchevski (eds.), *Ethics of Media*, pp. 72–88. Houndmills, UK: Palgrave Macmillan.

Derrida, Jacques. 2000. *Of Hospitality: Anne Dufourmantelle Invites Jacques Derrida to Respond*. Trans. Rachel Bowlby. Stanford, CA: Stanford University Press.

——. 2001. *On Cosmopolitanism and Forgiveness*. Trans. Mark Dooley and Michael Hughes. London, UK: Routledge.

Gert, Bernard. 2004. *Common Morality*. Oxford, UK: Oxford University Press.

Hanitzsch, Thomas, Patrick Lee Plaisance, and Elizabeth A. Skewes. 2013. 'Universals and Differences in Global Journalism Ethics', in Stephen J. A. Ward (ed.), *Global Media Ethics: Problems and Perspectives*, pp. 30–49. Malden, MA: Wiley-Blackwell.

Malloch-Brown, Mark. 2011. *The Unfinished Global Revolution*. Toronto, ON: Penguin.

Mason, Andrew. 1995. 'The State, National Identity and Distributive Justice', *New Community*, 21/2: 241–254.

Miller, David. 2007. *National Responsibilities and Global Justice*. Oxford, UK: Oxford University Press.

Nussbaum, Martha C. 1996. 'Patriotism and Cosmopolitanism', in Joshua Cohen (ed.), *For Love of Country: Debating the Limits of Patriotism: Martha C. Nussbaum with Respondents*, pp. 3–17. Boston, MA: Beacon Press.

Pogge, Thomas. 1994. 'Cosmopolitanism and Sovereignty', in Chris Brown (ed.), *Political Restructuring in Europe: Ethical Perspectives*, pp. 89–122. London, UK: Routledge.

Rawls, John. 1992. *A Theory of Justice*. Oxford, UK: Oxford University Press.

——. 1999. *The Law of Peoples with 'The Idea of Public Reason Revisited'*. Cambridge, MA: Harvard University Press.

——. 2003. *Justice as Fairness: A Restatement*. Cambridge, MA: Harvard University Press.

Scanlon, Thomas M. 1998. *What We Owe Each Other*. Cambridge, MA: Harvard University Press.

Shapcott, Richard. 2010. *International Ethics: A Critical Introduction*. Cambridge, UK: Polity Press.

Shue, Henry. 1996. *Basic Rights: Subsistence, Affluence, and U. S. Foreign Policy*. 2nd edition Princeton, NJ: Princeton University Press.

Singer, Peter. 1972. 'Famine, Affluence, and Morality', *Philosophy and Public Affairs*, 1(3): 229–243.

Stewart, Rory and Gerald Knaus. 2011. *Can Intervention Work?* New York, NY: Norton.

Tamir, Yael. 1993. *Liberal Nationalism*. Princeton, NJ: Princeton University Press.

Ward, Stephen J. A. 2005. *The Invention of Journalism Ethics: The Path to Objectivity and Beyond*. Montreal, QC: McGill-Queen's University Press.

——. 2010. *Global Journalism Ethics*. Montreal, QC: McGill-Queen's University Press.

Wiredu, Kwasi. 1996. *Cultural Universals and Particulars: An African Perspective*. Bloomington, IN: Indiana University Press.

3
Global Justice and Civil Society

Clifford G. Christians

Justice means giving everyone in society their appropriate due. Retributive and distributive justice in procedural terms are the standard framework for elaborating that definition. For the ethics of social justice to work productively in an international context, the meaning of justice must be given a different conceptual formulation and fundamentally new orientation than the way that retributive and distributive justice have been conceived up until now. The news media ought to base their rationale and mission on this alternative understanding of justice.

V. I. Lenin is correct about cultural transformation: Without a revolutionary theory, there is no revolutionary movement. There are multiple explanations of the news media's failure to see the faces and hear the voices of those who are wronged. We typically loathe the perpetrators of injustice and often we are overwhelmed by the magnitude of injustice. But the long-standing structures and practice of the liberal press may prevent us 'from acknowledging those that come before us bearing a claim upon us' of what is their due (Wolterstorff 2008, p. 1).

When justice is grounded in the inherent dignity of the human species, the ethics of justice shifts from the political domain to civil society. Civil society is where restorative justice is experienced most deeply and known in the vernacular. The extensive work on civil society in Latin America, the Middle East, China, in young democracies, and more established democracies like India indicates that transnational collaboration on justice has the greatest possibilities in this domain. India's version originated with the Gandhian tradition of volunteerism, and it illustrates many forms of activism for social justice. Reporters who take civil society seriously will come to understand the meaning and practice of restorative justice, to the same extent as the press' preoccupation with the law-and-order system has oriented it to procedural justice.

Justice as right order

The conception of justice as right order has dominated the Western intellectual tradition. Justice is present when members of a society receive from its institutions the goods to which they have a right. When Union Carbide's chemical plant in Bhopal, India, spewed poisonous fumes into the air, it deprived the residents of the valley of a good to which they had a right, namely the good of having non-noxious air to breathe. The residents were wronged; they were treated unjustly (Wolterstorff 2008, p. 25).[1]

Plato's version of justice, developed principally in the *Republic*, is a right-order account. Plato delineated a social order that is 'founded and built up on the right lines, and is good in the complete sense of the word' (121; 427e). He takes it as obvious that such a social order will exhibit justice. The social order is structured by differentiated roles (economic roles, defense roles, and governance roles in particular). To occupy one of these roles is to enter a structure of required ways of treating and of being treated by others. In a social order 'built up on the right lines' everybody will be doing their 'proper work' (139; 441d), performing their 'proper function' (140; 441e). What makes a social order just is that it measures up to the objective norms understood by Plato as the Forms.

In a just society there will be rights conferred on members of the social order by the legislation, the social practices, and the speech acts of human beings. For the right-order theorist, every right is conferred by institutions. This juristic understanding of rights became 'part of the medieval *jus commune*, the common law of Europe, that would in turn inform the polemical works of William of Ockham and the writings of early modern philosophers and theologians – figures as diverse and seminal in their own right as John Locke and John Calvin' (Reid 1991, pp. 39–40).

Justice as right order in democratic liberalism is typically procedural. Procedural justice requires due process and by definition concerns the fairness of decisions and administrative mechanics. Principles and procedures for justice are the outcome of rational choice. When rights and resources are distributed, and appropriate steps are taken to rectify wrong, justice is done. Rawls' *Theory of Justice* has dominated the formal terms and categories of procedural justice in Western democracies since its publication in 1971. While distinguishing three versions of procedural justice himself (perfect, imperfect, and pure), the pure model has gained the greatest traction (what constitutes a just outcome is the procedure itself). For the principles of justice to be fair, they must be developed in a situation that is itself fair. Lebacqz says, 'Justice applies not to the outcome, but to the system' (1986, p. 39). Rawls' method derives principles of justice without asserting any goal or making justice dependent on that goal. For Rawls' democratic liberalism, and for the mainstream media who presume it, humans are considered free, rational, and equal.

Michael Sandel (1998) challenges the individualistic biases of Rawls' theory. He disputes Rawls' theory of justice as depending on an 'unsubstantiated notion of the choosing self' (Lebacqz 1986, p. 41). For Rawls, there are not overriding ends that direct the choices made. The self becomes invulnerable – it is not changed by its experiences, nor by its cooperation with others. This limited view of the self does not account for important aspects of community and self-knowledge.

Sandel's argument can be summarized this way: In Rawls' procedural democracy, the process of fairness has priority over a conception of the common good. But we can accept such a priority only by presuming that individual identities can be established in isolation from history and culture. Liberal political theory supposes that people are distinct from their ends. Our selves are understood to be constituted antecedently, that is, in advance of our engagement with others. But, Sandel asks, 'who is the shadowy "person" that exists independently of, and able freely to choose, the ends that give her life meaning and value?' As Sandel says, we typically see ourselves 'as members of this family or community or nation or people, as bearers of this history, as sons or daughters of that revolution, as citizens of this republic' (1998, p. 179). Such social attachments are involuntary and rational choice has played no role. Some dimensions of justice are based not on agreements but on 'enduring attachments and commitments which taken together partly define the person I am. To imagine a person incapable of constitutive attachments' is to describe someone 'of no moral depth' (p. 179). Our moral obligations are not invented by individuals, but they are located within the social worlds that we enter and within which we live. The liberal concept of persons who invent their own conceptions of the good does not square with our actual moral experience. Contrary to the Lockean (1894/1690) dualism between individuals and society, we know ourselves primarily as whole beings in relation.[2]

Habermas' *Moralbewusstsein und Kommunikatives Handeln* (1990) develops a procedural model of community discourse. Justification of community interests 'is tied to reasoned agreement among those subject to the norms in question' (1990, p. viii). The overriding issue is whether a community's linguistic forms reflect the moral consciousness of its members. Competing normative claims can be fairly adjudicated in the public sphere under ideal speech conditions such as reciprocity and openness. He doesn't take for granted a liberal democratic political philosophy, but he argues that moral consciousness must be nurtured under the social and technocratic conditions that stifle autonomous action in the public arena.

Nancy Fraser's view (1992, 1997) – that Habermas' public sphere is not deeply holistic, gender inclusive, or culturally constituted – is well known. Foucault's (1984) critique centers on Habermas' right-order proceduralism. Foucault questions the very existence of autonomous citizens who are said to engage in rational discourse. Self-reflexivity is impossible for Foucault without emancipation from the prevailing regime of oppressive practices. From his perspective, we ought to struggle against the economic and ideological state violence that constitute us as moral subjects.

Regarding international justice, Rawls and Habermas present a liberal right-order theory of justice, though with different emphases. They agree that national sovereignty must be limited by respect for universal human rights and that differing peoples must be allowed to interpret these rights according to their own political traditions.

In his essay, *The Law of Peoples* (1999), Rawls argues for mutual respect and 'common sympathies' for human rights, just war principles, and economic assistance to burdened nations. But these transnational conceptions are to be organized around territorial states. Rawls speaks here for news professionals who frame their stories about international justice and injustice in these terms.

In *The Inclusion of the Other* (1998) and *The Postnational Constellation* (1998), Habermas, like Rawls, insists that rights are empty, apart from their unique constitutional venues. While noting the positive role played by nationalism in struggles for liberation and democracy, he recognizes that nationality today has all too often justified illiberal forms of nationalism that suppress dissident minority groups and other sub-nationalities. While advocating the idea that nations represent stable units of collective agency, he concedes that this stability is being discredited by the multicultural migrations set in motion by globalization.

As Allen Buchanan (2000) observes, Rawls overestimates the extent to which states are 'economically self-sufficient' and 'distributionally autonomous', while at the same time idealizing the degree to which they are 'politically homogeneous' without internal political divisions.

Habermas, by contrast, tends to view international justice as an extension of domestic justice, whereby relationships of mutual dependency presume something like a basic structure requiring rectification vis-à-vis principles of distributive justice.

Martha Nussbaum (2006) agrees that theories of justice should be abstract. They need the power of generality that enables them to reach beyond political conflicts. But right-order theories of justice in the Western tradition cannot solve 'today's urgent problem of extending justice to all world citizens.... Because all the major Western theories of social justice begin from the nation-state as their basic unit, new theoretical structures' are required 'to think well about this problem' (2006, p. 2). The 'old theoretical structures' cannot merely be applied to the new global situation (2006, p. 4). 'Economic and political developments have begun to reposition the nation as the basic ingredient of international politics', and the news media facing transnational conflicts and diasporic communities are being reoriented 'in relation to the state and national identity' (Kunelius 2009, p.139).

Wendy Willems (University of the Witwatersrand) calls for a new perspective in African terms:

> Since media studies began in the 1970s, its object of study has changed in fundamental ways. Media were at first conceptualized almost wholly within the frame of the nation-state, its policies and culture. The bulk of academic research on media and communication in Africa has studied media through the lens of media–state relations, hereby adopting liberal democracy as the normative idea and focusing on the potential contribution of African media to development and democratization. This approach has insufficiently looked at the actual role of media in African societies. Instead of understanding media on the continent in its own social terms, scholars have often produced ahistorical accounts that posture as negative imprints of Western models of media–state relations.
>
> (Call for Papers, 'Beyond Normative Approaches', 04/10/2011)

Sonia Livingstone (2012) rightly accuses the field of 'methodological nationalism' instead of the mapping of transnational flows. 'The field of media and communication – its phenomena, questions, and concerns – is focused on clearly demarcated, tradition-bound, institutionally-integrated countries widely recognized and referred to by their self-identified publics, media and culture' (2012, p. 416). 'In an age of globalization the nation-state is no longer the automatic starting point for comparative research, for media and communications flow within and across nations' (2012, p. 420). 'In political terms, cross-national research is critiqued for inadvertently privileging the dominant norm over the norms of others' (2010, p. 422).

Though justice as right order has dominated the West and is the standard formulation in the media, a different definition is necessary for working out a credible global justice as the standard for the international news media today. Theories of justice of the right order kind have generally centered on advanced, industrial democracies. Working on justice in terms that include young and developing democracies, and authoritarian systems also, moves the press and the world's citizens away from the right-order formulation.

Philosophical anthropology and justice

Philosophical anthropology centers on the nature of the human, on what are the necessary and sufficient conditions of being a member of the human species. This domain of philosophy concerns the nature of our humanness. It deals with the characteristics that are both common and unique to human beings as such (Ricoeur 1967).

Philosophical anthropology points us in a different direction. It critiques the definition of the human that right order presumes and sees primary justice as inherent in our humanness. Rights are not conferred and maintained as entities of a particular sort, but are inherent.

On account of possessing certain properties, all humans have worth. And that worth is sufficient for having rights we are owed. There does not have to be something else that confers those rights (Wolterstorff 2008, p. 36). On account of a person's worth, someone comes into my presence bearing claims against me. Receiving one's due arises from one's intrinsic worth; it is not a privilege for which one has gratitude. The universal generalization that torture of humans is unjust arises from humanity's intrinsic value, not because right order has been established in criminal law. On account of our worthiness, every human being is under obligation not to torture any human being (Wolterstorff 2008, p. 37). Intrinsic worth is ontologically prior to mechanisms of conferral.

Augustine

A prominent example of primary justice as inherent in our humanity is Augustine (354–430). For him, the public order of just transactions is impossible unless there is 'the right order within people themselves'

(*City of God*, XIX, 4, B.A. 37–68). Justice begins within. Augustine emphasizes intrinsic worth as preliminary to social order. If there is no order within human beings per se, 'then there is certainly no justice in an assembly made up of such members. As a result, there is a lacking... of people whose commonweal is a commonwealth' (*City of God*, XIX. 21, pp. 138–145). He rescued justice from identification with the law or *jus* of the nation-state and thereby released citizens from slavish subordination to the state. Above the state and its laws there is an absolute to which rulers and citizens cannot rightly be opposed. Hence no citizen need obey an unjust law.

Social justice helps to realize in each person the specific perfection of his or her humanity. Therefore, social justice is first and foremost a matter of loving one another, with love the motivation to give to others what is their due. In the *Confessions* (X.6–7 and XI.8), Augustine perceived justice as God's giving to all creatures what they are owed as beings. Justice is not juridical – the result of a common acknowledgment of rights and duties or the result of common interests – but the expression of people's love for God as God ought to be loved, and of people's love for their neighbor as they love themselves.

Love is what drives our efforts for justice. In Augustine's view, to be human is to love. We are born into and destined to love. It is our nature to love. We can choose what to love; we cannot choose whether to love. Compassionate joy over the moral and religious excellence of one's fellow human beings and compassionate grief over their turpitude is what Augustine urges. 'Although a man who is sorry for the sufferings of others deserves praise for his charity, nevertheless, if his pity is genuine, he would prefer that there should be no cause for his sorrow.... Sorrow may therefore be commendable but never desirable' (*Confessions*, III.2). When we love our neighbors as we love ourselves, we treat them according to their intrinsic worth and, thereby, justice is done.

When evil befalls our neighbors, 'a burning sorrow' then 'afflicts our hearts' (*City of God*, XIX.8). It is an anthropology different from the Stoics. The emphasis of the Stoics was on the intellectual side of the self; Augustine's emphasis was on the affective side. 'Some of the Stoics, with a vanity as monstrous as it is rare, are so entranced by their own self-restraint that they are not stirred or excited or swayed or influenced by any emotions at all. A thing is not right merely because it is harsh, nor is stolidity the same thing as health' (*City of God* XIV.9).

In *Upheavals of Thought* (2001), Martha Nussbaum interprets Augustine as a 'major philosophical achievement and a decisive progress beyond the Platonic accounts, because it situates ascent within humanity and renounces the wish to depart from our human condition' (2001, p. 547). She introduces Augustine's thought this way: In Augustine's love, space has been reopened 'within which fear, and anxiety, and grief and intense delight, and even anger, all have their full force. And correct love promises no departure from these other emotions – if anything, it requires their intensification' (2001, p. 530). For Nussbaum, in Augustine's working out a justice that is restorative, he restores compassion along with other emotions to a place of centrality (2001).

Hannah Arendt

Hannah Arendt (1906–1975), under the philosopher Karl Jaspers, wrote her PhD dissertation on the concept of love in Augustine: *Love and Saint Augustine* (1929/1996). *Caritas* is given various definitions, following Augustine, but caring as love for neighbor receives the premier emphasis. This version of *caritas* grounds human love in our common descent from Adam. The reason that we should love our neighbors is that we are fundamentally equal and share a common past. Loving action is tied to 'beginning', to the human ability to start something new in the world – in Augustine's terms, the creative capacity humans share and need to exercise for love to have an existential context (*City of God*, XII.20).

Arendt's *The Human Condition* is premised on a fierce love of the world. This neighbor-love is a property of social life, distinguishing it from the political. Labor, for example, is in the realm of the social, that is, in associational life which is prepolitical. Human social life is found in all societies, since the social is a dimension of human nature, but the political domain is constructed later and only by some societies. Freedom is opposed not to authority or coercion but to biological necessity. Where justice is done so that relationships are non-hierarchical, members of the public are also non-homogenous: 'All are the same in such a way that nobody is ever the same as anyone else who ever lived, lives, or will live' (Arendt 1958, p. 8).

Arendt insisted that the political should be blocked off from the *vita activa*, the maintenance of biological life for the survival of the species. 'The common world is what we enter when we are born and what we leave behind when we die. It transcends our life-span into past and future alike; it was there before we came and will outlast our brief sojourn in it. It is what we have in common not only with those who live with us, but also with those who were here before and with those who will come after us' (Arendt 1958, p. 55). Arendt borrowed the concept of 'world' from Martin Heidegger, though her understanding of it as the life on earth given to the human species is not identical to his.

Many reviewers of Arendt's work have criticized her distinction between the political and the social, and the exclusion of the latter from the former. But in maintaining the distinction, Arendt allows for a company of people who enjoy public happiness and freedom. She thereby emphasized the role of cultural factors as well as the importance of economic independence. Only when associated with one another by approval, agreement, and respect is public happiness possible. A friendship-based company, where all are given what they are owed, is the necessary condition for the rise of a political domain of diverse and independent equals. In helping journalists rethink justice, Arendt's *The Human Condition* is a valuable resource. Augustine may be remote for media professionals, but Arendt's socio-political orientation provides a familiar background for understanding the restorative justice most appropriate cross-culturally.

Contemporary notations

Ronald Dworkin in *Justice for Hedgehogs* (2010) establishes the justice-as-inherent argument in contemporary terms. What truth is, what life means and morality requires, and what justice demands are different aspects of the same large question. Human values in all their forms are unified around one big idea: dignity. Confusion and disarray in human life and cognition do not define the species; this one all-encompassing value attaches to all things on earth. Dignity is the centrifugal human nerve, the value that controls all values.[3] Thus some things are morally right and other things are morally wrong. How you live your life and construct a political state depends on this one norm of human existence.

Dworkin in *Justice for Hedgehogs* does not focus on his usual legal and political philosophy, but instead he focuses on the larger philosophical defense of the unity of value and the possibility that people come to know ethical truth. Rather than base ethical truths on metaphysics as referring to things out there, ethics is its own self-contained form of truth. In living the good life, dignity is indivisible. We expand to others the realization of one's own dignity. In the self-respect of taking my own life seriously, we define and circumscribe the decent behavior we owe to others. People have an ethical duty to themselves to live well and meaningfully, and simultaneously a duty owed to others.

Christian Smith's *What Is a Person?* (2011) argues against reductionist theories of human personhood and agency. 'What is a person' is the fundamental question of philosophical anthropology, but for Smith it ought also to be the social scientist's starting point. To interpret and explain social life scientifically requires a social theory that does justice to the humanistic vision of people and society. A theory of personhood centered on intrinsic human worth opens a pathway between the extremes of positivism and relativism and serves as a model for working with the concept of justice in a global society.

Primary justice and civil society

Primary justice belongs first of all to civil society. Civil society is the human domain outside government and business, at least relatively free from the political and commercial. Our customs, values, and life's meaning are learned and negotiated in the civil society of home, schools, religion, neighborhoods, voluntary associations, charities, civic groups such as a Residents' Welfare Association, and NGOs. Humans are moral beings, so civil society is a moral order. It is here where morality is nurtured and the home of justice as intrinsic worth receives its understanding and application. *Arche* in Greek is the appropriate term – *arche* meaning 'beginning' and simultaneously 'direction'. Civil society is where primary justice is experienced and known, and where justice gives us ongoing orientation to the world. For journalists who are preoccupied with the procedural justice of the courts, law enforcement, and imprisonment, the challenge is to immerse themselves in the theory and practice of civil society, where restorative justice is primary.

The pivotal historical figure in developing the concept of civil society was G. W. F. Hegel. In the early 19th century, in his *Philosophy of Right* he identified self-supporting citizens with their own centers of gravity as entities distinct from the political state (Reidel 1984). Charles Taylor (1992) puts Hegel's notion in the context of other political theorists, principally Locke and Montesquieu. For Kaviraj and Khilnani, Hegel is the basis of contemporary understandings of civil society (2001, p. 23), while they remind us that it is an old term entered into the English language via the Latin *societas civilis*. In addition, their comprehensive review locates other traditions besides the German strand running from Hegel, such as those of the Scottish and French Enlightenments (2001, chs. 4–5). Kaviraj and Khilnani also describe how intellectuals in various non-Western countries are 'infusing new and complex life' (2001, p. 12) into the concept – in India, Latin America, the Middle East, China, and Southeast Asia (2001, chs. 8–14).

When the press reconceives the notion of justice as inherent to our humanity and nurtured first and foremost in civil society, it gives priority to the facilitative role of the press rather than the monitorial one. The media facilitate civil society. They actively support and strengthen democratic participation in neighborhoods, churches, and organizations outside the state and market. This is a normative claim, in that the media do not simply report on civil society's activities and institutions but seek to enrich and improve them. In the process, the media are accountable to the widely shared moral frameworks that orient the civil society in which they operate and are given meaning.

The media reflect the political order in which they are situated, and the logic and rationale for their facilitating public life are primarily that of civic democracy. In this perspective, only within active communities do we discover goods together that we cannot know alone. Public opinion arises from deliberation and is not antecedent to it. Rather than an aggregation of personal preferences generated by the innermost self, public opinion on social justice is collective wisdom based on open debate. Citizens are taken seriously in clarifying and resolving public problems. Civic democracy understands civil society as constituted by interaction, and therefore public communication cultivates shared interests and common goals.

India

Civil society is a well-known concept in Indian media and everyday life, originating with the Ghandian tradition of volunteerism (Mukherjee 2001). 'Though the term NGO became popular in India only in the 1980s, the voluntary sector has an older tradition. Since independence from the British in 1947, the voluntary sector has had a lot of respect in the minds of people – first, because the father of the nation Mahatma Gandhi was an active participant, and second because India has always had the tradition of honoring those who have made some sacrifice to help others' (Chatterjee 2001, p. 23). Samuel Gregg of the Acton Institute calls these intermediary associations 'little platoons' that mobilize people without subsuming them into the state and that have 'the capacity to assist people to look toward the higher ends of truth, beauty, and the good' (*IndiaRealTime* 2011).

The primary role played by voluntary organizations, upon India's independence, was to fill in the gaps left by the government. 'Volunteers organized handloom weavers in villages to form cooperatives through which they could market their products directly to the cities. Similar cooperatives were set up to market diary products and fish' (Chatterjee 2001, p. 23).

In the 1980s, the voluntary movement largely turned into specialty groups known as non-governmental organizations (NGOs). Committed to development, various NGOs began running literacy programs in the villages. They encouraged farmers to experiment with crops and developed clinics for children. Typically, the NGO staff became a part of the community where they worked and promoted projects left out of government policy and action. 'There are many examples of voluntary organizations of this kind running very successfully in India for the last five decades. Perhaps the most celebrated example would be the treatment center for leprosy patients run by Baba Amte in central India' (Chatterjee 2001, p. 23).

The gaps left by the government in a huge country like India are 'sometimes by intention, sometimes due to lack of funds, sometimes due to lack of awareness' (Chatterjee 2001, p. 24). Some NGOs may work

> in areas that the government does not want to get into – like fighting discrimination based on caste. Most Indian politicians do not really want to upset the existing caste hierarchy in his or her constituency, because the politician depends for votes on the dominant castes of that particular constituency. In the process, laws prohibiting discrimination on the basis of caste are often ignored unless there is an NGO working in that area that is willing to take up the cause of those being discriminated against.
>
> (Chatterjee 2001, p. 24)

Healthcare is one area where NGOs play an important role in India's civil society. In addition to supplementing government efforts by providing health clinics, NGOs raise awareness of injustices like child malnutrition. Injustices such as the neglect of female children – even their feticide or infanticide – are no longer unnoticed or ignored.

The Center for Human Rights and Development (CHRD) is a non-profit organization based in Delhi. It pays special attention to human rights violations in marginalized communities, such as Dalit, Adivasis, and Muslim. Authoritarian religious brutality has caused the deaths of thousands in recent years. In CHRD's focus on marginalized communities where injustice is not attended to politically, CHRD not only raises awareness but assists on-the-ground action projects, develops networks of solidarity, and provides publicity of particular cases to the news media. The Dalit movement and the women's movement are examples of marginalized groups getting empowered on behalf of justice as human worth.

The history of South Asian civil society strongly underscores its active role in the region's struggle for social justice. Civil society has been successful in fulfilling its role; but, as the news has made clear, 'the continuing feudal character of South Asian states, polity, and society also reflects the limitations of civil society in the region. Similarly, in spite of the role of civil society – of engaging society with a trans-formative agenda – it has experienced serious limitation due to the state-centric social and political discourse of these countries' (Behar 2009). The challenge for the media is to enable their readers and audience to re-imagine civil society, to keep the idea vital and productive in the face of unprecedented changes in the region across society, polity, and the economy.[4]

Conclusion

Justice as right order is the mainstream conception in industrial democ-racies and generally in their media institutions. That definition carries with it the legal and policy agenda of the democratic nation-state and is therefore unacceptable for developing global justice. Being released from the proceduralism of retributive and distributive justice is a necessary first step for the press.

When primary justice is rooted in intrinsic worth, its natural home is civil society. Restorative justice becomes the focus. The criminal jus-tice system charges the accused with having committed a crime against the state; if convicted, the state punishes the criminal. Restorative jus-tice brings back into the picture the breach of the moral relationship between the accused and the victim, and rehabilitation into the social order is the aim. The media around the world can take their cue from those young, transitional democracies where civil society organizations are especially vital. When primary justice and its role in civil society are represented well in the news media, there is the possibility of cross-cultural engagement and understanding regarding humanity's intrinsic worth to which we owe our due.

Notes

1. My formulation in this chapter benefits from Wolterstorff (2008, chs. 1, 2).
2. Sen's similar concepts of justice as procedural and substantive (*nyaya* and *niti*) are elaborated in Shakuntala Rao's chapter following this.
3. In the same sense, the universal sacredness of life is considered a pre-theoretical protonorm (Christians 2010).

4. While illustrating restorative justice through civil society in India, examples can be found around the world. And through them, journalists understand more clearly the role of the press in facilitating restorative justice.

As the truth commissions of Argentina and Chile, and South Africa's Truth and Reconciliation Commission, make clear, commissions 'can be compatible with trials and punishments' (Crocker 2000, p. 104, Hayner 2002). However, their rationale is not criminal justice per se but the morally ambitious goal of providing restorative justice (Rotberg and Thompson 2000). When done with depth and sophistication, while having no power to execute punitive justice, systems of communication institute 'corrective moral justice by putting the record straight' (Villa-Vicencio 2001, p. 36). 'Truth commissions have struggled with basic questions about what justice requires .... Out of these struggles are emerging new vocabularies of truth and justice as well as new institutional repertoire for pursuing them' (Kiss 2000, p. 70).

On April 17, 2008 President Lee Myung-bak of South Korea, on the eve of his summit with President George W. Bush, decided to open the market to American beef – after the government had banned imports of American beef since 2003 when a case of mad cow disease was found in the United States. Lifting the ban mobilized the majority of South Korea's people. Tens of thousands began to hold candlelight vigils in Seoul. These vigils spread to other cities and the number of participants expanded to hundreds of thousands of people. The South Korea government used police force to stop the protestors, but the candlelight vigils continued to take place on a nearly daily basis for more than four months.

The peaceful demonstrations were not organized by organizations with a policy agenda. The vigils were not arranged by Korea's political society, its professional politicians, legal experts, and market strategists. The people were articulating their own values, creating solidarity, and advancing their own sphere outside commerce and the state. Mass demonstrations of civil society have a long history, originating during the rule of the authoritarian military regime. The press' coverage of peaceful protests such as the candlelight vigil are the ongoing means of keeping the idea of restorative justice vital among the citizenry as a whole.

References

Arendt, Hannah. 1996 [1929]. *Love and Saint Augustine.* Edited with an Interpretive Essay by J. S. Scott and J. C. Scott. Chicago: University of Chicago Press.

Arendt, Hannah. 1958. *The Human Condition.* Chicago: University of Chicago Press.

Arendt, Hannah. 1963. *On Revolution.* New York: Viking.

Behar, Amitabh. 2009. *Reimagining Civil Society.* November. http://infochange india.org/agenda/civil-society/re-imagining-civil-society.html

Buchanan, Allen. 2000. 'Rawls's *Law of Peoples:* Rules for a Vanished Westphalian World', *Ethics,* 110(4): 697–721.

Chatterjee, Patralekha. 2001. 'Civil Society in India: A Necessary Corrective in a Representative Democracy', *Development and Cooperation,* November/December: 23–24.

Christians, Clifford. 2010. 'The Ethics of Universal Being', in S. J. A. Ward and H. Wasserman (eds.), *Media Ethics Beyond Borders: A Global Perspective*, pp. 6–23. New York: Routledge.

Christians, Clifford, Theodore Glasser, Denis McQuail, Kaarle Nordenstreng, and Robert White. 2009. *Normative Theories of the Media: Journalism in Democratic Societies*. Urbana: University of Illinois Press.

Crocker, David A. 2000. 'Truth Commissions, Transitional Justice, and Civil Society', in R. J. Rotberg and D. Thompson (eds.), *Truth v. Justice: The Morality of Truth Commissions*, pp. 99–121. Princeton, NJ: Princeton University Press.

Dworkin, Ronald. 2010. *Justice for Hedgehogs*. Cambridge, MA: Harvard University Press.

Foucault, Michel. 1984. 'On the Genealogy of Ethics: An Overview of Work in Progress;' 'Politics and Ethics;' and 'An Interview', in Paul Rabinow (ed.), *The Foucault Reade*, Trans. C. Porter, pp. 340–380. New York: Pantheon.

Fraser, Nancy. 1992. 'Rethinking the Public Sphere: A Contribution to the Critique of Actually Existing Democracy', in Craig Calhoun, (ed.), *Habermas and the Public Sphere*, pp. 109–142. Cambridge, MA: MIT Press.

Fraser, Nancy. 1997. *Justus Interruptus*. New York: Routledge.

Habermas, Jürgen. 1990. *Moral Consciousness and Communicative Action*. Trans. C. Lenhardt and S. W. Nicholsen. Cambridge, MA: MIT Press.

Hayner, Priscilla B. 2002. *Unspeakable Truths: Facing the Challenge of Truth Commissions*. New York: Routledge.

IndiaRealTime. 2011. 'Politics Journal: Who Makes Up India's "Civil Society"?' June 20.

Kaviraj, Sudipta and Sunil Khilnani, (eds.) 2001. *Civil Society: History and Possibilities*. Cambridge, UK: Cambridge University Press.

Kiss, Elizabeth. 2000. 'Moral Ambition within and beyond Political Constraints: Reflections on Restorative Justice', in R. I. Rotberg and D. Thompson (eds.), *Truth v. Justice: The Morality of Truth Commissions*, pp. 68–98. Princeton, NJ: Princeton University Press.

Kunelius, Risto. 2009. 'Lessons of Being Drawn In: On Global Free Speech, Communication Theory and the Mohammed Cartoons', in A. Kierulf and H. Rønning (eds.), *Freedom of Speech Abridged? Cultural, Legal and Philosophical Challenges*, pp. 139–161. Göteborg, Sweden: University of Gothenburg Nordicom.

Lebacqz, Karen. 1986. *Six Theories of Justice: Perspectives from Philosophical and Theological Ethics*. Minneapolis, MN: Augsburg.

Livingstone, Sonia. 2012. 'Challenges to Comparative Research in a Globalizing Media Landscape', in F. Esser and T. Hanitzsch (eds.), *Handbook of Comparative Communication Research*, pp. 415–430. New York: Routledge.

Locke, John. 1894. *Essay Concerning Human Understanding*. Vol. 1. Oxford, UK: Clarendon Press (original publication 1690).

Mukherjee, Asha, S. Sen, and K. Bagchi. 2001. *Civil Society in Indian Cultures: Indian Philosophical Studies*. Council for Research in Values and Philosophy. Washington, DC.

Nussbaum, Martha. 2001. *Upheavals of Thought: The Intelligence of the Emotions*. Cambridge, UK: Cambridge University Press.

Nussbaum, Martha C. 2006. *Frontiers of Justice: Disability, Nationality, Species Membership*. Cambridge, MA: Harvard University Press.

Rawls, John. 1971. *A Theory of Justice*. Revised edition 1999. Cambridge, MA: Harvard University Press.

Reid, Charles J. 1991. 'The Canonistic Contribution of the Western Rights Tradition: An Historical Inquiry', *The Boston College Law Review*, 33:1, pp. 37–92.

Reidel, Manfred. 1984. *Between Tradition and Revolution: The Hegelian Transformation of Political Philosophy*. Cambridge, UK: Cambridge University Press.

Ricoeur, Paul. 1967. 'The Antinomy of Human Reality and the Problem of Philosophical Anthropology', in N. Lawrence and D. O'Connor (eds.), *Readings in Existential Phenomenology*, pp. 390–402. Englewood Cliffs, NJ: Prentice Hall.

Rotberg, Robert and Dennis Thompson, (eds.) 2000. *Truth v. Justice: The Morality of Truth Commissions*. Princeton, NJ: Princeton University Press.

Sandel, Michael J. 1998. *Liberalism and the Limits of Justice*. 2nd edition Cambridge, UK: Cambridge University Press (first edition published 1982).

Smith, Christian. 2011. *What Is a Person? Rethinking Humanity, Social Life, and the Moral Good from the Person Up*. Chicago: University of Chicago Press.

Taylor, Charles. 1992. 'Civil Society in the Western Tradition', in E. Groffier and M. Paradis (eds.), *The Notion of Tolerance in Human Rights*, pp. 117–136. Ottawa: Carleton University Press.

Villa-Vicencio, Charles. 2001. 'Communicating Reconciliation: In Pursuit of Humanity', *Media Development*, 48(4): 31–37.

Wolterstorff, Nicholas. 2008. *Justice: Rights and Wrongs*. Princeton, NJ: Princeton University Press.

4
Social Justice and Citizenship in South Africa: The Media's Role

Herman Wasserman

This chapter will focus on some specific issues pertaining to media ethics, democracy, and citizenship in South Africa. As a postcolonial, 'new' democracy marked by huge socio-economic inequalities, while at the same time emerging as a regional economic growth point, South Africa's struggles to deepen democracy via media may suggest some similarities with other emerging economies, for instance India, one of its partners in the BRICS (Brazil, Russia, India, China, and South Africa) alignment of states. The growing socio-economic inequalities that accompany South Africa's rise as an emerging economy bear resemblance to the double-edged story of 'unprecedented success or extraordinary failure' that can be told about contemporary India (Dreze and Sen 2011) and also characterize countries like Brazil, where contradictions between economic growth and internal inequalities are also stark. Comparisons between India and South Africa have indeed been suggested by scholars working in comparative political studies (e.g. Heller 2009), as well as scholars in the field of 'Indian Ocean Studies' (e.g. Moorthy and Jamal 2009), who studied the socio-cultural exchanges between these two countries and their neighbors in early stages of contemporary globalization. Some research has also been done in comparative media ethics between South Africa and India (see Rao and Wasserman 2007, Wasserman and Rao 2008).

In countries with high inequalities like South Africa and India, it is not uncommon to find a schizophrenic clash of realities presented by the media. The well-known Indian development journalist P. Sainath (2004) has pointed out how the Indian media are quick to tell the 'feel-good' story of India's rise – 'India Shining' – but neglect to tell stories of the struggles of the majority of the country's citizens. As an exemplar, Sainath recalls how hundreds of journalists covered the 2003

International Fashion Week in Mumbai, while stories on farmer suicides, drought, food security, and access to clean drinking water were much harder to find in the Indian media.

Similar patterns of coverage can be noted in the South African media. The demise of the 'alternative' media that under apartheid were funded by donor agencies and provided coverage of grassroots movements meant that the media landscape in the democratic era has become dominated by commercial media that follow market imperatives. The public broadcaster, the South African Broadcasting Corporation (SABC) only derives a small part of its income from government support and license fees, and it is therefore also reliant on advertising and commercial ventures for its sustainability (to boot, the broadcaster has been hampered by serious management issues and claims of government interference in editorial content). The community media, which receive some support from the Media Diversity and Development Agency aimed at providing a counterbalance to the commercial media, often struggle to sustain itself or attract audiences away from the mainstream. Furthermore, the notion of 'development journalism' is often resisted by South African journalists, as this is frequently associated with an uncritical, 'collaborative' (Christians et al. 2009) form of journalism that does not hold government to account. The result is that although South Africa, as a new democracy, needs an inclusive public sphere where vigorous debate about developmental issues can take place, neither is this sphere widely accessible to all South Africans nor can it escape the commercial pressures where investigative journalism often succumbs to funding cuts and entertainment of interest to a suburban elite takes precedence over news that is of relevant to the everyday lives and developmental priorities of the majority of the country's citizens (Friedman 2011).

Perhaps even more importantly, a view on these issues from the perspective of the poor and socially marginalized is largely absent from the news. While some of the topics, like the lack of service delivery, might make it onto the agendas of investigative journalism programmes on the public broadcaster or satellite television (like *Third Degree* or *Carte Blanche*) or onto the pages of 'quality' newspapers like the *Mail* and *Guardian*, very few news reports make use of ethnographic methodologies to allow the voices of those whose everyday lived experience is that of poverty, unemployment, and marginalization to be able to speak for themselves.

There remains a vast distance between the everyday lives of the majority of people in this most unequal country in the world and the ways in which most media represent them. However, South African media can certainly not be understood as a monolith: it spans a range of newspapers, magazines, television, and radio channels, both public and private. The mediated public sphere in South Africa remains fragmented across race and class, and it would be difficult for any media outlet to claim to represent 'the public interest' in any simplistic way. The huge social inequalities and the asymmetrical media attention that issues affecting people in different parts of South Africa receive raise the following question: What ethical response may we expect of the media that operate in this society?

This normative question has been asked frequently and the possible answers to it debated heatedly since the advent of democracy in 1994. The South African media have been a heavily contested terrain, with strong differences of opinion as to what the role of the media should be in a transitional, postcolonial democracy. This chapter will attempt to provide a response to the question as follows: First, the chapter will provide some context with regard to the South African media's position within broader issues of democracy, citizenship, and marginalization. The relation between media and citizenship will form the framework within which media ethics will be examined. I will then proceed to recap and critique some of the salient normative frameworks that have been constructed for the media since the end of apartheid, especially the contrast between 'watchdog' and 'developmental' journalism, before suggesting an alternative ethical framework, that of an 'ethics of listening', within which to think about the media's relationship to citizenship, marginalization, and participation in the post-apartheid society. The question of justice, especially social justice in the South African society which is still scarred by the legacy of apartheid, underpins these discussions.

Media, marginalization, and citizenship in South Africa

Despite the many challenges facing the country, post-apartheid South Africa has emerged as a rising power in the new global figuration of BRICS states. The invitation it received in December 2010 to become part of this group of emerging powers (Seria 2010) underlines its role as an economic leader on the African continent. As a function of its globalized economy, the South African media are technologically sophisticated and well developed in comparison to other African countries. Some of its media houses like Naspers (see company profile at www.naspers.com) have made their mark on the global media landscape, penetrating not only markets elsewhere in Africa but also in countries such as China, India, and Brazil. In a process that has been called the 'interpenetration' of media capital (Tomaselli 2000), South African media have not only been expanding on the continent and globally but also been on the receiving end of foreign investment, for example, by the Irish-based Independent group that now controls a significant share of the South African print media.

The advent of democracy has, therefore, brought about greater freedom for the South African media to operate within a larger global environment. Domestically, it also enjoyed unprecedented freedom, with constitutionally guaranteed rights to freedom of expression. However, since democratization the South African media constantly had to redefine its role, domestically marked by severe class inequalities and competing normative expectations of what the media's role in the new democracy should be (for a discussion of these various normative positions, see Wasserman 2006). A double repositioning has, therefore, been going on in the South African media – a kind of reorientation toward the global media landscape, as well as a rethink of its ethical roles and responsibilities within the country and the paradigms within which journalism is being practiced (cf. Berger 2008).

This normative reorientation has not always gone smoothly. While the South African media escaped the frequent interventions experienced by other transitional countries (Sparks 2011, p. 14), there are increasing signs of pressure from the African National Congress (ANC) government. Most recently, calls for a statutory 'Media Appeals Tribunal' with stronger powers of sanction than the current self-regulatory system, and the drafting of a Protection of Information Bill that would allow for information deemed sensitive to national security to be classified as secret, have been seen as creating an increasingly hostile environment for the media to operate in. (A special issue of *Ecquid Novi: African Journalism Studies*, published in 2011, addressed some of the wide-ranging implications for such a statute.) Central to these debates have been the following questions: How good is the South African media for its democracy (cf. Jacobs 2002) and the participation of all of its citizens in democratic life? What are the ethical responsibilities of the South African media in a country marked by poverty, inequality, and bearing the scars of history of racial and class conflict?

The link between media and citizenship in post-apartheid South Africa is further complicated by the fact that the very notion of citizenship itself is a contested one. While democratization has restored the legal and political rights to citizenship denied to the majority under apartheid, the continued exclusion from economic equality and the realization of social empowerment have resulted in a widespread experience of marginalization from the public sphere (Von Lieres 2005, p. 23). Heller (2009, p. 134), in his comparison of South Africa and India as postcolonial democracies, has pointed out that South Africa has consolidated the formal institutions and processed of its constitutional democracy, but has created very little capacity for its subaltern citizens to shape public policy (2009, p. 134). He characterizes the post-apartheid public sphere as marked by the lobbying of powerful interests on the one hand, using formal channels such as the media in putting issues on the agenda, and by a subaltern majority who have to resort to 'inchoate' local protests in an attempt to make their voices heard. Heller refers to this situation as a 'bifurcation of civil society' (2009, p. 144).

That this bifurcation is racialized should be no surprise given South Africa's history.

Despite attempts at transformation of the media industry, many commentators have remarked on the fact that the changes to the racial composition of newsrooms have changed the way the media look, but not the way they act; that although the majority of mainstream newspaper editors in the country are now black, the extent to which they can effect change is circumscribed by the market model within which they operate. A public war of words between the editor of the Sunday newspaper *City* Press, Ferial Haffajee, and a *Sowetan* columnist, Eric Myeni, underlined how the right to speak in the public sphere often takes on an essentialist character. Myeni accused Haffajee of being a 'black snake in the grass' that practised journalism 'for the white masters' after her paper published an article on how the controversial leader of the ANC Youth League, Julius Malema, acquired his wealth. The view that such criticism represents an assimilation of black editors into a 'white' discourse, in which attacks on government are not balanced by recognition of government's achievements, is a pervasive one (see Mgibisa 2011). Although usually dismissed by journalists as an attempt by government to persuade them to engage in the kind of developmental journalism that holds back on its criticism of government while praising its accomplishments ('sunshine journalism', Kuper and Kuper 2001), the critique does merit closer investigation, as it may suggest a more widespread disillusionment with media's ability to represent broader South African society.

This essentialization of discourse also takes place in the other direction. While black critics of government have been stereotyped as 'coconuts' ('black' on the outside but 'white' on the inside), white critics have also felt excluded from an essentialized African identity that has become the hallmark of the 'authentic' citizen (Chipkin 2007, Mangcu 2008). This framing started already under former President Thabo Mbeki's tenure, with his remarks to journalists that they were 'Africans before they became journalists' (for a discussion, see Wasserman 2005). The double effect of this narrowing of the designation of 'citizen' is that both subaltern South Africans – who are excluded from public debates due to lack of access to media channels or the wherewithal to utilize the institutions like courts in order to enact their citizenship – and elites – who do have the economic power to participate in public debate – find themselves delegitimized on essentialist grounds.

The intersection between media and citizenship in post-apartheid South Africa has to be understood more widely, however, than just the ability to participate in mediated public debates. Access to the media has been the focus of many political economy critiques of the post-apartheid media (e.g., Olorunnisola and Tomaselli 2011). The Habermasian-influenced emphasis on the structural dimensions of transformation such as ownership, staffing, and content tends to neglect the everyday cultural contexts within which media are produced and consumed.

What is needed is a greater understanding of how citizens make meaning from media in everyday life, how media are used – or not used – to guide political decisions, and what part media play in the way citizens negotiate their way through the often precarious social conditions they encounter every day. It will be argued later in this chapter that it is through such a cultural, dialogic understanding of media in everyday life that richer and deeper notions of citizenship and of the ethical imperatives of media in post-apartheid South Africa may emerge.

We can draw a parallel between the structural versus the cultural views of media use and Heller's (2009) distinction between the 'status of citizenship' and the 'practice of citizenship'. Heller points out that while all South Africans have nominally been granted citizenship rights with the establishment of democracy in 1994, they are not always in the position to practice that citizenship in a way that makes an actual difference to their lives. Subaltern citizens have very little capacity to shape public policy and are seen by an increasingly market-oriented state as clients rather than as participants. Instead of deliberation, citizens have to resort to protests (usually framed narrowly by the media as 'social delivery protests' rather than acts of resistance against the very nature of the political dispensation) to be heard momentarily. Heller's emphasis on the lack of practiced citizenship supports Von Lieres' (2005) view that, for the majority of South African citizens, the dominant post-apartheid experience has been one of exclusion from social and economic structures, even as they have nominally been granted political inclusion as rights-bearing citizens. Similarly, it may be said that while the structure of the post-apartheid-mediated public sphere – measured in the number of media outlets and the range of media platforms – has increased markedly as a result of democratization coinciding with glob-alization of the South African media (as described by Tomaselli 2000), this greater pluralism of the media industry does not necessarily imply a commensurate pluralism of perspectives or actual greater engagement by citizens with the media in making meaning of their everyday.

So, despite the technological sophistication of the South African media and the proliferation of channels and platforms, the ability of the media to facilitate greater participation by citizens in the post-apartheid public sphere is not self-evident. The extent to which the South African media's normative frameworks allow it to contribute to 'democratic deepening' (Heller 2009) has therefore been a recurring issue of debate in the 20 years of democracy. Let us briefly look at some of these debates.

Normative frameworks and contestations

In the debates around the ideal role of the media in post-apartheid South Africa, the ethical roles envisaged have frequently been reduced to a dichotomy consisting of the liberal-democratic 'watchdog' or 'Fourth Estate', monitorial paradigm (see Christians, Glasser, McQuail, Nordenstreng, and White 2009) on the one hand, versus a collabora-tive, developmental one on the other, which has mostly been advocated by representatives of government and politicians. The dominant frame-work espoused by the South African media can be said to be the former (for more detailed discussions of these frameworks, see Wasserman 2006, 2010a). While the media have largely derived their dominant frameworks from media systems theory developed in the Global North, counter-arguments for more 'Africanized' ethics have frequently either lapsed into essentialist identity politics (see Wasserman 2005, Banda 2007; Fourie 2008, Tomaselli 2011) or a crude view of developmen-tal journalism that defines it as uncritical toward authority and telling only positive stories about government accomplishments – hence the derogatory reference to 'sunshine' journalism (see Kuper and Kuper 2001).

While significant amounts of energy have gone into the development of a formalist ethical system (Christians 2010, p. 173) of self-regulation, centering around a Press Council and accompanying ethical codes befitting the newly democratic era after apartheid (Kumwenda 2011), these structural rearrangements have not laid to rest the bigger questions about the media's role in post-apartheid society nor the ways in and the extent to which citizens integrate media use into their daily lives in actually existing public spheres.

The result has been a normative impasse with media ethics being seen largely in formalistic terms, as a strategic ritual to protect an increasingly commercialized, corporatist media paradigm on the one hand, and crude political economic critiques and attempts to co-opt an uncritical media into political power projects on the other. In *procedural* terms, South African media ethics post-apartheid have therefore made great strides in setting up systems that facilitate the 'right' rational moral reasoning, but in *substantive* terms there is not yet agreement on what the media's role would be in constituting the 'good life for purposes of human flourishing' (Caldwell 2011, p. 61). The ethics of the relationship between media, citizenship, social justice, and the deepening of democracy have therefore up until now largely been addressed in terms of *procedures*, but there has been less agreement on what the *substantive outcome* of these procedures should be and what the *material effects* of ethical media practice in post-apartheid South Africa should be (Caldwell 2011, p. 61). In other words, what is the ultimate 'good life' that the South African media should contribute toward a society that is so unequal, where political agreements remain precarious and where 'the public interest' is so divergent and fragmented? How should the media conceive of its ethical role to make a difference in people's everyday material existence and not only on the level of abstract and rational debates?

In the post-apartheid era, two main normative views have crystallized. The dominant professional ideology of the post-apartheid media, within a liberal consensus of the media's role as 'Fourth Estate', is that of being a 'watchdog'. Opposing that view is one which may be characterized broadly in terms of Christians et al.'s (2009) notion of the collaborative role, with the media supporting the government's nationalist project and striving toward vaguely articulated goals of indigenization/ 'Africanization'. The post-apartheid brand of watchdog journalism is partly based on normative frameworks of adversarial journalism inherited from the West, but it is also a response to the ANC's dominance of the political landscape, which is perceived to be a threat to the evolution of a multiparty democratic system; the media are therefore seen as a countervailing political force (see Wasserman [2010, 2011b] for a discussion of journalists' professional identities, and Wasserman [2006] for a discussion of normative frameworks). The post-apartheid media therefore can be seen as a political player in its own right (cf. Jacobs 2002). This normative framework of watchdog journalism has led the post-apartheid media to be highly adversarial. Framed in a discourse of serving public interest, the South African media's dominant mode of engagement is that of attack.

This dominant assumption among media professionals that the media should be a vigilant and fierce protector of democracy leads them to view criticism (such as those coming from the ANC) as fundamentally based on a misunderstanding of the media's role in post-apartheid society and its potential to facilitate public participation in democratic processes.

However, those critics that call into question the inherent link between media, democracy, and transformation in the South African media post-1994 are not always acting out an exaggerated sensitivity for the media's exposure of post-apartheid government corruption, lack of service delivery, and defense of the public interest. Citizens for whom social and economic marginalization remain the dominant experience of everyday life in post-apartheid South Africa might not share the media's own sense of its centrality in democratic participation and its contribution to the substantive 'good life'. The media often claim in *procedural* terms as succeeding in its democratic role because they provide the information citizens need to perform their democratic roles and duties, and they serve as a space where citizens can deliberate to form public opinion and influence policy. The claim made most often by the South African media in deflecting attacks from the state or indifference from certain publics is that the media – especially journalism – should be considered as 'synonymous with democracy' (Papacharissi 2009, p. vii). The mainstream South African commercial media 'repeatedly depicts itself as a source of knowledge which is the property of the entire society, and therefore presumably reflects a common social reality' (Friedman 2011, p. 107), while in fact most media platforms (with the exclusion of community media and tabloid newspapers; see Wasserman 2010b) only do so for an elite, middle-class readership and not for the broader public.

As Amner and Lunga (2011) have pointed out, the adversarial stance of most media has translated into an 'anti-ANC bias and ideological orientation towards neoliberalism', which led not only to the neglect of the poorer sections of the citizenry but also to the 'privileging of freedom of the press over the rights to dignity, reputation and privacy'. This stance has led to a 'disconnect' between the ANC government and the media. This 'master narrative' of a corrupt officialdom and inept politicians has bred cynicism and public disengagement among media audiences and growing mistrust among citizens of what is seen by critics as a self-righteous and arrogant adversarial media (Amner and Lunga 2011).

But because the media can point to its obligation to procedural ethical aspects such as accuracy, factual truth, and balance (cf. Caldwell 2011, p. 74), policed by a self-regulatory system, it could avoid addressing the substantive question of what exactly the outcome of this adversarial stance is meant to be other than fulfilling vague notions of 'the public interest' or 'democratic debate'.

On the other hand, the counterclaims, made mostly by the ANC-led government, that the media should be less adversarial and more collaborative also fail to clearly conceptualize the substantive 'good' that the media should contribute to in everyday life. Although these counterclaims are often couched in culturalist terms of communitarianism, *Ubuntu* and African identities, the notion of community upon which these claims rest seems to be an essentialized and romanticized racial or cultural identity that seems to narrow down rather than open up the possibilities for social conviviality. The 'good life' seems often to be conflated with political allegiance; the public interest with national interest.

It is indeed clear that neither the antagonistic 'watchdog' model nor the subservient development model – which often lapses into uncritical collaborative journalism – is the answer to the normative contestations in a transitional democracy such as post-apartheid South African media (Kuper and Kuper 2001, p. 357). From their study of audience attitudes toward the media, Kuper and Kuper (2001, p. 357) reach the conclusion that while the watchdog model 'amplifies the friend–foe dichotomy by representing the government or other groups as the enemy', the sunshine model might exaggerate the extent to which social cohesion and development are in fact taking place. Both these approaches give citizens the sense of losing control over their lives – the poor feel helpless, and without a future, the rich feel removed from the social aims of the government (Kuper and Kuper 2001, p. 357). In order for the media to enable people to feel in control of their lives, they will have to tell the stories that affect their daily lives. As Kuper and Kuper (2001, p. 371) point out, enabling people to feel in control would not mean for the media to be less critical, but for this criticism to be more considered, and bottom-up. However, Kuper and Kuper (2001, p. 371) seem to suggest that the media could do this by catering for each social group on their own terms, in order to allay their fears about the future and confirming their sense of belonging in the country.

I would differ from this point of view, as such an approach could merely entrench the existing social inequalities and fragmentation exacerbated by market segmentation. A media landscape differentiated according to social class and/or racial and ethnic markers will limit the extent to which it can contribute to a greater mutual understanding of social groups that have forcibly been living in ignorance of one another for centuries of colonialism and apartheid. Ethically, there is therefore the imperative for media to not remain prisoners of their market segments but strive to contribute to greater social cohesion and the overcoming of the polarizations of the past which still resonate in the post-apartheid era due to material inequalities.

Instead, I would argue that the media in a country such as South Africa have the responsibility to attempt to redress the social and cultural divides brought about by the history of colonialism and apartheid. At the same time, if it claims to have a role to play in deepening the fledgling democracy, it would also work to prevent new exclusions – such as those brought about by economic inequality or essentialized identities – to emerge. The substantive 'good life' to which the procedural ethics of a self-regulated, independent, and professional media should contribute is one in which healing of the past can take place via the reconstruction of human dignity on a material, everyday and ontological level. The 'good life' cannot merely be constructed in terms of allowing different and disembodied voices to speak in rational debate. A substantive media ethics for post-apartheid South Africa would be one which enables the media to actively listen to these voices and respond to them in a way that would support the capacity of human beings to relate to one another, not only in rational, cognitive terms, but on an ontological level as holistic human beings that have material and emotional needs, human beings that are not atomistic individuals but are rooted in communities with specific histories.

A proposed response

In their discussion of the globalization of the notion of 'social responsibility', Christians and Nordenstreng (2001) propose that a global media ethics based on social responsibility should instead be based on the universal protonorms of dignity, truth-telling, and non-malfeasance. When related to the current situation in South Africa with regard to democracy and citizenship as discussed above, these protonorms give rise to various ethical imperatives for the media.

The protonorm of human dignity would require the media to seek ways to contribute to the redress of human dignity among a citizenry still scarred by a history of dehumanizing racism (which dehumanized both the oppressor and the oppressed) and to work toward social cohesion by healing the divisions of the past.

The protonorm of truth-telling gives rise to the ethical imperative of deepening democracy by 'speaking truth to power', that is, resisting new imperialisms and exclusions, be they political, economic, or social in nature. This imperative includes the contribution toward a more inclusive mediated public sphere, characterized by a diversity of voices.

The protonorm of non-malfeasance would mean not merely a distanced, 'objective' media that are satisfied by 'minimizing harm' but a media actively striving to undo the damage of the country's apartheid past by seeking social and economic justice for the majority of citizens who, despite their status as citizens, continue to experience marginalization from the practice of citizenship (in Heller's 2009 terms).

However, these norms and imperatives still have to be given concrete content within the context of media practice. To avoid a top-down defining of media roles and responsibilities by the media that runs the risk of enlarging the gulf between a media elite and citizens, the protonorms and their related imperatives would have to be given meaning within the everyday lives of South African citizens. This can only happen if the narratives of ordinary people are allowed to emerge. What is called for is not a speaking-on-behalf-of in the narrow sense of watchdog journalism but an ethics of listening, which would seek to hear how citizens experience everyday life in the post-apartheid democracy and how they see the media contributing to the deepening of democracy, not only in the language of elite politics, but in the concrete circumstances of their daily existence. This process of collaborative ethical meaning-making would be rooted in an ethnographic understanding of morality, that is, the realization that 'morality is rooted in everyday experience and gains multiple levels of complexity' (Christians 2010, p. 178). Seen in this way, the meaning of ethical concepts – such as truth-telling and human dignity – can only emerge within specific social, political, and historical contexts and cannot be imported or imposed from above. Instead of paternalistically presuming to speak on behalf of the public, or to 'give voice to the voiceless', the media could allow the content of these ethical norms to emerge by actively listening to the narratives of everyday life.

Through the narratives of everyday life it will become clear what truth-telling and human dignity would mean for South African citizens in the current historical juncture. In a highly unequal country such as South Africa, the meanings emerging from these narratives may differ vastly, but together they may contribute to a richer, textured, 'thick description' (in Clifford Geertz's well-known formulation) of what the media's ethical response should be in the specific post-apartheid context.

Christians, linking to James Carey's notion of 'communication as culture', explains how narrative provides a path to moral understanding (2010, p. 181):

> Narratives are linguistic forms through which we argue, persuade, display convictions, and establish our identity. They contain in a nutshell the meaning of our theories and beliefs. We tell stories to one another about our values and concerns, and our aspirations.

Following MacIntyre, Christians (2010, p. 179) argues for a perspective on media ethics rooted in 'the way humans actually experience life and how they interpret it, that is, in narrative'. Moral action arises out of 'our life narratives lived out in a historical context' (2010, p. 179), and so a 'shift from principle to story, from formal logic to community formation, is appealing' (2010, p. 180).

At the moment, this listening to the narratives of everyday lives is not happening in the South African media. The mainstream news media especially have taken on an elite position which assumes the ability to articulate the interests of a broad South African public, yet does not critically reflect on its own positioning and the limits of its own representations. A certain arrogance is discernible in the depictions of popular/populist political leaders like Julius Malema, controversial leader of the Economic Freedom Fighters and former president of the ANC Youth League. Payi (2011) observes this attitude as follows:

> What we have observed (and really here I'm using Julius [Malema] as an example of a much broader problem) is that opinions and views which come from the uneducated or the poor are disregarded as howling voices of ineptitude. 'How can they tell us anything if

they never passed woodwork, or even peered through the window of an institution of higher learning?'

This arrogance in the guise of detached, 'objective' watchdog journalism runs the risk of broadening the social and political gulfs in post-apartheid South Africa, and it is likely to result in a greater mistrust of and cynicism toward the media, thus limiting the media's ability to interrogate power relations – in other words, actually undermining the very 'watchdog' function they proclaim to be playing.

An ethics of listening would not mean a retreat from critical engagement. The stance required is not a passive, docile one but one that enables an active listening to Others. It takes courage, not timidity, to respond to what the Other tells us. In her work on whiteness, Samantha Vice (2010, p. 335) proposes that white South Africans adopt the virtues of 'humility and silence'. While this call might be problematic when it sees virtue necessarily in a disengagement from political debate (and our current discussion is not on the area of racial politics per se), her argument for a virtuous silence that 'would not be passive' (2010, p. 335) is worth considering in this context. The silence and listening Vice proposes is one that provides the listener with the opportunity to reflect on their own positioning and assumptions but does not paralyze them or exclude them from a conversation. Crucially, for a country such as South Africa, where the public sphere is fragmented and mediated discussions are often solipsistic within existing, historically constituted groups, such a listening-in-dialog will actively seek to cross borders:

> And as Plato knew so well, self-knowledge is often reached in dialogue with others; you find your own voice and allow others to find theirs in sincere, truth-directed conversation. So silence should not rule out conversation, with those who are both familiar and, probably more importantly, unfamiliar to us.
>
> (Vice 2010, p. 336)

Vice (2010, p. 336) quotes Paul Taylor about the kind of listening that constitutes an active participation in dialog:

> Silence, on this reading, is the complement to *the other's voice*; it signals one's willingness to receive the other's struggle to find words both for his or her experiences and for the self that those experiences have conspired with the act of expression to create. Silence ... is part of listening for a voice.

An active listening on the part of the media would enable a 'shift from principle to story' (Christians 2010, p. 180), in that it would see dialog not in procedural terms as an end in itself, where principles are debated on a conceptual level, but in substantive terms as the space within which human beings can give meaning to protonorms such as human dignity, truth-telling, and non-malfeasance, as these take shape in their real, embodied, everyday lives. The dialogical ethics required from the post-apartheid South African media would have to extend beyond the procedural notion of the public sphere as a space for rational debate facilitated by a professional and self-regulated media. The proposed ethics of listening that seeks to use dialog as a way of contributing to substantive ethical outcomes would be rooted in a framework of care and compassion.

An ethics of listening, rooted in the values of care and compassion, would see humans as always in relation to one another, existing interdependently within communities rather than as atomized, independent individuals (as viewed by liberal democratic approaches) or as collectives of individuals (the assumption underpinning utilitarianism).

The feminist ethics of Carol Gilligan, for instance, goes beyond the injunction against harming others, to the imperative of actively caring for and nurturing our fellow human beings. For Nel Noddings, ethics implies a caring relationship with others that does not remain at good intentions but extends to actual encounters with them (Christians et al. 2009, p. 23).

What would this mean in practice?

In a country such as South Africa, with more than the average share of trauma, an ethics of care may lead the media to act out their social responsibility in a way that goes beyond the enumeration of the statistics of poverty, the political debates around HIV/AIDS, or the horror stories of crime to good, contextual stories that open up possibilities for greater understanding and compassionate action. Sanders (2003, p. 95) distinguishes between 'pity', associated with condescension, and compassion, which refers to the desire to relieve another's suffering by supplying what they need. Compassion can be considered the emotion associated with an ethics of care that sees the media's role as one of engagement rather than distance and detachment; a lack of compassion can be 'at the heart of some of the more unsavoury journalistic practices' like ambush interviews and pack journalism (Sanders 2003, p. 95). Pity, on the other hand, even when sincere, can construct a kind of 'spectatorship of suffering' (Chouliaraki 2006) that merely confronts audiences with images of distant hunger, disease, and death without enabling them to do anything about it. Such simplistic reporting leads at best to a kind of 'compassion fatigue' (Moeller 1999) and at worst to a kind of voyeurism which makes it acceptable and even predictable for audiences to consume images and narratives of a suffering Other. Audiences are then turned into morally ambivalent or neutral spectators, with no moral compulsion to imagine themselves in a relationship of care and responsibility toward an Other.

An ethics of care, one which actively listens and responds to the stories of fellow human beings, would be concerned primarily with how the media can build and heal, rather than protect and attack. Instead of distance we would see immersion, instead of the epistemology of rational deliberation we would see a move toward more ethnographic methodologies, instead of market-driven segmentation of audiences we would see the courage to move beyond the own group to actively listen to the narratives of Others.

An ethics of listening would go beyond the kind of public journalism that remains underpinned by the notion of audiences as 'consumers' or result in stereotypical villain–victim narratives (Amner and Lunga 2011) that might just reinforce the separation between different publics (Amner 2011). Such a journalism will not be a place for people in a hurry (Nyamnjoh as cited in Wasserman 2009), but it will instead be characterized by a certain slowness. Gess (2012) describes 'slow journalism' as follows:

> Perhaps it is time to look at the potential of a 'slow journalism' movement, one that challenges the assumptions and ethics of 'fast journalism' – one that rethinks journalism as an enterprise that provides a different sort of media to its consumers, a media that builds community sustainability, resilience and adaptability.

An example of the ethics of listening which is prepared to relinquish control over narrative and seek input from audiences might be the call put out by the Grahamstown community newspaper *Grocott's Mail* in which it asked for reader suggestions as to how the 200th anniversary of the town should be celebrated on its pages. This call was also marked by the acceptance of the slowness of this process, which goes against the journalistic dictum of providing 'history in a hurry'. As a settler town, the city has a history of conflict and polarization, and therefore celebrating its history is not uncontroversial. In an editorial comment (Grocott's 2011), the paper asked its readers:

> Deciding how to observe this significant landmark is tricky though, because the residents of this town come from a critically divided past – so how can we seek unity if we have widely divergent perspectives? There is no quick answer to that question, but that doesn't mean that we should shy away from it. Difficult questions have the potential for provoking more fascinating answers.

This approach does not mean a retreat from the political or a disengagement from public debate. An ethics of listening, rooted in dialog, would however seek to facilitate a grassroots politics in which citizens are enabled to use media from the bottom-up rather than impose political opinion upon audiences. New media technologies have provided media with myriad ways of listening to audiences and facilitating political subjectivity through, for instance, mobile phones, social networking, and blogging. Recent examples of political uprisings through new media, ranging from the 'Arab Spring' to the Occupy movement and the Indignados, have given cause for optimism about the ability of new media to facilitate political participation. However, the relationship of these technologies with politics should be understood in a nondeterministic fashion and their limits also be acknowledged (Wasserman 2011c).

Conclusion

It is good that the South African media have demonstrated their commitment to ethical journalism through the setting up of self-regulatory structures and the vigorous resistance to attempts to curb their freedom. But the question must still be asked in more depth as to what the outcome of these processes are meant to be – how exactly a free, independent, and fair media could contribute to the 'good life' in a society marred by vast material inequalities that manifest themselves in a range of social problems ranging from unemployment and poverty to violent crime, HIV/AIDS, continued racism, sexism, and xenophobia. This chapter has suggested that a dialogical media ethics enabled by procedures that enable rational debate in the public sphere should not be an aim in itself. Rather, such dialog should take the form of 'active listening', a seeking out of lesser heard, marginalized, and subaltern voices with the aim of finding ways in which healing can take place and social justice be brought about.

The lack of consensus around normative frameworks in post-apartheid South Africa should not be cause for an attempt to move 'beyond' normativity, or refusing to engage with moral questions in the light of postmodern fragmentation and diversity. Rather, a cultural approach to normative media ethics is required that sees ethics as located within the narratives of people as holistic beings. As Caldwell (2011, p. 62), drawing on the work of Charles Taylor, points out, the modern condition assumes various separations as natural – theory from practice, body from mind, self from other, procedure from substance, rational thought from emotions. By a cultural approach is meant not the reductionist and essentialist views of belonging and the right to speak that have often marred Afrocentric normative approaches, but an ethics that will listen to humans as rational and emotional, conceptual as well as material beings.

Such a normative approach to media will resemble an ethics of care, in which media practitioners emerge themselves in the life-worlds of citizens to listen to everyday experience and suspend their own assumptions in order to engage in relationships with communities. It will further draw on the notion of narrative ethics, where the media's role is not to presumptuously act as a watchdog on behalf of a vaguely articulated public interest, nor to unreflexively claim to represent 'the people'. Especially, in a highly unequal country such as South Africa, still scarred by histories of polarization and subordination, the notion of 'the public interest' is highly problematic. Instead of rushing to speak, attack, and defend, the media might better serve the substantive 'good life' in post-apartheid South Africa if they care enough to stand still to listen. And then have the courage to respond.

References

Amner, R. 2011. 'Paper Bridges: A Critical Examination of the *Daily Dispatch's* "Community Dialogues"', *Ecquid Novi: African Journalism Studies*, 32(1): 25–48.

Amner, R. and Lunga, C. 2011. Send in the Mongrel Newshounds! Exploring Hybridised Normative Models of Press Conduct for Public Problem Solving in SA. *Paper Presented to the Sacomm Colloquium on Media, Democracy and Transformation*, Pretoria, 29 August.

Banda, F. 2007. 'Kasoma's Afriethics: A Reappraisal', *The International Communication Gazette*, 70(2): 227–242.

Berger, G. 2008. 'A Paradigm in Process, What the Scapegoating of Vusi Mona Signalled about South African Journalism', *Communicatio*, 34(1): 1–20.

Caldwell, M. 2011. 'Between Proceduralism and Substantialism in Communication Ethics', in N. Hyde-Clarke (ed.), *Communication and Media Ethics in South Africa*, pp. 58–75. Cape Town: Juta.

Chipkin, Ivor. 2007. *Do South Africans Exist? Nationalism, Democracy and the Identity of 'The People'*. Johannesburg: Wits University Press.

Chouliaraki, L. 2006. *The Spectatorship of Suffering*. London: Sage.

Christians, C. G. 2010. 'Communication Ethics in Postnarrative Terms', in Linda Steiner and C. G. Christians (eds.), *Key Concepts in Critical Cultural Studies*, pp. 173–186. Urbana: University of Illinois Press.

Christians, C. G., Glasser, T. L., McQuail, D., Nordenstreng, K. and White, R. A. 2009. *Normative Theories of the Media*. Chicago: University of Illinois Press.

Christians, C. G. and Nordenstreng, K. 2001. 'Social Responsibility Worldwide', *Journal of Mass Media Ethics*, 19(1): 3–28.

Dreze, J. and Sen, A. 2011. 'Putting Growth in Its Place', *Outlook India*. Retrieved November 15, 2011 from http://www.outlookindia.com/article.aspx?278843

Grocott's Mail. 2011. 'Leader Article: How Do We Observe 200 Years of Grahamstown?' 25 October, p. 4.

Heller, Patrick. 2009. 'Democratic Deepening in India and South Africa', *Journal of Asian and African Studies*, 44(1): 123–149.

Leibbrandt, M., I. Woolart, and H. Bhorat 2001. 'Understanding Contemporary Household Inequality in South Africa', in H. Bhorat, M. Leibbrandt, M. Maziya, S. Van den Berg, and I. Woolard (eds.), *Fighting Poverty – Labour Markets and Inequality in South Africa*, pp. 1–20. Cape Town: UCT Press.

Fourie, P. J. 2008. 'Moral Philosophy as the Foundation of Normative Media Theory: Questioning *Ubuntuism* as a Framework', in S. Ward and H. Wasserman (eds.), *Media Ethics Beyond Borders: A Global Perspective*, pp. 105–124. Johannesburg: Heinemann.

Friedman, S. 2011. 'Whose Freedom? South Africa's Press, Middle-Class Bias and the Threat of Control', *Ecquid Novi: African Journalism Studies*, 32(2): 106–121.

Gess, H. 2012. 'Climate Change and the Possibility of "Slow Journalism" ', *Ecquid Novi: African Journalism Studies*, 33(1): 54–65.

Heller, P. 2009. 'Democratic Deepening in India and South Africa', *Journal of Asian and African Studies*, 44(1): 123–149.

Jacobs, S. 2002. 'How Good Is the South African Media for Democracy? Mapping the South African Public Sphere After Apartheid', *African and Asian Studies*, 1(4): 279–302.

Kumwenda, O. 2011. 'Press Councils and the Democratic Political Landscape in South Africa', in N. Hyde-Clarke (ed.), *Communication and Media Ethics in South Africa*, pp. 117–135. Cape Town: Juta.

Kuper, A. and Kuper, J. 2001. 'Serving a New Democracy: Must the Media "Speak Softly"? Learning from South Africa', *International Journal of Public Opinion Research*, 13(4): 355–376.

Lee, C. 2010. 'Die Antwoord Prompts a Big Question', *Los Angeles Times*, October 25. Retrieved October 31, 2011 from http://articles.latimes.com/2010/oct/25/entertainment/la-et-die-antwoord-20101025

Mangcu, Xolela. 2008. *To the Brink: The State of Democracy in South Africa*. Scottsville: UKZN Press.

Mgibisa, M. 2011. 'Black Journalists' Voices Blowing in the Wind?', *The Media Online*. Retrieved on September 14, 2011 from http://themediaonline.co.za/2011/09/black-journalist-voices-in-the-wind/

Moeller, S. D. 1999. *Compassion Fatigue*. New York: Routledge.

Moorthy, S. and Jamal, A. (eds.) 2009. *Indian Ocean Studies: Cultural, Social, and Political Perspectives*. London: Routledge.

Nevill, G. 2011. 'Come Dine With Me SA Has Viewers Eating out of Its Hand', *The Media Online* October 26. Retrieved on October 26, 2011 from http://themedia online.co.za/2011/10/come-dine-with-me-sa-has-them-trending-on-twitter/

Olorunnisola, A. and Tomaselli, K. G. (eds.) 2011. *Political Economy of Media Transformation in South Africa*. Creskill: Hampton.

Papacharissi, Z. (ed.) 2009. *Journalism and Citizenship: New Agendas in Communication*. London: Routledge.

Payi, X. 2011. 'Intellectual Arrogance Poses a Greater Danger than Intellectual Inferiority', *Daily Maverick*. Retrieved October 28, from http://dailymaverick .co.za/opinionista/2010-10-22-intellectual-arrogance-poses-a-greater-danger -than-intellectual-inferiority

Rao, S. and Wasserman, H. 2007. 'Global Journalism Ethics Revisited: A Postcolonial Critique', *Global Media and Communication*, 3(1): 29–50.

Sainath, P. 2004. 'The Feel Good Factory', *Frontline*. Retrieved February 5, 2013 from http://www.frontlineonnet.com/fl2105/stories/20040312007800400.htm

Sainath, P. [n.d]. 'On Media', *Why Democracy?* Retrieved October 26, 2011 from http://www.whydemocracy.net/film/34

Seria, N. 2010. 'South Africa Is Asked to Join as a BRIC Member to Boost Emerging Markets', *Bloomberg*. Retrieved April 22, from http://www.bloomberg.com/news/2010-12-24/south-africa-asked-to-join-bric-to-boost-cooperation-with -emerging-markets.html

Sparks, C. 2011. 'South African Media in Comparative Perspective', *Ecquid Novi: African Journalism Studies*, 32(2): 5–19.

Sanders, K. 2003. *Ethics & Journalism*. London: Sage.

Tomaselli, K. G. 2000. 'South African Media 1994–7. Globalising via Political Economy', in J. Curran and M.-J. Park (eds.), *De-Westernizing Media Studies*, pp. 247–259. London: Routledge.

Tomaselli, K. G. 2011. '(Afri)ethics, Communitarianism and the Public Sphere', in N. Hyde-Clarke (ed.), *Communication and Media Ethics in South Africa*, pp. 76–95. Cape Town: Juta.

Vice, S. 2010. 'How Do I Live in This Strange Place?', *Journal of Social Philosophy*, 41(3): 323–342.

Von Lieres, B. 2005. 'Culture and the Limits of Liberalism: Marginalisation and Citizenship in Post-Apartheid South Africa', in S. Robins (ed.), *Limits to Liberation after Apartheid: Citizenship, Governance and Culture*, pp. 22–32. Oxford: James Currey.

Wasserman, H. 2005. 'Talking of Change: Constructing Social Identities in South African Media Debates', *Social Identities*, 11(1): 75–85.

Wasserman, H. 2006. 'Globalised Values and Postcolonial Responses, South African Perspectives on Normative Media Ethics', *The International Communication Gazette*, 68(1): 71–91.

Wasserman, H. 2009. 'Extending the Theoretical Cloth to Make Room for African Experience: An Interview with Francis Nyamnjoh', *Journalism Studies*, 10(2): 281–293.

Wasserman, H. 2010a. 'Freedom's Just Another Word? Perspectives on Media Freedom and Responsibility in South Africa and Namibia', *International Communication Gazette,* 72(7): 567–588.

Wasserman, H. 2010b. *Tabloid Journalism in South Africa: True Story!* Bloomington: Indiana University Press.

Wasserman, H. 2011a. 'The Presence of the Past: The Uses of History in Contemporary South African Normative Journalism Discourses', *Journalism Practice,* 5(5): 584–598.

Wasserman, H. 2011b. 'Towards A Global Journalism Ethics Via Local Narratives: Southern African Perspectives', *Journalism Studies,* 12(6): 791–803.

Wasserman, H. 2011c. 'Mobile Phones, Popular Media and Everyday African Democracy: Transmissions and Transgressions', *Popular Communication,* 9(2): 146–158.

Wasserman, H. and Rao, S. 2008. 'The Glocalization of Journalism Ethics', *Journalism: Theory, Practice, Criticism,* 9(2): 163–181.

5
Paying for Journalism: An Ethics-Based and Collaborative Business Model

Lee Wilkins

Journalists need others to get their jobs done. They require sources, documents, and access to people and institutions to report stories. To massage that raw information into news and distribute it to others, they need a team – editors, photographers, layout and design professionals, web designers, editors, and programmers. Some modes of doing journalism foreground cooperation. Producing broadcast news – both radio and television – has always required a team. Despite a resurgent myth that focuses on the lone individual, producing journalism historically has been a cooperative activity, whether that cooperation is likened to a factory assembly line or a more densely networked effort. In contemporary journalists' daily lives, cooperation, while sometimes filled with small frictions (all reporters clash with editors), is the norm.

Yet, journalism has never been financially self-sufficient. As media economist Robert Picard (2010) notes, news has never been the sort of thing that – by itself – has made money. It has always required outside support and the organization to garner it, whether in the form of political party (the era of the US partisan press which is reflected in contemporary, European media systems) or the most contemporary support mechanisms: advertising, reader and listener pledging, or the financial power of enormous corporations. This kind of cooperation is more subtle, is often unacknowledged, and sometimes challenges individual understandings of best practices. Historically, individual journalists have balanced these tensions ethically by emphasizing individual independence and autonomy (Black, Steele, and Barney 1997).

This chapter seeks to bring these two sorts of cooperative arrangements – the cooperative task of producing journalism and the equally cooperative, although often unacknowledged, task of paying for it – together. The Internet and its impact on the financial health of media organizations now requires individuals and their organizations to think more expansively about the normative foundations of their work and financial arrangements. Using the insights of the daily lives of journalists as they cooperate to produce journalism, this chapter argues that those same insights can be used to develop new business models for paying for that process. Furthermore, by using ethical concepts as a foundation for building and then evaluating collaborative financial arrangements, a template for best practices emerges. These potential – and some actual – arrangements are reviewed in the latter portion of the chapter.

Thinking collaboratively adds notions of reciprocity and justice to the core professional values of autonomy and independence. But, there is also a larger community, a profession-wide connection – what Sandel calls a 'sense of belonging to an extended community over time' (p. 235). Such a community requires an ethics of professional collaboration. For contemporary journalism, collaborative efforts need to move from within the newsroom walls, where collaboration is a way of life, to the connections between the newsroom, citizens, and the financial arrangements necessary to support professional work. As Borden notes, such efforts 'must redefine bad journalism as a social problem; it must construct internal consensus around the practice's standards of excellence and demand accountability from news executives; and it must persuade citizens, officials, and non-profits to alter the political and economic conditions most hostile to journalism's best traditions' (Borden 2007, p. 120). Thus, this chapter examines collaboration and reciprocity at the individual and organizational levels; it also links these understandings to profession-wide goals. Financial arrangements for paying for professional work influence individuals and organizations at multiple levels of analysis. Those financial arrangements must be evaluated at multiple levels as well.

In the case of collaboration, predominant in this project is the acknowledgment of a fruitful tension between the collaboration necessary to produce professional work and the necessity, within that collaborative environment, to maintain journalistic independence and autonomy both individually and organizationally. The daily lives of journalists have produced normative understandings about what it means to work together toward a common goal. Political philosopher Michael Sandel refers to this as the 'obligations of solidarity and membership [that] point outward as well as inward' (Sandel 2009, p. 234.)

Historically, these understandings have included various ways of paying for the news.

Examining the daily lives of individual journalists, beginning with the 'lived experience' as feminist epistemology suggests, provides important insights into thinking about cooperation and collaboration. 'This ethic is grounded in community so that research serves the community, reflects a community's multiple voices, and enables participants to act to transform their social world' (Steiner 2009, p. 372). Feminist ethicist Nel Noddings notes that an epistemological commitment to the context in which decisions occur allows for principles to emerge from life rather than imposing principles on living. 'Moral decisions are, after all, made in real situations, they are qualitatively different from the solution of geometry problems' (Noddings 1984, p. 3). Principles – rules of the road – arrived at in the way feminist epistemology suggests are, of necessity, somewhat messy and inclusive of internal tension rather than definitional and reliant on more formal rules.

Definitions

In modern English, collaboration has two opposing meanings. For historical and political reasons, collaboration can be defined negatively: cooperate with or willingly assist an enemy of one's country and especially an occupying force. In certain contexts, for example collaboration with the Nazi's during World War II or collaboration with various powerful elites during the genocides of the 20th century, collaboration includes elements of coercion and betrayal. Collaboration of this sort implies an unequal distribution of power, the substitution of one party's ends for another's, and an inability to withdraw from the relationship. Collaboration of this sort demeans autonomy and independence, substitutes force for solidarity, and undermines distributive justice among citizens and within societies.

However, collaboration also has a positive definition: to work jointly with others or together, especially in an intellectual endeavor; to cooperate with an agency or instrumentality with which one is not immediately connected. This definition of collaboration at a rudimentary level describes the lives of journalists today. It honors autonomy and independence but adds notions of solidarity around a goal and a more equal distribution of power – reciprocity – among the collaborating parties. Working together toward an intellectual goal also implicates professional capabilities. Collaboration defined this way seeks justice as reciprocity and capability; these two ethical concepts become instrumental in achieving professional ends. Articulating clearly what they mean in professional life can provide the basis for establishing collaborative agreements of all sorts – particularly, but not exclusively, those that provide financial support for journalists and their organizations and for superficially new methods of 'gathering' news. Clarity about philosophical foundations can thus provide a template for best professional practices.

Reciprocity: The obligations of affirmative duties

Reciprocity as an ethical concept begins with Aristotle and continues through contemporary philosophers, including feminist ethicists and work in African ethics. Reviewing the highlights of this philosophical base is essential but by necessity somewhat superficial. However, it is important to note that understandings of reciprocity, while amplified, have been remarkably consistent through the millennia and focus on a core set of concepts and principles.

Aristotle (1987) linked reciprocity to distributive justice within political society. For Aristotle, justice was attached to agreements people entered of their own free will, and he acknowledged that different people might contribute differently to agreements, but that justice itself might still be served. 'Justice then is a sort of proportion; for proportion is not peculiar to abstract quantity but belongs to quantity generally, proportion being equality of radios' (Aristotle 1987, pp. 151–152). Linking reciprocity with justice, voluntary agreements and some rough form of proportionality persists to the present day.

The voluntariness of the concept and its connection to 'fairness' in terms of proportionality are a central feature of John Rawls' conceptualization of the term. Reciprocity, particularly behind the veil of ignorance in the 'original position', is a central feature of Rawls' work on justice as fairness. In Rawls' construction, citizens are free (autonomous) to act in specific ways, with the resulting assumption that in the original position people will be able to obey laws – and to have laws enforced – because they apply to all. 'In justice as fairness, on the other hand, persons accept in advance a principle of equal liberty and they do this without a knowledge of their more particular ends. They implicitly agree, therefore, to conform their conceptions of their good to what the principles of justice require, or at least not to press claims which directly violate them' (Rawls 1971, p. 31). This insistence on equal liberty between/among parties without knowledge of particular ends is crucial to understanding potential collaborative arrangements involving journalists. Such a definition of equal liberty does not infringe on journalistic autonomy, but rather it links that autonomy to a more abstract end: justice as fairness. Justice therefore becomes a shared end. An end of justice places collaborators on the same 'side', instead of occupying some sort of adversarial position. In Rawls' conceptualization, reciprocity is unstated but implicated. The agreements behind the veil of ignorance are reciprocal in nature; they apply to all stakeholders. Proportionality is also a component of such understandings; while some – the weaker party – may get 'more' out of the agreements, all parties benefit.

Linking reciprocity with justice is also a central feature of transitional justice – the sort of political arrangements typified by the truth and reconciliation commissions of South Africa. Reciprocity within the framework of transitional justice connotes forgiveness for past wrongs and the elevation of the weaker party, for example, the victims of war crimes or of various sorts of structural discrimination, to the moral level of those who committed or perpetuated these denigrative social arrangements.

Reciprocity in transitional justice fuels deliberative democracy, that is, a discussion of policy and political alternatives that is informed by history, culture, emotion, and fact. It is important to note that a feminist interpretation of transitional justice acknowledges both its rational and emotional side. In the actual workings of truth and reconciliation commissions, it is a change in the emotional understanding of the impact of a racist history and/or specific acts, a truth about injustice that provokes an emotional response to superficially logical social and political arrangements that constrain individual lives and relationships, that promotes reconciliation. Reconciliation in this deep way is an empathetic response that couples emotion and logic. This sort of empathy is based on a logical understanding of the racist (or other unethical) choices, but without granting them moral sanction. It is this lack of moral sanction that allows for the ethically informed imagining of a 'different' way to proceed among individuals and to develop institutions that will promote different sorts of – and more ethically vibrant – relationships, social, and political structures. Emotion and logic power the transition to justice.

Transitional justice is thus founded in equality and dialog – it argues for agreements openly arrived at which consider, but are not constrained by, the history between the two parties. Reciprocity in this context implies the ability to come to common agreement – it requires dialog as a preliminary step toward a more just outcome. Further, such dialog is public; it meets the test of publicity as it is understood in applied philosophy (Bok 1983). Transitional justice, more so than the works of Rawls or Aristotle, explicitly acknowledges the role of history and past cultural experience in arriving at 'more just' social and political arrangements.

Contemporary writing about reciprocity has noted the connection between theory and practice implicit in the concept. Implementing reciprocity requires individual virtue. 'That we should return good for good in proportion to what we receive, that we should resist evil, that we should make reparation for the harm we do, and that we should be disposed to do these things as a matter of moral obligation' is how one scholar summarizes a robust view of reciprocity (Becker 1986, p. 16). This definition lodges reciprocating firmly in the present, but it also asserts that present actions respond to history, thus melding ethical action with the sort of transitional justice that truth and reconciliation represent. In this sense, reciprocity may be one normative mechanism that supports changes in long-standing but problematic social, political, and economic arrangements. Reciprocity as both a virtue and as moral obligation, then, could promote the development of new arrangements. In Becker's rendering, these arrangements have an element of justice at their core.

The role of the present in thinking about reciprocity has also led to both criticisms and interdisciplinary insights that help to deepen the concept. Sociobiologist E. O. Wilson emphasized the importance of the future – the long view – when he theorized that reciprocity can span many years and multiple interactions, noting that reciprocity requires both a 'subtle and complex' memory. Wilson's work, of course, was foreshadowed by game theory, where the response of 'tit for tat' has found to be a robust predictor and stabilizer of cooperative systems (Axelrod 1984). Combining these two bodies of work suggests that while it may take collaborative arrangements a while to develop, once they do they may be robust even in the face of serious assault. This insight certainly applies to the collaborative relationships between journalistic organizations and advertisers – a system that has withstood the test of time for more than a century and is unlikely to be completely abandoned even in the present day.

Other scholars have been less certain about the explanatory power of even a robust notion of reciprocity, particularly when the central 'good' in question is a common rather than an individual one. Putnam (1988) notes that, when the issue becomes common goods held over time, it is difficult to know how to reciprocate or expect a return on 'one's own efforts'. Putnam, in response to Becker, also notes that it is difficult – except in theory – to articulate and then fulfill reciprocal obligations to future and past generations, both of which are responsible for the continuing production of many public goods.

Putnam finds the link between reciprocity and justice – particularly when collective goods are at issue – a weak one, and one that, at the level of practical application, is fraught with problems for which theory has no easy response. Putnam's doubts, which emerge from a body of theory that is top-down in nature, are reflected in the tension and sometimes conflicts that independent journalism can produce when individual journalists or their organizations relate to non-journalistic entities. In an entirely capitalistic marketplace, journalism is a product that comes at a price. But Putnam's reasoning also suggests that journalism can be considered a 'common good', something that is necessary for democratic functioning but not linked specifically with particular individuals or organizations. Journalism is instrumental to democratic functioning, even more essential to a mature democracy where citizens require liberty, justice, and community. Journalism in democratic societies functions as a common good at the institutional level, and the problems of financial support, either public or private, that have plagued the institution for most of the past decade are representative of the sort of problems Putnam outlines for public goods more generally. The market constitutes a poor response to the instrumental professional role. In the context of public goods, reciprocity represents an incomplete response to furthering justice.

Thus, the philosophical literature links reciprocity imperfectly with justice. Reciprocity is voluntary and applies to all stakeholders, although the application itself may be proportional in nature. It also demands conversation that focuses around agreements and their nature, and such conversation needs to be public – at least if a sort of transitional justice is the common goal. Such agreements may persist through time; indeed, extended periods of reciprocity among parties can be a key to robust collaborative environments. When the issue becomes public or common goods, however, extending reciprocal agreements through time can become tenuous. The contemporary international debate over how much debt individual political societies can sustain, for example, provides a troubling illustration about the fissures that may develop in contractual and reciprocal arrangements that extend over decades and generations. Any attempt to articulate reciprocal arrangements that support the development of political and social discourse through a media system that is both private and for profit as well as publicly supported raises similar issues. Connecting notions of virtue and duty, which in the philosophical tradition are intensely individual and personal in nature, with institutional arrangements makes for a particular knotty element of the problem. But, considering the practical nature of the lived journalistic life today, connecting the individual to the organizational is imperative. And, considering the lived experience of journalists themselves, for financial arrangements to work, they need to be reciprocal and hence collaborative.

The foregoing discussion thus moves from individual and interpersonal agreements to structural arrangements. It should be noted that such arrangements are not exclusively unidirectional; for example, South Africa's truth and reconciliation commissions are structural in nature, rely on individual virtue, yet combine both in an attempt to provide the normative energy to alter political structure in long-lasting ways. Justice, distributive justice, and fairness therefore find a potential philosophical home in contractualism, where an emphasis on specific agreements and the distribution of commonly valued goods is crucial. Ward notes that the dominant understanding of contractualism is an ethical approach that specifies what is ' "right", "obligatory", or "wrong" in any domain of society determined by principles that define a reasonable co-operative framework... the object of a suitable agreement between equals' (Ward 2011, p. 29). Central to contractualism is communication that results in formal agreements between and among the parties involved, including central actors and the public. Time, too, becomes important, for memory of unjust acts – coerced collaboration – needs to be supplanted with a more equitable foundation and contracts can be extended over time. For justice to result from such arrangements, autonomy and reciprocity must receive equal weight. How that happens – both in theory and in fact – demands one more ethical principle: promise keeping.

Promise keeping is an ethical duty implied in Aristotle's discussion and which is explicitly discussed in contractual thinking. There are almost certainly implied promises in what one will and will not do upon emerging from behind Rawls' veil of ignorance. But, for practical efforts in the real world, the work of W. D. Ross gives the best account of the subtleties of application. Ross' conceptualization of duties works well for professionals, who must balance competing roles, obligations, and stakeholders. What makes Ross so applicable to professional arrangements is that unlike Kant or Mill, who relied on a single principle, Ross allows for multiple duties which can sometimes come into conflict. Ross' list of six duties emphasizes the affirmative role that community and relationships play in thinking through ethical acts (Ross 1930).

Ross theorized that there were two sorts of duties, 'Prima facia duties are broad and abstract; actual duties are specific and contextual' (Meyers 2003, p. 85). Meyers, in his elaboration of Ross, notes that Ross does not provide an a priori way of weighing competing duties. At the level of practical application, Ross asks ethical decision-makers to consider the potential consequences of the fulfillment of the various duties without abandoning the very personal nature of duty itself. 'For the estimation of the comparative stringency of these prima facia obligations, no general rules can...be laid down' (Ross 1930, p. 41). Ross goes on to add that, all things being equal, a 'great deal of stringency belongs to the duties of "perfect obligation"', promise keeping among them. But, as Meyers notes, in the real world, things are almost never precisely equal. He urges adapting Ross' notion of perfect obligation to specific circumstances, acknowledging that specific circumstances will bring their own 'hierarchies of duty'.

Specific circumstances in the journalistic case would certainly include collaborative arrangements. The perfect obligation of special circumstances also suggests that there is not a single, ideal collaborative arrangement, but a potential series of such arrangements. Practical variations around 'paying for journalistic work' might include differing levels of financial support, the length of time that support is expected, non-financial means of support (e.g. help with issues ranging from access to office space), and what happens should the journalists and/or the journalistic organizations involved failed to fulfill the professional obligations publicly and cooperatively agreed to. Outside of the financial realm, new journalistic arrangements also could emerge. The normally hierarchical understanding between journalists and their sources – I'm the journalist and you tell me things and I decide what to make public – is subject to a similar reinterpretation, one that is collaborative, reciprocal, and demonstrates a more equal and potentially just distribution of power, even in the professional domain.

It is important to note that, for these sorts of arrangements to work for journalists and the normative journalistic role, non-performance cannot focus on specific news content but rather on the process of collecting that content. That financial support and professional relationships support a process of journalism, not a specific and predetermined outcome. The concept of multiple options also reflects the daily lives of journalists as they have existed for decades as well as the potentials for new arrangements that have not yet been incorporated into the daily experience. These arrangements need to meet the test of publicity. The arrangements themselves must be distributive – in other words, not all parties involved need to benefit equally so long as all parties do benefit. A thick understanding of reciprocity outlines the potential benefits involved, even though reciprocity by itself may not provide a sufficient theoretical base for collective goods. However, reciprocity and promise keeping provide an ethical foundation for the sort of collaborative arrangements that journalists and their news organizations have entered into historically. The goal here is justice, and in the case of journalism, the potential to arrive at new arrangements that will sustain the work of the commonweal. It is to this potential that this effort now turns.

Collaboration and justice as capabilities

The foregoing account of the nature of collaboration and reciprocity requires flexibility about the nature of various agreements as well as an ethically based but practically oriented commitment to adhere to those agreements. The nature of justice is assumed to be the dominant end at the most abstract level, but as Rawls, among others, notes, justice itself can be a sort of 'moving target', because the impact of protecting the weaker party while maximizing liberty for all means that individual arrangements themselves will change over time – but always toward more just as opposed to the less just end. Collective goods represent a particular problem, precisely because they need to continue over time. However, collective goods tend to focus on the sorts of things that will enhance human flourishing. That enhancement of life may provide one theoretical approach to thinking about reciprocity as a foundation of collective well-being in a philosophically different light.

Philosopher Martha Nussbaum (2006) has built on this insight with what she calls 'the capabilities approach to justice'. Nussbaum notes, 'the basic intuitive idea of my version of the capabilities approach is that we begin with a conception of the dignity of the human being, and of a life that is worthy of that dignity – a life that has available in it "truly human functioning" the sense described by Marx in his 1844 *Economic and Philosophical Manuscripts'* (Nussbaum 2006, p. 74). Nussbaum does not intend the capabilities approach to provide a complete account of social justice, but rather to help explain the 'minimum core social entitlements' (Nussbaum 2006, p. 75) that thinking about human dignity in the form of capabilities promotes.

As part of this process, Nussbaum outlines ten capabilities as 'central requirements of a life with dignity' (Nussbaum 2006, p. 75). She argues that her list of capabilities protects pluralism and is fully universal. Numbers six and seven on the capabilities list are articulated as follows:

'practical reason – being able to form a conception of the good and to engage in critical reflection about the planning of one's life.... and 7. Affiliation: being able to live with and toward others, to recognize and show concern for other human beings, to engage in various forms of social interaction; to be able to imagine the situation of another (protecting this capability means protecting institutions that constitute and nourish such forms of affiliation, and also protecting the freedom of assembly and political speech)' (Nussbaum 2006, p. 77). Nussbaum intends her capabilities approach to justice to apply to all of humanity in daily life. Since part of daily life includes work, in this specific case, professional roles, capabilities are applicable in that sort of human endeavor as well.

Nussbaum's articulation of capabilities implicates journalism and news; indeed, it summons a certain type of journalism which, not coincidentally, is both expensive to produce and, because particularly of the financial decline of newspapers which were the primary provider of investigative work, increasingly less common. The necessity for journalistic story-telling to provide the capability to imagine the situation of another makes the continuance of a certain kind of journalism essential for the development of individual capacities. In Nussbaum's language, it promotes affiliation through freedom of assembly and political speech. Although Nussbaum (2000, 2006) intended for her work to be applied to individual development, her articulation of it specifically discusses political society and therefore the efforts of organizations, including, but not restricted to, the support of government. Government is a common good, and it is reasonable to apply the notion of capabilities to other common goods, among them the political speech understood broadly that journalism represents.

Nussbaum (2000) specifically links capabilities with justice; indeed, she argues that justice is served only when human capabilities are tended and flourish. Although her project focuses on individual capabilities, there is much in its articulation that focuses on how individuals relate to – and even need – institutions to achieve those capabilities. For Nussbaum, connecting human capabilities to dignity and flourishing allows for the 'imagining' and then creating of different sorts of institutional arrangements. As long as those arrangements promote justice, understood at a very individual and human level, then new arrangements themselves are worth attempting. In Nussbaum's work, institutions can collaborate with individuals to achieve a more just end.

Journalism scholars have themselves envisioned a journalism of capabilities, one where relationships are founded on mutuality (reciprocity) and the professional product itself is committed to building a more just community that moves toward social transformation (Christians, Ferre, and Fackler 1993, pp. 13–18). Capabilities and reciprocity, thus, provide a deep meaning to the concept of professional collaboration – one that is reflected in the daily lives of journalists but can also be used as the basis on which to build new financial arrangements to support a journalism of justice, particularly in democratic political society.

A template for financial collaboration with journalists

For working journalists, the foregoing discussion is heavy in philosophical theory and somewhat opaque in practical application. This section of the chapter, thus, takes that philosophical theory and applies it to the daily circumstances of working journalists. The initial application, just as does the philosophical theory from which it emerges, is focused on democratic societies with developed media systems. However, emerging democracies may find some or all of these applications pertinent to contemporary media systems which grow and change in response to the changing political context. These applications also acknowledge that because of the Internet's world-wide reach, these collaborative principles of funding journalism in some ways need to speak to global professional standards. Those standards are still very much in the process of being negotiated, although, as Borden notes, the emerging standards of professional journalistic solidarity appear to have foundational support among journalists themselves but far less consistent support, let alone approval, from the organizations for which journalists work and the nations in which they do the bulk of their professional work. Considering the foregoing, the following abstract criteria should characterize journalistic collaborative agreements:

1. Collaborative arrangements need to fund human-based but professionally expressed capabilities. They need to promote the sort of journalism that allows journalists themselves as well as readers, viewers, and listeners to imagine the situation of another.

- This condition for collaborative agreements is directly linked with the human capability to nourish affiliation and protect political speech. As such, it forms the baseline or foundational maxim for all collaborative agreements involving individual journalists and news organizations. Others of the capabilities outlined by Nussbaum are, of course, fundamental to human flourishing. However, when human flourishing is placed in the professional, journalistic context, this quality of flourishing needs to inform the actions of all parties at every step and level of involvement.

- Specific collaborative agreements should be targeted at developing the sort of journalism that is difficult to accomplish, either because it is expensive – for example, investigative or international journalism – or because it requires extensive team efforts – for example, some forms of documentary film or differing kinds of relationships with sources.

2. Collaborative agreements need to privilege the protections of the weaker party while maximizing liberty. This conceptualization of justice as fairness can apply to both methods of story selection and specific cooperative arrangements themselves.

- Journalists need to retain both autonomy and independence, particularly in reporting and editing, within collaborative arrangements.
- Journalists also need to keep the promises that reciprocity implies, including, but not limited to, producing the high-quality professional work that is being supported, and keeping professional promises – for example, sharing credit for reporting/editing/publishing – the results of those efforts.
- Non-journalistic collaborators may be expected to enter into collaborative agreements based on reciprocity and proportionality. For example, financial support of journalistic efforts should not be tied to editorial control.
- Non-journalistic collaborators may reasonably expect that the journalistic project itself can support the more abstract goals of the collaborating individual or organization, an articulation of reciprocity. For example, the Robert Wood Johnson Foundation may reasonably expect that the goal of a journalistic effort would be to improve public health without specific approval of specific projects or the results of those projects. Those who support journalism in this way should not be expected to agree with all the specific results of all journalistic projects. However, reciprocity implies that non-journalism organizations have reasons to expect that every professional effort is made to collect, organize, and publish such work.

3. Collaborative agreements should be publicly arrived at and capable of withstanding third-party scrutiny. While these agreements may

vary in specific terms, in general they should reflect the same set of understandings, specifically reciprocity, promise keeping, and promoting professional capabilities.

- Individual collaborative agreements may vary. However, the broad outlines of those arrangements should be public to the individual journalists involved as well as the organization providing financial or other sorts of support. Individuals or organizations providing support to journalists should not expect 'special' status, either in the nature of the specific collaborative agreements or the results of such professional work. Thus, government funding of journalistic work becomes possible, but only when government relinquishes editorial control.
- Individual collaborators should not be able to determine who should and should not be allowed to collaborate with journalistic organizations.

4. Collaborative agreements can be ended, and the ability to end such agreements should be reciprocal. How collaborative agreements can be concluded should be public and apply equally – which is not to say identically – to parties involved in individual agreements. There should be no 'special rider' status for concluding collaborative agreements.

5. While the foregoing outlines what are colloquially called 'one-off arrangements', both journalistic and collaborative organizations should be asked to consider longer-term continuing support. Taking this longer view acknowledges what both philosophers and game theorists call 'the shadow of the future' as well as the problems associated with collective goods as outlined by Putnam. Longer-term continuing support provides the foundation of new social and political arrangements that promote the best traditions of journalism as well as current inventions that promote good work.

- News organizations should consider asking collaborators to provide some portion of financial support for continuing journalistic efforts that will not be confined to the specific project(s) outlined in the collaboration agreement.
- In many ways, this sort of investment in a form of collaboration characterizes the role that advertising has played in providing financial support to the news industry or that subscriber support has played for magazines such as *Ms.* or *Consumer Reports*. It should be noted here that such support is not without its continuing tensions and

problems, but that the general approach is not without some long-term virtues. The same may be said of long-standing collaborations among newspapers, for example, the Associated Press.

- This sort of collaborative financial arrangement can also be applied to public support of specific organizations, for example, individual listener support for individual National Public Radio stations or for the Corporation for Public Broadcasting. Subscriber support is also not without tensions, but it does move collaborative arrangements away from individual projects and toward the institutional journalistic project in important ways.

- Less well known in the United States, but perhaps as pertinent, is that financial collaboration can come in the form of tax support. While this approach is inconceivable to Americans, it has worked in other nations (Picard 1986).

Changing the relationship between journalists and sources: Crowdsourcing

Journalists and sources collaborate all the time. But, that collaboration is seldom a relationship of equals. Most often it is a dance for power and control, with journalists employing the ethical values of independence and autonomy to retain the exclusive ability to develop media content – the news – while sources seek control over that same content so that their points of view and experiences will be published unfiltered. Often this jockeying for position is gentle, but in partisan politics it becomes contentious and fierce. Theoretically, this has led to what mass communication scholars refer as 'source dependency', meaning that news content is almost entirely shaped by specific sources and journalistic access to them. Normatively it means that audience members, particularly those who have less political and economic power, too seldom find themselves and their experiences reflected in the news. When politics is the focus, journalists are skeptical to the point of cynicism of what their sources have to say and their motivations for saying it. The result is too often news accountants that are hollowed of any human core. People – the ones whom news is designed to represent to each other – become absent from content.

Crowdsourcing has become one response to this tug over content between journalists and their sources. The term has many definitions, almost all of which have emerged from professional practice rather than top-down principles. Crowds can check – and hence source – the accuracy of news accounts, acting as editors and fact checkers. Crowds can also originate content: when journalists cannot be present to cover events, or when events are so large that even teams cannot provide something accurate or systematic, the crowd steps in. Crowds can also provide tips on what might be news, if only there were a journalist there to see and understand it. For purposes of this chapter, crowdsourcing is defined as journalists' use of content originated by citizens to further news accounts. Content can be verbal as well as visual; it may produce additional information or serve as a method to verify information the journalist has already obtained. Crowdsourcing is not the unfiltered use of social media as a method of information transmission – for information to be crowd sourced, a journalist must act as a gatekeeper at some point in the information transmission process.

Crowdsourcing is problematic. Crowds can forward rumors, which can be inaccurate and potentially harmful. Crowds are often concerned with the trivial; there is more mobile phone video of violent weather sent to broadcast outlets than reports of parent–teacher association meetings that influence how schools, teachers, parents, students, and taxpayers relate to one another. There is mounting evidence that few members of the crowd are interested in the routine of governing; many in the crowd are interested in what they believe is government corruption. Many members of the crowd can only incompletely support what they think they 'know' with fact. Crowdsourcing is often seen as a market response to the institutional economic woes. The crowd will look for itself – or at least its individual members – in the news, and hence be willing to pay for it. Some scholars have labeled the crowd as 'first informers' to distinguish their role from the role of journalists who have responsibilities for truth-telling and verification – the concept of earned information – that extend beyond the crude first-person facticity that crowdsourcing represents (Wilkins 2013).

Yet, stripped of its dance for power and control, journalists and their sources simply have to collaborate to make news possible. Democratic governing accepts that those who govern must respond to those who are governed, and the most common, frequent, and generally effective way to do that is through the news media. So, if collaboration is a requirement for 'doing' journalism, how might the process of crowdsourcing benefit from the application of the ethical principles of recipriocity and promise keeping with the longer-term goal of promoting the justice of capabilities?

- First, crowdsourcing needs to be employed in such a way as to allow readers, viewers, and listeners – as autonomous individuals – to imagine what Nussbaum calls 'the situation of another'. For such imagination to be full-throated, it must be lodged in community, and journalists will have access to that community, in part, through the crowd.
- In crowdsourcing, the crowds' view must not be substituted for professional acumen. Rather professional judgment is informed by multiple sources. The exchange of information is reciprocal. The resulting understanding is shared and subject to revision by all.
- Crowdsourcing and the content it produces must withstand public scrutiny. Who is included in the crowd and under what arrangements need to be transparent and capable of third-party scrutiny. Crowdsourcing is not used as a means to the end of profitability, the most common rationale in the industry today, but as a way of furthering the instrumental role of political speech in a democracy. It represents more people speaking, and speaking in ways that, over time, engage the imagination of all. Distributing the capacity for political speech as both information source and receiver furthers traditional notions of justice.
- Crowdsourcing also needs to become part of journalistic routines, even though this will alter traditional routines that favor fewer and more readily accessible sources. Journalists need to develop routines that will allow sources to include the 'crowd'. When the crowd becomes a part of journalistic routines, standards of completeness and accuracy also will shift.
- Crowdsourcing does not eliminate some of the proportionality inherent in justice. As the crowd takes on the role of 'first informers', journalists will assume the role of verifying, analyzing, and placing raw information into a meaningful context. This journalistic role will include holding the 'crowd' to account for accuracy and truth-telling; rumors and misinformation can be tolerated no more in crowd-sourced news stories than in traditionally sourced ones. Crowdsourcing will allow for much finer role distinctions between the act of collecting information and understanding it and conveying it in a meaningful way. For the past 200 years, journalists have performed both these role-based functions.
- This sort of collaboration with the crowd will foreground reciprocity and capability. The promise kept is a civic one, and by making the crowd a much more equal partner in the work of journalism, it is the kinds of collaboration that may help democracy remain robust.

Does the financial template inform reality?

Because this project begins with an epistemological approach grounded in the lives of journalists, it is realistic to expect that the result should, at least in some specificity, resemble emerging financial arrangements that support a variety of journalistic efforts, from nascent news organizations such as the St. Louis Beacon to the Pulitzer Center and ProPublica. These organizations have demanded editorial independence and autonomy when seeking outside funding and have developed a variety of mechanisms to insure individual journalists provide high-quality work with no interference with the directions and the conclusions of the work itself. Similarly, collaborations among news organizations themselves, while less frequent at this time, also adhere to many of the suggestions outlined above, particularly with regard to the sharing of the results of reporting efforts and the sharing of journalistic credit, as well as a sharing of the financial costs of doing professional work.

The biggest gap is that there is simply not enough money to support the sort of in-depth, high-quality and occasionally experimental journalism that either journalists themselves believe needs to be done or that others believe is necessary for continuing democratic functioning. To a certain extent, this has always been the case. But, one result of the current financial debacle in the news industry is that there is perceptibly less money to support journalism and that the result is that news organizations themselves are retrenching or, in the case of the newspaper industry, ceasing to exist. This financial meltdown has continued for more than a decade, and while there are a host of experiments to fund journalism, the impact of the trend itself is likely to be felt for decades and may continue to intensify.

That is one reason that, going forward, news organizations are going to have to build the 'shadow of the future' into their collaborative financial arrangements. This may mean that organizations are going to have to ask potential donors/supporters to provide a certain amount of funding over and above that devoted to specific projects so that other important, but in some ways more mundane, works get done. From any perspective, such a request is likely to be a very difficult 'ask'. In addition, trying multiple forms of collaborative arrangements lessens the potential that the demise of any particular arrangement will scuttle important journalistic work. Phrased more pointedly, news organizations do not need to repeat current history of becoming dependent on a single financial model which has every possibility of changing radically over the long term.

Collaboration with government: Important boundary work for crowdsourcing

In their revisiting of *The Four Theories of the Press*, Christians et al. (2009) outline a collaborative role for the media – where the primary collaborator is government. They note that, in theory, collaboration with government most often occurs in new nations, but that even in robust democracies, media collaboration with government is sometimes born of emergency (think severe weather warnings) or necessity (think covering electoral debates). They also note that the collaborative role, and the others the authors outline in the book, 'take us directly to the dilemmas and complexities that lie at the heart of any body of normative theories of the media' (Christians et al. 2009, p. 127). Other scholars are much less charitable (McChesney 1999), noting based on substantial empirical evidence that journalism, particularly in the United States, is often the handmaiden of government rather than of a partner or a critic. Government coercion through capitalistic market economics summarizes this view.

Keeping these important insights in mind, it is at the institutional rather than the individual or organizational levels that collaborative arrangements are at their most fragile. This does not mean that institutional-level collaboration is always inappropriate or impossible, just that it becomes much more difficult to foreground reciprocity and capabilities – both of which promote justice – at the institutional level. It is as a bulwark against institutional coercion that crowdsourcing may be a partial remedy, at least when harnessed to investigative and more routine political news. Multiple points of view and deeper involvement in the conversations of democracy do make it more difficult for coercion to succeed. Whether there is or can be a more positive effect on the political imagination is more difficult to forecast.

And, it is justice, as understood through the lens of reciprocity and capabilities, that provides an ethically informed but practical foundation for ongoing collaborative agreements. Such agreements are not going to provide sufficient financial support for all journalists and news organizations, but they can – and in many ways already are – become a much more important 'player' than in previous eras. Thinking through an ethical approach to what collaboration should look like has at least the potential of allowing those arrangements to be long-lived and productive, to support journalism that remains a public service, and to allow those who understand the need for that service to have an impact on the political community of which all actors are a part.

References

Aristotle. 1987. *The Nicomachean Ethics*. Trans. J. E. C. Welldon. New York: Prometheus Books.

Axelrod, 1984. *The Evolution of Cooperation*. New York: Basic Books.

Becker, Lawrence C. 1986. *Reciprocity*. London, Boston: Routledge & Kegan Paul.

Black, J., Steele, B., and Barney, R. 1997. *Doing Ethics in Journalism. Society of Professional Journalists*. New York: Allyn & Bacon.

Bok, S. 1983. *Lying: Moral Choice in Public and Private Life*. New York: Random House.

Borden, Sandra L. 2007. *Journalism as Practice: MacIntyre, Virtue Ethics and the Press*. Aldershot, UK: Ashgate.

Christians, Clifford, G., Ferre, John, and Fackler, Mark. 1993. *Good News: Social Ethics and the Press*. Oxford: Oxford University Press.

Christians, C., Glasser, T., McQuail, D., Nordenstreng, K., and White, R. 2009. *Normative Theories of the Media: Journalism in Democratic Societies*. Champagne, IL: University of Illinois Press.

McChesney, R. 1999. *Rich Media, Poor Democracy: Communication Politics in Dubious Times*. Urbana: University of Illinois Press.

Meyers, Christopher. 2003. 'Appreciating W. D. Ross: On Duties and Consequences', *Journal of Mass Media Ethics*, 18(2): 81–97.

Noddings, Nel. 1984. *Caring: A Feminine Approach to Ethics and Moral Education*. Berkeley: University of California Press.

Nussbaum, Martha. 2000. *Women and Human Development: The Capabilities Approach*. Cambridge: Cambridge University Press.

Nussbaum, Martha. C. 2006. *Frontiers of Justice*. Cambridge, MA: Harvard University Press.

Picard, Robert. 2010. *Value Creation and the Future of News Organizations: Why and How Journalism Must Change to Remain Relevant in the Twenty-First Century*. Lisbon: Media XXI.

Picard, R. 1986. *The Ravens of Odin: The Press in the Nordic Nations*. Ames, Iowa: Iowa State University Press.

Putnam, R. 1988. 'Reciprocity and Virtue Ethics', *Ethics*, 98(2): 379–389.

Rawls, John. 1971. *A Theory of Justice*. Cambridge, MA: Harvard University Press.

Ross, W. D. 1930. *The Right and the Good*. Oxford, UK: Clarendon Press.

Sandel, M. 2009. *Justice: What's the Right Thing to Do*. New York: Farrar, Straus and Giroux.

Steiner, Linda. 2009. 'Feminist Media Ethics', in L. Wilkins and C. Christians (eds.), *The Handbook of Mass Media Ethics*, pp. 366–381. New York: Routledge.

Ward, Stephen J. A. 2011. *Ethics and the Media: An Introduction*. Cambridge: Cambridge University Press.

Wilkins, L. 2013. 'I Don't Do the News: If Anything Important Happens, My Friends Will Tell Me About It on Facebook', in Berrin Beassley and Mitch Haney (eds.), *Social Media and the Value of Truth*, pp. 65–82. Lanham, MD: Lexington Books (Rowan & Littlefield).

Wilson, E. O. 2000. *Sociobiology: A New Synthesis*. Cambridge: Harvard University Press.

6

News for Sale: 'Paid News', Media Ethics, and India's Democratic Public Sphere

Vipul Mudgal

It is difficult to theorize the practice of 'paid news' in routine democratic discourse. As such, sociologists have been skeptical of media's objectivity or selective perceptions, but even by those standards putting a price tag on news coverage is the new low for India's thriving quality press. Ample literature has been written on how media is linked to the exercise of power and hegemony, how it helps in manufacturing consent and steering of public opinions, or how concerns of the marginalized citizens seldom make news (Gramsci 1971, Adorno and Horkheimer 1979, Herman and Chomsky 1988, Entman 1989, Nimmo and Combs 1990, Entman and Bannett 2001). More specifically, some research is now available on the awesome spread of the Indian media, particularly in the language market, and also on its pro-urban and pro-market predispositions (Jeffrey 2000, Ninan 2007, Thakurta 2009, Mudgal 2011, Krishnan 2012). But the issue of selling editorial space by the 'free press' still baffles the believers and the skeptics alike. What is now (in)famous as 'paid news' in India is the practice of charging a fee, in cash or equity, from politicians, film stars, businessmen, or from private companies, for presenting biased and one-sided news items to be passed off as routine news coverage. Its occurrence goes up during elections, when individual candidates or their parties could do with orchestrated hype, or when a private company enters the equity market or even when a new movie is about to be released.

During India's 15th parliamentary elections in 2009, many candidates made complaints to the Election Commission (EC) about their rivals paying for media hype as well as to black out news about them as opponents. According to P. Sainath, the rural affairs editor of one of India's largest circulation English Dailies, *The Hindu*, whose reports first exposed the scam in the state of Maharashtra in Western India, the newspapers in question fixed a rate for news slots, where news items apparently supplied by the 'buyers' would be published without editing. The whole operation was mostly illegal and was transacted in 'black' or unaccounted money, with serious implications for holding democratic elections. During the 2014 elections to the 16th Lok Sabha, the EC has issued 3100 notices to individual candidates for having indulged in 'paid news' and out of which it has confirmed 787 cases as those of 'paid news', Indian Express reported quoting EC sources.[1]

After the exposure by Sainath, the Press Council of India (PCI) commissioned a report on the subject, apparently under moral and public pressure. The Council later declined to make the report public, apparently under pressure from media barons or their representatives who are its members. (The composition of the PCI is such that the owners of publications, and the managers/journalists appointed by them, have a majority in the 28-member council.) In theory the members can come to the council from different nomination routes, but the owners do exercise more power over the Council than any other group. The report was later made public only on the intervention of the Central Information Commission under the citizens' Right to Information (RTI). The report,[2] now available on the Press Council of India's official website, notes: 'The phenomenon of "paid news" goes beyond the corruption of individual journalists and media companies. It has become pervasive, structured and highly organised and in the process, is undermining democracy in India.'

The matter has attracted nationwide shock and outrage in India, ostensibly because the common people still have high expectations from their media. The practice has profound legal, moral, and ethical implications. It violates the basic principle of media ethics such as the sanctity of facts, impartiality, and even rudimentary notions of professionalism and objectivity. In legal terms it breaches the statutes of the bourses and their regulatory bodies like the Securities and Exchange Board of India (SEBI), the rules and regulations of the statutory Election Commission of India, and the Income Tax laws. The PCI report calls the practice a 'deception' or 'fraud' and calls it an open violation of media, election, and tax laws.[3]

In a country where some election or the other to 29 State Assemblies, seven Union Territories and thousands of rural or urban local bodies takes place round the year, 'paid news' has a direct bearing on the state's responsibility to provide a level playing field to all candidates and also on the individual voter's right to make informed choices. The candidates or their parties are free to buy advertisement space in the media, subject to the EC's expenditure limits. But eyebrows are hardly raised at these or at media's ideological positions in favor of a party or an individual because the readers have learnt to expect – and factor – all kinds of affiliations, kinship, or even prejudices in a multi-cultural and multi-lingual country of India's size and diversity. There are hardly any expectations from dubious publications either. However, 'paid news' evokes outrage when the 'quality press' deliberately passes off advertisements as news. Obviously, besides offending readers, it tinkers with the process of political communication in ways that compromise democracy.

Some of these dangers are already being felt and discussed in India. The PCI sub-committee report quotes Mr Madabhushi Sridhar, Director of the Centre for Media Law and Policy, Hyderabad: 'earlier, politicians used to hire musclemen with huge amounts of money and train them in booth rigging. Now...candidates are training media pens instead of mafia guns to "rig" the minds of people with constant opinion bombarding.'[4]?

This chapter attempts to theorize India's practice of 'paid news' in the context of political communication, where on the one hand a market-driven media shuns even basic notions of professional ethics, while on the other an incremental mediaization of politics tends to render democratic processes vulnerable to motivated distortions. It also argues that despite elemental flaws in commercial media systems, the practice can be tackled to a large extent by implementing the rule of law, strengthening citizen oversight, and by reinforcing professional ethics through mature democratic institutions, a watchful civil society, and the presence of a plural public sphere.

Political communication, mediation, and passive publics

The core business of politics – from acquiring power to policymaking and from negotiating controls to allocating resources – requires delicate and constant communication at every stage. That is why a politician is only expected to use all means to connect with his constituency in order to try and influence public opinion, of course without violating the law, or more precisely, without being caught violating the law. Political parties, celebrities, and even nations are increasingly being seen as brands in the cultural marketplace with semiotic depiction of the values/ideologies they represent. Scammell (2007) argues that branding is the new hallmark of political marketing. In a paper which examines the rebranding of Labour Party prime ministerial candidate Tony Blair in the run up to the 2005 UK elections, Scammell maintains that branding has now replaced market research, spin, and advertising which were seen as the key signifiers of political communication in the 1980s and 1990s. Indian National Congress, one of India's main political parties, was the first one to use a professional advertising agency in the 1980s, heralding a new beginning in political communication in India. Almost all political parties ever since have been using professional agencies and newer communication technologies for marketing and brand-building in the subsequent elections involving big money and some of the biggest names in the advertising world (Karan 2009). However, the brand-building exercise was taken to newer heights by Bharatiya Janata Party's (BJP) Narendra Modi, the then Chief Minister of the Western Indian State of Gujarat, who used 3D audio-visual technology to 'address' several virtual public meetings simultaneously. The 3D holographic video projection was put up by the British firm Musion and the opposition leaders put the price tag at somewhere around INR 250 crore (USD 45 million), even though the BJP played it down. Modi's hi-tech campaigns, first in Gujarat in 2012 and then in entire India as BJP's prime ministerial candidate in 2014, set up media war rooms to harness social media and mobile platforms in order to build brand-Modi as something bigger than his own party, in what is described as India's most expensive and most polarized election so far.

The trend clearly shows that the use of emerging technologies, political marketing, and brand-building strategies is on the rise. However, 'paid news' comes across as a crude retail option for candidates who may not be able to afford refined and expensive devices. A successful politician has to learn the whole range of political communication, from pleading to bullying and selling dreams to delivering hate speeches. Eric Louw (2005) puts it most succinctly: 'Political communication is a multi-dimensional multi form phenomenon, e.g. speech, body language, memoranda, media releases and political violence. The spectrum of communicative possibilities is endless – including one-on-one deal making with colleagues/allies; negotiating with opponents; making promises to win support; making threats...; and threatening and unleashing, coercion and violence.'[5] A vital sub-text of political communication is persuasion by any means – even through real or threatened violence. Schmid and Graaf (1982) have studied many forms of violence as means of political communication: 'violence aims at behavior modification by coercion. Propaganda aims at the same by persuasion.

Terrorism is a combination of the two.'⁶ Some parts of political communication, such as the use of threats and hate speech, are routine for politicians who have profound understanding of commercial media's news selection criteria. A fuller picture of this phenomenon lies as much in the nature of sectarian politics as in the functioning of the mass media.

For a politician willing to take a minor risk, 'paid news' offers affordable communication solutions in the times of exorbitant brand-building campaigns. It is well known that many rabble-rousers are invited to TV studios for the traction of their outrageous statements, but the 'paid news' opens up newer vistas even for them. The art of running strategic electoral campaigns would normally require them to get ahead in the persuasion game. For an extra buck the permutations and combinations of options under 'paid news' allow candidates to steal a march over rivals, while simultaneously arranging negative exposure for them. It is like a 'poor man's impression management tool' available in the retail market. They can build and demolish a straw man by amplifying statements of petty rivals or even make a multi-corner contest look like a two-horse race. Just like the high-value brand-building exercise, 'paid news' also has the potential to alter the texture of political communication as we have known it so far.

For the news media, however, selling 'spurious' news amounts to willfully keeping those unsuspecting audiences who believe that the news stories are based on verifiable facts and have passed through experienced hands in the dark. In their own advertising, media houses claim to be in the business of telling the truth. The readers therefore expect professionalism from the media outlets they patronize. For the audiences unaware of compromised 'paid news', it is like an 'unfreedom' which prohibits their informed choices and adversely affects their right to expect quality services from their chosen service providers.

It will be oversimplification to look at the sale of editorial space as a complete departure from existing practices. Journalism, like any other vocation, relies on a set of professional practices, and the end product passes through a standard production process, in this case, akin to cultural assembly lines. There is no denying that journalists in reputed media organizations try not to take sides and are encouraged to work professionally. However, despite observing a degree of detachment, they have to deliver crisp copies, obviate legal hassles, score a point over competition, earn credibility, and, in the long run, help build (profitable) media brands. All this, however, does not negate the fact that journalism operates like a work of fiction (Manoff and Schudson 1986).

It is not that they close their eyes and imagine stories. Journalists use professional skills to construct stories block by block and often filigree their creations by nuances, juxtapositions, visuals, data, file-footage, and other canned material which is not germane to the issue at hand.

Plainly put by Schudson (2011), 'News, like bread or sausage, is something people make. Scholars emphasize the manufacturing process.' The course of such wholesale construction has its own systems of almost automatic inclusions and exclusions. Tuchman (1978) believes that not just news but all sorts of public documents follow discourses unique to them. Cohen, Adoni, and Bantz (1990) describe the process of everyday construction of reality as a dialectical process 'in which the human beings act as creators and as products of their social world. This is a consequence of a special human faculty of externalization and objectivation of one's own internalized and subjective meanings, experiences and actions.'[7] That is why a large part of political communication will be understood through the practices which produce it in the first place rather than through the larger message it intends to convey (Golding and Elliot 1979). It will also be unraveled through a 'consumer model' rather than a 'mass media model' (Scammell 2007).

Any understanding of political communication will be incomplete without studying aspects of meaning construction by the real or intended receivers of the messages. The worldviews of the citizens – who largely depend on media for news and who tend to be second hand consumers of politics – are principally media-tized worldviews with ample scope for tinkering. In the world of bespoke media solutions for branded political products, messages could be professionally flavored with enhancements or distortions, through a variety of new-age crafts and emerging technologies. In this perspective, 'paid news' can be seen as just another bespoke media solution meant for marquee clients. Plain vanilla advertisements are passé and the new marketing managers in successful media companies have to get into their clients' skins to be able to provide 'solutions' and extra mileage for political branding. All this, in the long run, adds to hegemonic endeavors and control mechanisms of the dominant sections and classes.

'Media-tization' of politics has far-reaching impact on both politics and media, where TV studios overshadow established institutions like the court or the parliament. The new direct-to-home technologies allow the media to assemble artificial publics and then market other derivatives based on their numbers or purchasing powers. It is well known that the modern commercial media are primarily in the business of selling audiences to advertisers rather than selling news to consumers, as is fondly believed. The advent of newer technologies, particularly the mobile-phone-based news platforms, is bound to hasten this process in future. The possibilities of enhancement and spin allow mass struggles to be replaced by proxy political battles fought not in the streets but in the newspaper columns and TV studios.

Thus the 'second-hand reality' that the audiences consume in mediated societies has serious implications for political communication. By this logic, the members of the public(s) are mostly passive participants in political processes around them. Nimmo and Combs (1990) argue that most American citizens don't encounter politics in a first-hand manner. The media create synthetic 'publics' by aggregating 'atomized' individual members of the audience who may not be linked to one another through socially significant ties even though they serve as homogenous sets (of socio-economic groups) ready to be bundled together and 'sold' to advertisers. Conversely, the inclusion of publics in political processes around them should work as an antidote to mediation and media-tization, opening new possibilities in participatory politics and the expansion of a democratic public sphere, but we will come to that later.

Just as the politicians need to market their brands during elections, companies entering the stock market through Initial Public Offerings (IPOs) require professional communicators to attract as much public money as possible in the shortest possible time. Individual stockholders are mostly passive consumers of vital information about the companies they are investing in, just as the citizens are often passive consumers of second-hand politics. Their relationships with the goods and services they invest in remain highly vicarious. It is hardly an exaggeration that a considerably large section of investing publics in the retail share market depend entirely on the mass media for information. Hence, just like questionable election reporting, news about companies and share market operators is often 'rigged' with potentially disastrous consequences for shareholders, and ultimately for democracy.

This is where the blurring of lines between advertisements and editorials become significant. One of India's most profitable media companies, Bennett, Coleman and Company Limited (BCCL), pioneered inventive schemes like 'medianet' which offered publicity and hype in news columns to private entities, individuals, and movie stars for a price without giving the readers a fair idea of the paid-up content. Later, the BCCL, the publishers of the Times of India, branded many supplements of the paper as 'advertorial, entertainment promotional feature', ostensibly to evade legal traps of selling news space without proper disclosure.

The BCCL also launched 'private treaties' with fledgling companies to give them positive publicity for a price bartered in shares. Such private treaties come not only at the cost of the shareholders' interests but also at the cost of providing level playing field to other companies floating their IPOs.

Lobbyists, spin artists, and some willing collaborators

Some of India's powerful Public Relations and spin outfits got exposed almost accidentally when the 'Radia tapes' were leaked in 2010, ostensibly as a result of a corporate tussle between two competing industrial groups. The tapes were an assortment of telephonic conversations between a corporate lobbyist, Niira Radia, who was made famous by the sudden spotlight, her prestigious 'contacts' in the media, and her clients among India's top industrial houses. The conversations were recorded in 2008–2009 by the Income Tax Department as part of an investigation into suspected money-laundering and were later leaked to some media websites. The conversations show the who's who of Indian media, blatantly helping the lobbyist get access to top politicians. These included the top editors of several English newspaper and TV channels, top managers of publishing houses, and some of the country's most influential politicians. The PR agency successfully lobbied for appointments in the all-powerful union cabinet, planting motivated coverage about government policies on resource allocations concerning bandwidth for telecom industry, mining leases, and oil exploration blocks.

Although the media coverage 'arranged' through friendly scribes is, at best, a sophisticated form of 'paid news', it exposed the ease with which the corporate world uses and manipulates the media. While the tapes exposed some cozy relationships, what did not come out beyond circumstantial data, however, was the evidence of money being paid for the services provided. The murky story of Niira Radia creating an empire worth around USD 50 million through her PR operations definitely goes beyond the practice of 'paid news'. One of the obvious discoveries was the way in which the spin doctors, lobbyist, and some of the country's most highly placed – and highly paid – journalists were keenly promoting corporate interests, sometimes independent of their employers. The ease and the sophistication of the process in which the high and mighty were able to subvert the system made the everyday examples of 'paid news' look crude, like a highway robbery.

Vinod Mehta, editor-in-chief of the nationwide English news magazine *Outlook*, who first posted the audio tapes on his magazine's website, says in his memoirs (Mehta 2011): 'Even a fleeting hearing led to the unavoidable conclusion that India is up for sale.'[8] Mehta, who is no stranger to goings on inside the hallowed media portals said that 'the recklessness, the candour, the bargaining, the venality, the conviction that anything and everything could be fixed, took our breath away'.[9] Clearly, the Radia tapes brought the spotlight on India's layered political communication involving the troika of the political class, business houses, and the media. It is ironical that while some ministers had to face the humiliation, and unusually long jail terms, the media went back to 'business as usual' with odd apologies and half-clarifications.

Since the mid-2000s India has been witnessing a new trend of consolidation of media in fewer hands through large investments by leading corporate houses. The biggest of these include the Aditya Birla Group's investment, said to be over 27%, in the TV today Group that runs the Hindi TV news channel *Aaj Tak* and its English counterpart, the *Headlines Today*. India's biggest private company, Reliance Industries Limited, controlled by the Mukesh Ambani Group, took over the South India-based Eenadu Group, which controls a string of TV news and entertainment channels in many languages across the country, and simultaneously entered into an arrangement with the Network18 Group, which runs English TV channel *CNN-IBN*, Hindi channel *IBN 7*, and business and financial news channel *CNBC India* to create one of India's largest media entities. Another important channel, *NDTV* has close to 15% investment from the Oswal group.

A large number of Indian politicians and political parties too run newspapers, magazines, and TV news channels. The parties (or their key leaders) which directly or indirectly control sizeable news operations include the ruling BJP; the main opposition party, the Indian National Congress (INC); ruling parties in many states, like the Biju Janata Dal in Orissa, the Akali Dal in Punjab, DMK and AIADMK in Tamil Nadu and the Samajwadi Party and Bahujan Samaj Party in Uttar Pradesh; among many other parties in many other states. Even the two Communist Parties of India – CPI and CPIM – control networks of mass circulation newspapers and TV news channels in several Indian languages. However, not all such papers or channels are official 'organs' of the parties owning them.

Professionalism and public interest as defense mechanisms

Despite the gloomy picture of media ownership and the new trends, it is not uncommon to find stinging media scoops or investigative stories in the commercial news media. This is necessary to retain credibility which is the main currency of the business. In fact, media organizations take pride in, and make a show of, their investigative stories in avowed public interest. There are numerous instances of journalists reflexively resisting pressures, often at great risks to their careers and even lives. There are equally significant instances of the spin doctors falling flat on their faces, often due to such exposés. These instances are not a daily occurrence, but the fact that they are there can be the foundation for a sharper adversarial relationship between the media and the political powers. It is not my case to write off journalism as completely inconsequential, or beyond improvement, because of the industry's commercial nature. To lose all hope in the positive potential of journalism will be like throwing the baby out with the bath water.

A good way to appreciate the value of a commercial 'free' press is to compare it with those societies where the media is gagged or is an appendage of the ruling dispensation. It is reassuring therefore that media organizations' earnings commonly have a correlation with their credibility. The market logics can't negate the fact that the audiences place a premium on integrity and credibility, in a competitive environment of media diversity and pluralism. And that is why there is always some scope for the citizens to be able to intervene in ways that can make media more conscientious and accountable to society. As discussed earlier, a deliberative democracy, with institutional ways of public participation, can guard against media's excesses. It is true that media-tization hampers participation, but processes like devolution of power and governance through subsidiarity have the ability to create enabling environments. Just as a liberal democracy with all its flagrant flaws scores over most other systems of governance, a credible media that is commercial, yet, independent of the government is the citizens' best choice in the want of something better. This can even be a building block for something more constructive in the times to come. In future, one cannot rule out the possibility of a new model of public service media emerging out of new trends like coalition politics, citizen journalism, and emerging social media technologies.

In all this, the significance of pluralism, vigilant institutions, and a competitive environment cannot be overemphasized. For instance, even the best of PR and spin professionals often cancel out each other when working for divergent interests. The competing media organizations, often backed by rival political interests, also outdo each other in exposing corrupt dealings of those in power and their cronies. Some of India's most stinging exposés, including those of the 2G telecom scam, concerning questionable sale of telecom spectrum, and the coal block allocation scams, were possible because of the alert institution of the

Comptroller and Auditor General (CAG). Even in Britain, Prime Minister Tony Blair's main spin doctor Alastair Campbell was axed for 'sexing up' the intelligence dossier ('dodgy dossier') about Saddam Husain's nonexistent 'weapons of mass destruction' before the Iraq War, largely because of the power of investigative journalism.

Obviously, this kind of journalism can get occasional and opportunistic support from the antagonistic interest groups besides the forces and institutions that have stakes in strengthening democracy. The very fact that the Indian news magazines *Outlook* and *Open* were able to take on the high and mighty by posting the incriminating Radia tapes on their websites (and many blogs and independent sites followed up with detailed transcripts and interpretations) also managed to cock a snook at the establishment. Some of India's most influential corporate houses and even the government of the day did everything in their power to remove such material from open platforms on all kinds of pretexts, including violation of privacy, but failed in doing so mainly because the judiciary failed to oblige. Many other institutions like the EC and regulators like the SEBI, and the judiciary can go a long way in strengthening the extending the reach of the media.

Earlier, Bangaru Laxman, the president of the BJP which was leading New Delhi's ruling coalition in 2001, was captured on a camera sting accepting a bribe as advance payment of a bigger commission to be paid in return for facilitating a fictitious defense deal. In 2012, over a decade after the sting, carried out by investigative journalists Aniruddha Bahal and Samuel Matthew for Tehelka magazine, Laxman was sentenced to four years rigorous imprisonment by Delhi High Court for taking bribe. In another sting carried out by Bahal in 2005, ten high-profile members of parliament lost their seats for accepting cash in front of hidden cameras for asking questions in parliament. Controversial as they are, the 'sting operations' have not been called unlawful by the judiciary except in rare cases. In the court hearings of the cases filed following the Bahl exposés, and in many other similar cases, the Indian judiciary upheld the sting operations by exonerating journalists. It is significant that the Broadcasting Standards Commission of the United Kingdom has advised that the level of deception used in a sting should be proportionate to the alleged wrongdoing effectively justifying intrusion in a corrupt individual's privacy in 'public interest'. Aiden White, General Secretary of the International Federation of Journalists, said in an interview on Lok Sabha TV that one of the most honorable acts of sting was carried out in South Africa during apartheid when journalists bugged a meeting of the racist military leaders who were planning action against African National Congress leaders in which lives could have been lost.[10]

The exposés and other responses to 'paid news' in India

If there is anything spectacular in the Indian society's response to 'paid news', it was the country's shock and awe expressed from virtually every quarter, including from autonomous institutions like the EC, PCI, SEBI, and judiciary. Media diversity and pluralism have also played a leading role in the exposés that have rocked some of the mightiest media empires. The practice has been subsequently challenged, confronted, and denounced in public meetings, discussions, on social media and in court and parliamentary proceedings. Many rival newspapers, magazines and TV channels – who resisted the temptations of 'paid news' but whose business rivals were indulging in the practice – were the first ones to take a shot. The most scathing attack came from P. Sainath who blew the cover of some powerful politicians and media barons in his columns in *the Hindu*. Sainath named the Maharashtra Chief Minister Ashok Chavan for brazenly using 'paid news' during his election campaign and dared Chavan to sue him, and this, eventually led to his resignation.

In an elaborate expose, 'It is shameful to misguide people', Sainath wrote: 'Several newspapers published in Maharashtra between October 1st and 10th 2009 make fun reading. Sometimes, you find a page of mysteriously fixed item sizes, say 125–150 words plus a double column photo ... This was so because everything – layouts, fonts, and printouts came from the candidate seeking a slot.'[11] Another elaborate story in *Outlook* by Anuradha Raman in December 2009 quoted many politicians, including Haryana Chief Minister Bhoopender Singh Hooda, as corroborating charges of 'paid news'. It also quotes Congress Member of Parliament Sandeep Dikshit as expressing shock over a TV journalist negotiating a package deal of INR 2.50 lakh (USD 5,000 approx) per hour for live coverage of his party leader Rahul Gnadhi's visit during elections. Dikshit said that the channel offered to even arrange the crowds and shared his helplessness: 'You watch your opponent misusing the media and you are forced to part with money. I won't take names but everyone is involved.'[12]

On the face of it the EC does not deal with the media or its practices, corrupt or otherwise. But as a democratic institution with statutory powers it can take punitive action for electoral violations. This is how EC disqualified Uttar Pradesh legislator Umlesh Yadav, of Rashtriya Parivartan Dal, in October 2011 for not declaring the expenditure on 'paid news' in two Hindi dailies, against whom no action was taken. The EC disqualified Ms. Yadav, from contesting any election for Parliament or the State legislatures or Councils for three years, under Section 10A of the Representation of the People Act, 1951. Similar proceedings are also initiated against Chavan and the former Chief Minister of Jharkhand, Madhu Koda. Although the EC has managed to constitute Media Certification and Monitoring Committees in all constituencies to keep an eye on such cases, it is a travesty of justice that the cases against Koda and Chavan are still going on while the MPs completed their parliamentary terms and Chavan even got reelected to the 16th Lok Sabha in 2014.

While the democratic institutions are trying to assert themselves, the media owners and their inventive managers are trying hard to push advertisements into the 'sacred' domain of news. Most publications run elaborate advertorials where sponsored features are run as news under ambiguous tags like the 'media marketing feature' or 'impact feature' instead of straight 'advertisement' or even 'advertorial'. These, however, have not raised the hackles of the audiences, the civil society or the autonomous institutions because of the proverbial fig leaf of differentiation between sponsored and designated news.[13] However, the civil society has treated 'paid news' with the contempt worthy of spurious drugs or adulterated food. This is so because of a general belief that the consumers have a right to expect a reasonable quality of news from commercial media in the same way as they expect a reasonable quality of medical service or education from a commercial hospital or a private university. It is another matter, however, that unlike other paid services and products, the impact of a news story goes far beyond its immediate context and has a direct bearing on matters of politics, governance, and public opinion.

Prabhash Joshi, Chief Editor of the Hindi language broadsheet *Jansatta* said at a discussion organized by the Foundation for Media Professionals (FMP), an organization of journalists at New Delhi on October 28, 2009, that if the media owners consider newspapers to be just another product, they must fulfill the consumer logic of disclosing upfront ingredients like news, advertisements, and sponsored features, just as a box of corn flakes has to mention ingredients, or just as medicines have to disclose side effects. A summary of what became Joshi's last public discussion are available on Youtube and on the FMP website.[14] Joshi named three senior politicians, Harmohan Dhawan of the Bahujan Samaj Party (Chandigarh Constituency), Atul Kumar Anjan of the Communist Party of India (Ghosi constituency in UP) and Mohan Singh of Samajwadi

Party (Deoria Constituency, also in UP), all of whom lost their elections because of the use of 'paid news' by their rivals.

Many other prominent groups, among them the Editors' Guild of India, Delhi Union of Journalists (DUJ), International Federation of Working Journalists (IFWJ), and the India International Centre, deplored the practice in packed halls and urged the EC to take strong action against the violating media entities and politicians. Many civil society organizations, including the Mazdoor Kishan Shakti Sangathan (MKSS) and the Association for Democratic Reforms (ADR), demanded that media companies appoint ombudsmen to redress complaints about fairness or accuracy of news and a forum of all ombudsmen be created to further adjudicate unresolved complaints.[15]

It may be argued that due to citizens' pressure, assertions of norms by democratic institutions, and the fear of losing credibility and business, many media houses, including Hindi daily, Dainik Bhaskar, which earlier faced charges of 'paid news', launched a 'no "paid news" campaign' in 2012. (The group's English paper Daily News and Analysis (DNA) also brought out a code of ethics on the front page on the Republic Day edition, January 26, 2012.) The Editor-in-Chief of the Hindustan Times also declared in a signed editorial on the paper's front page in early 2013 that 'HT brings you real news not "paid news"', denying a report in the *Hindu* attributed to the Press Council of India making allegations of 'paid news'. Even the BCCL later started maintaining, rather categorically, that they do not sell editorial space in the main paper.

In lieu of conclusion: Ethics in the times of hi-tech pluralism and digital public sphere

Media are an integral part of India's democratic life. It is common to find at least sections of media pursuing anti-establishment campaigns at any given point of time. Boasting of 22 recognized languages, 29 states and 657 districts, each with an average population of close to two million, India's media universe is plural and diverse. The country has over 80,000 registered publications, about 250 radio stations, and 800 TV channels, until the last count in 2012. It is understandable, and pleasantly so, that such diverse media hardly ever speaks in one voice, except perhaps when the Indian cricket team wins a tournament! No wonder then that the practice of 'paid news' was first exposed by Indian media itself, notably the *Hindu*, Hindi daily *Jansatta*, and news magazines *Outlook*, *Tehelka*, and *Open*, among others, at different point of time. It is not clear, however, that these expose were borne out of professional considerations alone, or, for that matter, if these organizations would rise to the occasion every time ethical norms are violated.

The biggest casualty of the lack of codified ethical norms is enforceable standards of professionalism. A lack of ethical norms tends to reduce professionalism to contestable notions of fairness and objectivity. Such exalted notions have come under sharp criticism from media scholars for a very long time (Tuchman 1971, Schiller 1981, Herman and Chomsky 1988, Bagdikian 1992). However, the ideas of ethics/professionalism are more tractable and less nebulous compared to those of objectivity/fairness and the enforcement of the former can lead to a semblance of the latter. Those who pin their hopes on pluralism and media diversity believe that the commercial media can be made more ethical, professional or accountable to the citizens. Many democratic societies have also attempted to resurrect, successfully to varying degrees, versions of public service media to strengthen not-for-profit journalism and to give a healthy competition to their commercial counterparts.

How the citizenry, or, the competing multiple publics, will rein in the media will always be a tenuous proposition but a tug of war is usually on. The citizens choose the media outlets which reinforce their ideas and beliefs, and therefore, are deeply suspicious of the opposite. A small but growing number of younger media consumers are bypassing the conventional media for virtual media and other real-time, interactive options. A brand new and full-fledged discipline is emerging around a somewhat subversive notion of digital publics and digital democracy (Dahlberg 2011).[16] New types of counter-publics are forming around the digital and the virtual worlds and alternative media forms are already flourishing on the Internet. Consequently, the conventional media could be 'a narrative of decline' because of a profusion of citizen-operated blogs and the subsequent rise of opinion (Graeme Turner 2010).

Although the rise of the new media is far from throwing mainstream media out of business, its challenge is palpable for both the industry as well as the establishment. The conventional media is hedging its bets by using the Internet and mobile platforms as force multipliers but it has to compete against a multitude of smaller, and often smarter, players. An explosion of the hyper-local language press and the advent of social media have led to a dramatic expansion of the democratic public sphere even though the burgeoning volumes of audiences as content creators have led to a certain diffusion of the information universe. For instance, the fact that the new social media technologies allow fast interactivity and participation, they have a direct bearing on widening of the public sphere, often with healthy consequences like the formation of social capital, and sometimes with disastrous results like outbreak of rumors and eruption of sectarian riots. This form of communication and connectivity has serious implications for both media and politics. That is why the establishments like to monitor and control the virtual world.

Those who count on the power of pluralism in liberal democracies place their faith in the simultaneous presence of competing interest groups. They support an active citizenry and disagree that mediated societies are forever and that they would necessarily lead to the creation of passive publics. And therefore, it is a rational assumption that the advent of active citizenry, competing interest groups – and the presence of watchful institutions – would curb the power of governments and enforce ethical norms on all professions including journalism. If the ruling parties and the governments have stakes in secrecy, the opposition, sundry watchdogs and the civil society have equal stakes in transparency and accountability. A case in point is the success of the civil society and peoples' movements in pushing subversive legislations like the Lok Pal (anti-corruption ombudsman) Right to Information and Whistleblower Protection.

As a diverse media reaches out to more people at the bottom of the pyramid, through increasing localization of language papers, argues Sevanti Ninan (2007), more and more issues of vibrancy of the grassroots are reflected in the local coverage, expanding the local public sphere in ways considered unimaginable earlier.[17] Ninan believes that the new reach of the language papers has percolated India's party politics down to the *panchayat* level. The increase in circulation through the 90s is nothing short of an explosion (Jeffrey 2000) recording over 100% rise for six languages (Bengali, English, Kannada, Malayam, Marathi, and Urdu), over 200% for Hindi and Oriya, 372% for Telugu and 613% for Assamese.[18]

All this is bound to play a bigger role in the reinforcement of a democratic public sphere. If 'a portion of public sphere comes into being in every conversation in which private individuals assemble to form a public body', as argued by Habermas (1964), the presence of numerous forms of citizens' organizations should work against the domination of the state. It is significant that 'the state and public sphere do not overlap' and the public sphere mediates between the society and the state[19] and 'facilitates maximum public participation and debate',[20] Rajeev Bhargava and Helmut Reifeld (2005) argue that the public sphere is depersonalized and has a strong dimension of impartiality to it[21] and that the raison-d'être of the public sphere is to exert influence on public policy.

Besides democratizing public sphere, a plural polity also prevents any single entity from becoming perpetual ruling elite. The dynamics of competing interests – and the vibrancy of vernacular politics – paves the way further for a more accountable system. Professional ethics, and even self-regulation, have a better chance of working in environments where citizens and their institutions are both dynamic and diverse. In many countries where citizens' awareness levels are high it is common for competing media organizations to publicize their codes of ethics and conflict of interest policies on their websites, and declare their stakes in the companies being written about.

A relatively transparent system works like the saving grace of commercial journalism and helps individual journalists to evolve a working ideology for themselves around their organizations' self-avowed ethical and professional codes. It is akin to the difference between the doctor's profession and the business of running a profitable hospital. Even though the management of the hospital might want all patients to undergo expensive and unnecessary tests in the interest of the hospital's economy and its shareholders, medical ethics require doctors to keep their patients' interest above all such persuasions. Christian, Fackler and Rotzoll (1995) argue that the ethics of the media are inalienably linked to the society's overall social ethics. The authors predicate their big arguments about media ethics on social responsibility theory and take their inspiration from the thoughts and initiatives evolving out of medical ethics. Hence an idea of professionalism based on ethics provides some relative freedom to individual reporters and a degree of autonomy to the editors in the newsroom. This is essential to achieve a relatively more accountable, if not ideal, media.

The idea of locating commercial news media in the context of an active citizenry and an expanding public sphere puts the burden of at least some of the system's flaws on the society's failure to evolve and enforce higher values of social ethics, democracy, and the rule of law. This means that many of these flaws could be easily removed by effectively implementing the existing laws, creating a system of citizens' oversight of media functioning, putting reasonable restrictions on cross media ownerships, and encouragement to competition and diversity against monopolies. The individuals' rights do have public dimension in the context of the wider public sphere and therefore the exercise of freedoms and rights by those who value them has a bearing on the 'unfreedoms' experienced by fellow and less privileged citizens. It will therefore be hasty to write off the privately-owned media as something beyond recovery.

Issues of transparency, accountability to citizens, and normative ethical standards would therefore apply to almost all commercial public services in general and in particular to professions linked to privately owned universities, corporate hospitals, and commercial media organizations. Seen from this perspective the crisis of Indian media is linked to the crises of other professions and services. The commercial nature of the media and the pressure of their investors and shareholders would always push media companies to look for innovative ways to maximize profits, but an equal pressure of demands from the citizens and their institutions would constantly work as a counterweight. After all the shareholders of, say, private hospitals and media companies too are citizens with stakes in the system. The same principle applies to the civil society organizations which often depend on the state and the market forces for existence even though they equally often have to function as an antidote to both. An individual may be passive as a member of an audience, but the public dimension of her rights is significant for the public sphere. Both media and civil society contribute in the expansion of such public sphere by constantly pushing the boundaries and both gain significantly from its presence.

Notes

1. Indian Express, May 24, 2014 (http://indianexpress.com/article/india/india-others/paid-news-ec-issues-3100-notices-confirms-787-cases/) last visited on June 9, 2014.
2. Press Council of India sub-committee on 'paid news' comprising two members, Kalimekolan Sreenivas Reddy and Paranjoy Guha Thakurta was constituted On July 3, 2009, by the PCI exercising the powers conferred on the Council under Sections 8(1) and 15 of the Press Council of India Act, 1978. The report is available on the official PCI website: http://presscouncil.nic.in/HOME.HTM (last accessed on January 12, 2013).
3. Ibid.
4. Ibid., p. 61.
5. Eric Louw (2005, p. 14).
6. Schmid and Graaf (1982, p. 14).
7. Cohen, Adoni and Bantz (1990, p. 34).
8. Mehta Vinod (2011, p. 250).
9. Ibid.
10. Interview of Aidan White on Lok Sabha TV (India) on August 1, 2008, by Paranjoy Guha Thakurta quoted in Media Ethics (2009).
11. *The Hindu*, December 23, 2009.
12. *Outlook*, December 21, 2009.

13. The term 'civil society' is used several times here and its broad connotations are in terms of a moral civil community of individual citizens, non-state and non-market groups, unions and associations, social as well as peoples' movements, and entities that represent or speak for multiple publics. Rather than being a definition, this is meant to be a working understanding of the variously described term.
14. http://www.youtube.com/watch?v=ek3G3in7Mfo and the FMP website: http://www.fmp.org.in/index.php?p=799 (both sites last accessed on January 15, 2013).
15. Note submitted to the Parliamentary Standing Committee on 'paid news' in December 2010.
16. Lincoln Dahlberg (2011) presents four positions about the diversity of understanding of digital democracy in order to draw attention to different understandings of what extending democracy through digital media means, and to provide a framework for evaluation of digital democracy rhetoric and practice.
17. Sevanti Ninan (2007).
18. Jeffrey (2000) quotes the Registrar of Newspapers for India (RNI) figures to show that the with the growth in literacy from 30 million to 90 million in UP from 1980 to 2001, which is also the time when the Bahujan Samaj Party grew as a *dalit* political force, the circulation of daily newspapers trebled in UP.
19. The Public Sphere: An Encyclopedia Article (1964) by Jergen Habermas, New German Critique, No 3 (Autumn 1974).
20. According to Kellner (2000) 'After studying with Horkheimer and Adorno in Frankfurt, Germany in the 1950s, Habermas investigated both the ways that a new public sphere emerged during the time of the Enlightenment and the American and French revolutions and how it promoted political discussion and debate.'
21. Bhargava and Reifeld argue that in civil society people come together for restricted, personal ends but the public sphere includes the concerns of everybody.

References

Adorno, T. and Horkheimer, M. 1979. 'The Culture Industry: Enlightenment as Mass Deception', in T. Adorno and M. Horkheimer (eds.), *Dialectic of Enlightenment*, pp. 120–124. London: Verso.
Bagdikian, B. 1992. *The Media Monopoly* (fourth edition). Beacon Press: Boston.
Bhargava, R. and Reifeld H. (eds.) 2005. *Civil Society, Public Sphere and Citizenship: Dialogues and Perspectives*. London: New Delhi, Thousand Oaks, Sage.
Chomsky, Noam. 1989. *Necessary Illusions: Thought Control in Democratic Societies*. London: Pluto Press.
Christian, Clifford G., Fackler, Mark and Rotzoll, Kim B. 1995. *Media Ethics: Cases and Moral Reasoning*. USA: Longman Publishers.
Cohen, Adoni A. and Bantz, Charles R. (eds.) 1990. *Social Conflict and Television News*. London, NY: Sage Library of Research 183, Sage, Newbury Park.

Dahlberg, Lincoln 2011. *Reconstructing Digital Democracy: An Outline of Four Positions. New Media and Society*, 13(6). September 2011. LA, London, New Delhi, Singapore and Washington DC: Sage.

Entman, R. M. 1989. *Democracy Without Citizens: Media and the Decay of American Politics*. Oxford: Oxford University Press.

Entman, R. M. and Bannett, W. L. 2001. *Mediated Politics: Communication in the Future of Democracy*. Cambridge: Cambridge University Press.

Fraser, N. 1990. *Rethinking the Public Sphere: A Contribution to the Critique of Actually Existing Democracy, Social Text No 25/26*. Duke University Press. http://api.ning.com/files/hRwSaOzKhGD-wGyDZuJeNffJvQrETo9IizI7bNRisAQ_/RethinkingthePublicSphere.pdf

Golding, P. and Elliot, P. 1979. *Making the News*. London and New York: Longman.

Gramsci, A. 1971. *Selections from the Prison Notebooks*. London: Lawrance and Wishart.

Habermas J. 1964. *The Public Sphere, An Encyclopaedia Article (Originally Appeared in Fischer Lexicon, Staat und Politik)*. New Edition, Frankfurt Mam main 1964. pp. 220–226. http://links.jstor.org/sici?sici=0094-033X%28197423%290%3A3%3C49%3ATPSAEA%3E2.0.CO%3B2-Z

Herman, S. Edward and Chomsky, N. 1988. *Manufacturing Consent: The Political Economy of the Mass Media*. Pantheon Books: New York.

Hohendahl, Peter Uwe. 1979. *Critical Theory, Public Sphere and Culture, Jargen Habermas and His Critics*. New German Critique No 16 (Winter 1979). http://www.jstor.org/stable/487878 (last accessed on March 19, 2012).

Jeffrey, R. 2000. *India's Newspaper Revolution: Capitalism, Politics and the Language Press*. New Delhi: Oxford University Press (Third Edition 2010).

Karan, K. 2009. 'Political Communication in India', in L. Willnat and A. Aw (eds.), *Political Communication in Asia*, pp. 191–215. New York: Routledge.

Keane, J. 1991. *The Media and Democracy*. Cambridge: Polity Press.

Kellner, D. 2000. 'Habermas, the Public Sphere, and Democracy: A Critical Intervention' in Lewis Hahn (ed.), *Perspectives on Habermas* (eds), Chicago and La Salle, Illinois: Open Court Press.

Kellner, D. 2005. *Media Spectacles and the Crises of Democracy: Terrorism, Wars, and Election Battles, Paradigm*. Also see The Media and Social Problems at: http://www.gseis.ucla.edu/faculty/kellner/)

Krishnan, S. 2012. Urban Press Glosses over Rural Protests (Coverage Given to Anti-Nuclear Protests in Kudankulam) The Hoot/Books and Research http://thehoot.org/web/Urbanpressglossesoverruralprotests/6064-1-1-9-true.html (last accessed on January 12, 2013).

Kuhn, T. S. 1980. *The Structure of Scientific Revolutions*. Chicago: University of Chicago Press.

Locke, J. 1966. *The Second Treatise of Government*. Oxford: Basil, Blackwell.

Louw, E. 2005. *The Media and Political Process*. London, Thousand Oaks, New Delhi: Sage.

Manoff, R. K. and Schudson, M. (eds.) 1986. *Reading the News*. New York: Pantheon Books.

Mehta, Vinod. 2011. *Lucknow Boy: A Memoir*. New Delhi: Penguin Viking.

Mudgal, V. 2011. Rural Coverage in the Hindi and English Dailies, *Economic and Political Weekly*, XLVI(35), July 27, 2011.

Nimmo, D. and Combs, J. E. 1990. *Mediated Political Realities*. New York: Longman.

Ninan, S. 2007. *Headlines from the Heartland: Reinventing the Hindi Public Sphere*. New Delhi: Sage.

Sen, A. 2000. *Development as Freedom*. Oxford: Oxford University Press.

Scammell, M. 2007. 'Political Brands and Consumer Citizens: The Rebranding of Tony Blair', pp. 176–192, *Annals of the American Academy of Political and Social Science*, 611, The Consumption of Politics/The Politics of Consumption.

Schiller, D. 1981. *Objectivity and the News: The Public and the Rise of Commercial Journalism*. Philadelphia: University of Pennsylvania Press.

Schmid and de Graaf. 1982. *Violence as Communication: Insurgent Terrorism and the Western News Media*. Beverly Hills, CA: Sage.

Schudson 2011. 'Why Democracies Need an Unlovable Press', in Doris A. Graber (ed.), *Media Power in Politics*, pp. 33–44. Washington DC: C Q Press.

Thakurta, Guha Paranjoy 2009. *Media Ethics Truth Fairness and Objectivity: Making and Breaking News*. New Delhi: Oxford University Press.

Tuchman, G. 1971. 'Objectivity as Strategic Ritual: An Examination of Newsmen's Notions of Objectivity', *American Journal of Sociology*, 77 (4): 660–679.

Tuchman, G. 1978. *Making News*. New York: Free Press.

Turner, Graeme. 2010. *Ordinary People and the Media: The Demonic Turn*. LA, London, New Delhi, Singapore, Washington, DC: Sage.

7
Practices of Indian Journalism: Justice, Ethics, and Globalization

Shakuntala Rao

Globalization defines our era. It is what happens when the movement of people, goods, or ideas among countries and regions accelerates. In recent years, globalization has come into focus, generating considerable interest and controversy in the social sciences, humanities, and policy circles and among the informed public at large. Throughout most of history, the vectors that organized and gave meaning to human lives and human imaginations were structured primarily by local geography and topology, local kinship and social organization, local worldviews and religions. Today the world is another place. While human lives continue to be lived in local realities, these realities are increasingly being challenged by and integrated into larger global networks of relationships. Media are at the heart of such changes. The multidirectional flow of media and cultural goods is creating new forms of convergence and identities. These forms are often received either with exhilaration or panic (Mattelart 2002). Yet no one can disregard that there is an acceleration of media convergence exemplified by various intersections among media technologies, industries, content, and audiences.

If we are to consider justice and the institutions of justice to be key institutions that 'hold democracy together', an analysis of media globalization must include understanding the connections between journalism ethics, democracy, and justice (Muhlmann 2010, p. 222). While journalism is not necessary to democracy, where there is democracy, journalism can provide different services to bring about a just society. Those functions, Schudson (2006, p. 12) writes, could provide initiatives of justice, public interest, and accountability by 'informing the public, investigation, analysis, social empathy, public forum, and mobilization'. Journalism, thus, provides spaces of public reasoning from which understandings of justice could emerge (p. 12).

This chapter will focus on Amartya Sen's (2009) philosophy of justice as articulated in his book *The Idea of Justice*, in which Sen locates justice and injustice in the context of Hindu beliefs and Indian history. While Sen is well recognized, in and outside of India, as a public intellectual (having won the Nobel Prize for Economics in 1998), I limit my discussion to this book where Sen gives us a blueprint of a workable philosophy of justice. In my thinking through issues of ethics, justice, and injustice, I focus on Sen's analysis and expansion of two concepts from early Indian jurisprudence: *niti* (strict organizational and behavioral rules of justice) and *nyaya* (the larger picture of how such rules affect ordinary lives). Sen accounts for the role of media in the process of enacting *nyaya*. Media enable the public to hear diverse sections of the society, allow for reasoned deliberations, and communicate injustices. If indeed *nyaya* is integral to the democratic process, as Sen asserts, and if media and journalism can contribute much to the discursive construction of justice, this chapter addresses the following questions: 'What is the relevance of *nyaya* as articulated by Sen to journalism ethics and practices in the newly globalized and liberalized media in India?' and 'What is the relevance of *nyaya* in developing a workable philosophy of ethics for global journalism?'

Sen's interpretative use of *nyaya*

'Justice', writes Sen (2009, p. 19), 'is ultimately connected with the way people's lives go, and not merely with the nature of institutions surrounding them'. Sen argues that justice is relative to a situation and that instead of searching for 'ideal justice' (2009, p. 20), a society should strive to identify, ameliorate, and eliminate structural but redressable injustices, such as subjugation of women, poverty, and malnutrition. Sen takes issue with his predecessors, such as Rawls, who emphasizes the *niti*-oriented political philosophy, where justice is seen primarily in procedural terms (see Christians's chapter in this book). While Sen writes that his own approach can be understood as not a radical foundational departure from Rawls' own program, he draws on the Sanskrit literature and treatises by outlining the distinction between *niti* and *nyaya*. Both of these terms can be translated as justice, but *niti* refers to correct procedures, formal rules, and institutions; *nyaya* entails a broader, more substantive focus on the world that emerges from the institutions we create, and it is central to creating a sustainable and just society. The recognition, Sen observes, is that the realization of justice in the sense of *nyaya* is 'not just a matter of judging institutions and rules, but of judging the societies themselves' (2009, p. 20). Arguing for a 'realization focused perspective on justice', Sen wants a global citizenry to be not merely about trying to achieve, or dreaming about achieving, some perfectly just society or social arrangements but 'about preventing manifestly severe injustices or *anyaya*' (2009, p. 21). He writes, 'When people across the world agitate to get more global justice ... they are not clamoring for some kind of "minimal humanitarianism". Nor are they agitating for a "perfectly just" world society, but for the elimination of some outrageously unjust arrangements' (2009, p. 26).

In agreeing with Rawls that 'Democracy is an exercise in public reason' (2009, p. 323) and not just about elections and balloting, Sen writes:

> The crucial role of public reasoning in the practice of democracy makes the entire subject of democracy closely related to justice ... if the demands of justice can be assessed only with the help of public reasoning, and if public reasoning is constitutively related to the idea of democracy, then there is an intimate connection between justice and democracy, with shared discursive features.
>
> (2009, p. 326)

Here Sen critiques *niti*-oriented political philosophy which understands democracy in narrow organizational terms, focusing primarily on the procedures of balloting and elections. 'The effectiveness of ballot', writes Sen, 'depends crucially on what goes along with balloting, such as free speech, access to information, and freedom of dissent' (2009, p. 341). In formulating his close connection between *nyaya*, reasoned deliberation, and democracy, Sen critiques the claim that democracy, like reason, is a quintessentially European or Western idea. Sen gives the example of Emperor Ashoka, from third-century BC India, who had attempted to codify rules for public discussion by organizing meetings of Buddhist scholars. Similarly, by giving examples from *Akbarnama*, the recorded words of Mughal Emperor Akbar from the 15th century, Sen recounts that the path of reason or the rule of intellect was, for Akbar, the basis of good and just behavior as well as of an acceptable framework of legal duties and entitlements.

The history of *nyaya* philosophy has provided the concept of reasoned deliberation in India. Panini, the great grammarian, thought that the term '*nyaya*' came from the root '*ni*' and has the same meaning as '*gam*' which means 'to go' (Saha 1987, p. 107). Hence *nyaya* in the local sense of the word can be the same as *nigaman* or the conclusion of a syllogism. In Sanskrit different terms have been used to express the science of conclusions and logic: *Hetu castra* or the science of causes; *Avviksiki* or the science of inquiry; *Pramana castra* or the science of correct knowledge; and *Vadartha* or the science of discussion. *Nyaya* philosophy originated in the times of *Vedas* (ancient scriptures of Hinduism) and evolved in the disputations and debates among scholars trying to ascertain the meanings of the Vedic texts. Such studies resulted in the writing of *nyaya sutras* (books), written to discuss the conditions of valid thought and the means of acquiring true knowledge or *buddhi*. The *nyaya* philosophical tradition in India, in its 4,000 years of history, was comprised of various thinkers and texts such as *Nyaya sutras* of Guatama, *Bhasya* of Vatsyayana, *Nyaya Vartika* of Uddyotakara, and *Tarkasamgraha* of Annambhatta. Many of these *nyaya* texts, as in other schools of Indian philosophies, were *atman* (soul) centered. '*Nyaya* philosophy is *atman*-centric', writes Chatterjee (1950, p. 188); 'Everything originates from the *atman* and is dissolved in it. It is the center of interest, the central principle of metaphysics, psychology, ethics, aesthetics, and religion.' While the liberation of *atman* from pain and pleasure is the ultimate goal for *nyayayikas* (*nyaya* philosophers), the question, posed by Guatama, in the beginning of *Nyaya Sutra* was, 'What is the nature of knowledge?' (Saha 1987, p. 9). *Nyaya* philosophy, its logical and dialectical technicalities, breaks away from the existence of the ideal in Indian thought by showing that the external world does not exist independent of thought but that the world is intelligible; our reason could reach its reality and could know its true nature. The process of *nyaya*, for *nyayayikas*, was a multilayered path which began with *Anubhava* or presentation of facts through *Smirti* or memory; there existed a distinction between *Prama* or valid knowledge or *Aprama* or invalid knowledge; the recognition of *Yathartha* (truth) or *Ayathartha* (falsehood) in speech; reaching *Buddhi* was a process of *samcaya* (doubt), *Viparyyaya* (error), and *Tarka* (hypothetical argument) along with *Pratyaksa* (perception), *Anumana* (inference), *Upamana* (comparison), and *Sabda* (testimony). These levels and practices in speech and thinking gave a clear path to reasoned knowledge (D'Almeida 1973).

Sen takes *nyaya* philosophy away from its focus on *atman* and supreme happiness into the realms of the ethical-societal and of justice, but his interpretative and pragmatic use of *nyaya* as a path of reasoned deliberation closely resembles its historical formulations by Gautama and Vatsyayana. While making outstanding points of philosophical thought, especially against the more dogmatic and instrumental views of society in various traditions of Indian philosophy, *nyayayikas* have been critiqued for not reaching the most important and essential characteristic of human knowledge, namely its transcendence. Because the material and objective world is known through reason, critics argue, *nyayayikas* seem to treat knowledge as they would treat many physical phenomena. 'Knowledge reveals for us the facts of the objective world and this is experienced by us', writes Chatterjee. 'But that the objective world generates knowledge can hardly be demonstrated by mere experience. Knowledge is not like any other phenomena for it stands above them and interprets or illumines them all' (p. 55). Sen, in the line of other great *nyayayikas*, argues against trying to find an ideal justice and instead emphasizes for a more tempered *nyaya* position, recognizing and considering comparative and feasible alternatives, and choosing among them. He gives us a deceptively simple example of a pragmatic interpretation of *nyaya* when he writes:

> If we are trying to choose between a Picasso and a Dali, it is of no help to invoke a diagnosis that the ideal picture in the world is the Mona Lisa. That may be interesting to hear, but it is neither here nor there in the choice between Dali and Picasso. Indeed, it is not at all necessary to talk about what may be the greatest or most prefect picture in the world, to choose between two alternatives that we are facing. Nor is it sufficient, or indeed of any particular help, to know that the Mona Lisa is the most perfect picture in the world when the choice is actually between Dali and Picasso.
>
> (2009, p. 122)

For Sen, as for other *nyayayikas*, reflective and objective cognition (*Anuvyavasaya*) brings the self (*Manas*) in direct contact with the knowledge of the object and leads to knowledge, justice, and ethics. The comparative analysis of Picasso and Dali provokes a choice between two alternatives rather than invoking the presence of Mona Lisa as the ideal. The public reasoning and practice of *nyaya* envisions a just society, neither in its transcendental manifestations, nor in its search for *atman*-centered happiness. *Nyaya*, thus, stands away from the Western philosophies of reasoned deliberations as explicated in the works of Haberman and Rawls, wherein *nyaya* would be inclusive of class, gender, inequality, and other social and economic variants which make injustice visible and explicit. *Nyaya*, in its most empirical form, would be the practice of justice, not an effort to locate its transcendental use or measure its ideal manifestations.

Nyaya and *ananya* in Indian journalism practices

It is in the context of reasoned deliberation, and its significance for achieving *nyaya*, that Sen locates the importance of an 'unrestrained and healthy media' (2009, p. 254). The absence of free media, writes Sen, and the suppression of people's ability to communicate with each other have the effect of directly reducing the quality of human life even if an authoritarian state happens to be rich in terms of gross national product. Without media's ability to disseminate information, it would be difficult to engage in any form of public reasoning and deliberation and to achieve *nyaya*. A free and unrestrained media can directly contribute to free speech, allow for dissemination of knowledge and critical scrutiny, and provide a protective function in giving voice to the neglected and disadvantaged. If democracy is a history of people's participation in public reasoning, it is in a well-functioning media that one finds the most important space of public reasoning. Rejecting the idea of 'discussionless justice' (2009, p. 255), Sen asserts that it is a free, energetic, and efficient media in which one can facilitate the needed discursive process about democracy. 'Media is important', writes Sen, 'not only for democracy but for the pursuit of justice in general' (2009, p. 254). *Nyaya* – and the parallel focus on *anyaya* – journalism is distinct from the Western notion of 'watchdog journalism', which centralizes the role of the journalist as a purveyor of knowledge, as someone who investigates and uncovers. The *nyaya* journalist is not only committed to an 'unrestrained and healthy media' but, concomitantly, envisions the end result of the journalistic process as the removal of injustices and social justice as multifaceted and contextually connected to variants such as income, gender, caste, and other economic, political, and social factors.

Indian journalism practices and media environment have been radically transformed in the last two decades of dramatic economic globalization and privatization. While, immediately after independence, Indian journalists and publishers hoped and endeavored to fulfill the Gandhian vision of a free and independent press, the postcolonial Indian government was not as eager as these journalists to establish a free press (Ravindranathan 2005). Journalists battled, unsuccessfully, to add a 'free press clause to Article 19(1) (a) of the constitution', which gave the republic freedom of speech and expression but no guarantee of a free press (Natarajan 2000, p. 87). When Prime Minister Indira Gandhi declared emergency rule in 1975, her government began to strictly censor all political news and arrested and jailed more than 300 journalists.

Since the end of the emergency in 1977, print news media in India have functioned relatively free from government intervention and there have been no attempts to 'muzzle the press or expression of dissent' (Sonwalkar 2002, p. 825).

Television news, however, had remained under state control. Until recently *Doordarshan*, the state-operated television system, and the only one allowed to broadcast, started its modest operations on September 15, 1959. For 12 years, when the rest of the world's television media gained momentum in terms of quality content and freedom, India had a one-hour, twice-a-week experimental service in Delhi until the second television center began in Mumbai in 1972 (Bhatt 1996). Without any competition, *Doordarshan*'s news programming remained dull and uncontroversial, as the government approved and censored it; the news covered few stories about justice and injustice issues, and did not interest viewers. It was only with the deregulation, privatization, and commercialization of the broadcast industry in the 1990s that television news became an important source of information. In the past decade, commercial television has established itself as the vanguard in news-making though it has also been accused of 'copying US-style sensational journalism' with an entertainment-oriented news agenda (Thussu 1999, p. 129). There are now more than 300 cable news channels, broadcasting in 16 different languages, catering to vast audiences in the subcontinent and among South Asian diasporas (Guha Thakurta 2009). Having depended solely on *Doordarshan* to provide news, viewers have access not only to the major international cable television news stations such as *CNNI*, *BBC World*, *MSNBC*, *Bloomberg*, and *Headline News* but also to a plethora of Indian news channels such as *STAR News*, *Zee News*, *NDTV 24×7*, and *India TV*.

The use (and abuse) of hidden cameras

The new broadcast journalism in India has heavily invested itself in questions of democracy, democratic institutions, justice, and injustice. Broadcast journalism, in the age of privatization, liberalization, and globalization, has begun to address questions of social justice and political accountability. The rise in the use of hidden cameras in Indian journalism is one such example. Journalism practices have been transformed with the phenomenal rise of hidden cameras in the past decade. Indian news channels have aggressively used hidden cameras to gather news, calling resulting news-stories 'sting operations'. The television media have used hidden-camera revelations to expose violations of trust and abuses of power and to debate the morality of the activity captured in such stories and, thus, to further the practice of *nyaya* and democracy.

Tehelka.com (an online magazine) started the trend in 2001, airing video footage that revealed professional cricketers fixing matches and taking bribes. In another hidden-camera story, *Tehelka* sent two journalists, who posed as agents from a fictitious arms company called 'West End', and tried hawking a non-existent product – handheld thermal cameras – to politicians and bureaucrats. The journalists proffered bribes and prostitutes to push the deal through, captured all transactions on a spycam, and exhibited the footage at a press conference. In both of these two news-stories, hidden cameras revealed an abuse of power and forced influential men and women to surrender their power and reputations (Rao 2009). Democracy is well served by such stories, as, if it is indeed true that, as Sen contends, democracy succeeds not only by striving to have the most perfect institutional structure (*niti*) but also by integrating our behavior patterns and the direct contribution of press freedom into the quality of our lives (*nyaya*). In such a context, the use of hidden cameras to watch and freely and energetically critique immoral behaviors, justice becomes possible and helps strengthen the functioning of democracy.

One example of a hidden-camera story concerned Nithyananda Swami, a self-styled guru or holy man whose devotees included politicians and movie stars. Founder of the 'Life Bliss Spiritual Movement', Nithyananda headed *Dhyanapeetam*, a group of ashrams in Bengaluru and in other Indian cities. News channels received a hidden-camera video of Nithyananda having sex with two women, one of whom was an actress. The footage was first broadcast on Sun TV, a Tamil-language network based in Chennai; several news channels broadcast parts of the video. *NDTV 24×7*, a Delhi-based English and Hindi news network, ran a lengthy story entitled 'God men, good men, and bad men'. Prior to his arrest, *Zee News*, another Delhi-based Hindi news network, ran a story titled 'Tainted Swami tracked down'. In this news-story, the visuals show Nithyananda walking out into a hotel lobby followed by 20–30 journalists and videographers. Nithyananda appeared on camera to say, 'I will go into the vow of silence from now on to heal all the people and I don't wish harm to anybody...I feel only peace' (*Zee News*, March 30, 2010). The reporter continued, 'He might preach silence to the media but he will have to have a reply ready when he appears before a court in Bangalore...In a YouTube video [Swami] has admitted that the bedroom scenes with the Tamil actress were experiments...Vow of silence or not, the Swami has a lot of explaining to do.' Media coverage focused on the injustice of his violation of trust; *nyaya* was well served when he was exposed and arrested.

Another such 'sting operation', the SpyCam video footage of Narayan Dutt Tiwari, an 83-year-old veteran politician, and the governor of the southern Indian state of Andhra Pradesh, showed that hidden-camera coverage could expose a person's abuse of power and support the justice of such people's removal from power. The video, first broadcast on a local news channel, *Amoda Broadcasting Network* (ABN), was later broadcast on news channels around the country. In the video, Tiwari is seen with three young women performing various sex acts. The faces of the women were blurred and the broadcast had no audio. Despite first denying the authenticity of the video, Tiwari resigned two weeks later. In *a Zee News* story titled *'Tiwari ka antim sanskar'* (Tiwari's end) (*Zee News*, January 10, 2010), the reporter pointedly discussed the details of Tiwari's abuse of power. She says, '[Governor] was 83, and the women ranged between the age group of 17 and 25. It is reported that usually those girls were brought from different parts of the country to be employed in Raj Bhavan [Governor's mansion] giving them tax-payers money to provide a variety of sexual comforts. Radhika, a woman, has admitted that that she sent the young women on Tiwari's request. In return, she claimed, the Governor failed to keep his word to provide her a mining license in Andhra Pradesh.' The television news channels covered Tiwari's public denial and, subsequently, his resignation. *Zee News* ran a special titled 'End to a distinguished career: The life of N.D. Tiwari' and *Star News* broadcast a more provocatively special titled 'The Old man and Sleaze: The N.D. Tiwari scandal' (*Star News*, January 8, 2010).

In a special story titled *'Tasveer ka toofan'* (Photographs create storm), *Zee News* covered women's group protests in Hyderabad, the capital city of Andhra Pradesh. Visuals showed protestors standing in front of the governor's office, shouting slogans, and holding up placards reading, 'Tiwari must resign'. The voiceover of the reporter said, 'These voices are speaking out ... [the Tiwari] video is creating controversy in Hyderabad and women's organizations are protesting.' *Zee News* then interviewed a local women's rights activist, identified as Sandhya, who said, 'These women [in the video] it is shameful for them as to what has happened ... the women would be willing to come out in public if there is an inquiry but only under police protection.' Protests by women's groups and reporters against Tiwari's denial both stoked and reflected ordinary people's sense of outrage and injustice, and Tiwari's resignation seemed justified given he had abused the trust and power they had afforded him.

Nyaya is served in the coverage of Tiwari's and Nityananda's cases, where the behavior of each, their abuse of power, is harshly critiqued by a free and energetic media. If the hidden camera (in India) has become the 'weapon of the weak' (Rao 2008, p. 194), media practices in these two cases reflect its ability to bring about social and political justice (Rao 2008, p. 194). It is in media that justice should manifestly and undoubtedly be seen to be done, for there is a 'clear connection between the objectivity of a judgment and its ability to withstand public scrutiny' (Sen 2009, p. 394).

While Indian media have easily located injustices in corruption cases, they sometimes disagree on criteria for judging hidden-camera stories and, thus, to fully contextualize *anyaya*. In the case of the death of Srinivas Ramachandra Siras, a professor in the Modern Language Department at Aligarh Muslim University (AMU) in Aligarh, a city in Northern India, it was unclear as to who was the victim of injustice: the professor who had been unfairly fired and had died under mysterious circumstances, or a university which had employed a man engaged in immoral activities? Unlike in Tiwari's and Nithyananda's cases, reporters and producers determined the moral criteria of establishing the victim and perpetrators of injustice, which affected the ways in which the story was told. Professor Siras had been suspended by the university administration after they had been provided a videotape in which he was seen having sex with another man. The professor accused two independent video journalists, Adil Murtaza and Siraz, of surreptitiously entering his apartment and taping the sex act. None of the news channels broadcast any part of the tape. Siras was found dead in his university apartment weeks after he had been suspended from his job. Police reports first claimed that he had committed suicide, but later suggested that his death had been a case of homicide. While *NDTV 24×7*, in a report titled 'Fired for being gay?', suggested that unfair targeting of gays by the university and media's 'sting operation' had victimized Siras, *Zee News* suggested that the professor had been justifiably fired for 'molesting men in his university-provided apartment', and thus the men were victims. While the *NDTV 24×7* report described the sex as 'consensual sex', *Zee News* reported that it was 'molestation' (*NDTV 24×7* February 24, 2010; *Zee News* February 23, 2010).

Coverage of Siras' death suggests that *anyaya* remains ill-defined in the Indian media; a widely accepted cultural taboo against homosexuality affected media assessments of Siras' firing and death. This case highlights the often-invoked 'cultural values' which explain and even justify the deficiencies of public reasoning about minority rights. The media's obligation to give voice to the minorities, even sexual minorities whom the public despise and fear, suggests that a free media must challenge widely held cultural notions, such as homosexuality is an immoral act, and open up a discussion of human rights. According to Sen (2009, p. 254), a free press has and must fulfill a 'perfect obligation' not only to report about oppression and marginalization of minorities but also to prevent ways in which oppression takes place. In depicting competing claims of freedom, between those who assert majority cultural rights over those who seek individual minority rights, media can succeed in advocating public reason and *nyaya* only when journalists recognize inclusiveness as part of democracy and as a common principle.

Uneven injustices: Coverage of crime

While the highly censored *Doordarshan* news had rarely covered any types of crime, and seldom focused on injustice of any sort, liberalization and privatization of television news have resulted in a 24-hour, seven days a week continuous news, and have created a cycle of uninterrupted reporting about violent crimes such as rape, molestation, murder, assault, incest, and child abuse, but less coverage of poor victims and the victims' families than coverage of wealthy victims.

The first high-profile murder case widely covered in the post-liberalized Indian media was the 1999 murder of a fashion model, Jessica Lall, by Manu Sharma, the son of a wealthy politician, where journalists discovered that the police and judiciary had committed systemic injustices. Another high-profile murder, that of Aarushi Talwar, the 14-year-old daughter of a successful dentist couple, occurred in 2008, and like the Lall murder case, it garnered much and continuous coverage from television news past several years. On the morning of May 16, 2008, Talwar was found dead with her throat slit in her parents' home at Jalvayu Vihar in Noida, Uttar Pradesh, an affluent neighborhood on the outskirts of Delhi. Suspicion immediately fell on the family's live-in man-servant, Hemraj, who was found missing from the home. But, two days later, the police found the dead body of the missing man on the terrace of Talwar's residence. After a disorganized and drawn-out investigation, the police arrested Rajesh Talwar, the father of the deceased girl, and charged him with having committed the double murder. Rajesh Talwar, however, was released two months later because the police had failed to produce any credible evidence against him. The coverage of the Aarushi Talwar murder case focused on the police's failure to collect evidence, tampering with and losing physical evidence, and failing to follow viable leads. The Central Bureau of Investigation (CBI) took over the investigation in June 2008 in an attempt to solve the case. In December 2010, two years after the murders, the CBI closed their investigation without any new findings.

On the day of the release of the CBI report, all the news channels broadcast interviews with Aarushi's parents, who spoke fluently in English and Hindi. *Zee News* ran a story titled 'Rajesh Talwar: Justice has been denied to my daughter'; *Star News* ran a poll for its audiences and asked them to SMS (text message) the answer to the question, 'Has there been justice for Aarushi Talwar?'; *Star News* ran a story titled 'Aarushi's family and friends want justice'; *NDTV 24×7* interviewed a well-known Indian film star, Rani Mukherjee, who said on camera she was 'praying for justice for Aarushi' (*NDTV 24×7* December 30, 2010). Journalists interviewed Rajesh and Nupur Talwar, often in their spacious and markedly wealthy surroundings, such as in their living room and front lawn. Several journalists used the word *anyaya* (injustice) in their report. One reporter said, on camera, after covering the press conference conducted by the Talwar family, 'This is a story about injustice. It is also story [that] speaks to every family's heart. Parents want to know about the relationship between a child and parents. Children are interested to see what was happening to their peers.'

In the newly commercialized news media, it is not unusual to find stories about injustices against children. Some recent examples are *NDTV 24×7*'s footage of a nine-year-old drug addict seen beaten after having been tied to a tree; the report mentions that the mother of the child had asked for intervention from local goons after she had unsuccessfully tried to wean the child off drugs. *Zee News* did interviews with six-year-old Shah Rukh, who had been abandoned by his father on a train because he was suffering from a chronic disease. In one case, a ten-year-old girl, like Aarushi Talwar, also raped and stabbed, was found in the lower middle-class neighborhood in Delhi. The father, who, unlike the educated Talwars, spoke only in a rural dialect of Hindi, was interviewed briefly by *Zee News* and *Star News*. Television news channels frequently run stories of purposely blinded children turned into beggars, street children run over by cars, and children trafficked from Nepal.

While such television news coverage of crimes against children show the reporters', producers', and audience's continuing interest in and concern about *anyaya*, no one case received the kind of continuous and extensive coverage as the Aarushi Talwar case did. The class status of the victim or, if known, the victim's family, seems to have made a difference in the amount of coverage any case received. The intensity of the focus on injustice was mitigated by social class of the victims. Any case, such as the Aarushi Talwar case, in which the victim was wealthy, received far more coverage than similar crimes, in which the victim was poor. Crimes against poor children were widely reported as a systemic failure of the government, police, and judiciary to check abuses, but none received continuous or in-depth coverage. The media coverage of crimes against lower-class children showed neither commitment to nor consciousness of class equality, nor substantive analysis of the complicated issue of child labor in India. Such coverage, which treats violence against children as an individual psychopathy of abusers, supports Sen's (1999, p. 69) contention that 'the battle against class divisions has substantially weakened in India'. News coverage suggests that class stratification gets intensified in discourses of injustices. If news discourses can play a critically important role in facilitating public reasoning and if Sen's notion that justice ought to be theorized through our experience of injustice, media narratives about violent crime need to be contextualized and substantively analyzed in terms of class, gender, and sexual inequalities which underlie both crime and television news coverage of it. Further, in a country like India, where caste continues to pervade every aspect of social life, the media's inability to fully cover caste-based crimes keeps such experiences marginalized.

Nyaya in global media ethics

Journalism practices in India show us a complicated scenario in advocating *nyaya* and in addressing *anyaya*. For instance, in some cases hidden cameras have been successfully used to uncover the abuse of power by the powerful and to strengthen democratic institutions; other uses of hidden cameras seem to highlight the biases which underlie cultural experience. Cultural values, in certain instances, overshadow advocacy of public reasoning and minority rights. Similarly, the coverage of crime, which is omnipresent in India's commercialized news media, shows a troubling amount of coverage on injustices against the rich and powerful while ignoring injustices against the poor and weak. While the practice of *nyaya* in media coverage of crime and hidden camera stories in India remains uneven, I see the relevance of *nyaya* and *nyaya*-based journalism to discussions of global media ethics.

Grappling with changes in technology, globalization, and ethical theory during the past decade, journalism and media professionals have made various efforts to develop a philosophically rigorous and epistemologically sound ethics for the global media (Christians and Traber

1997, Couldry 2006, Silverstone 2007, Ward 2010). In one attempt to formulate global media ethics, the *Journal of Mass Media Ethics* published a special issue titled 'Search for a Global Media Ethics' (2003). In this issue, Callahan writes that the profession's global scope and transnational media provoke the question of whether there can be 'universal ethical standards for journalism to meet the challenges of globalization' (Callahan, p. 3). Similarly, Ward (2005, p. 4) states that a global media ethics would imply that responsibility 'would be owed to an audience scattered across the world', given the increasingly global reach of media corporations facilitated through new technologies. Christians and Nordenstreng (2004) have proposed a theoretical formulation which re-examines the search for global media ethics and proposes the social responsibility theory as a possibility for the press to adopt internationally. They offer the possibility of establishing several universal principles which they ground in 'a morality rooted in animate nature' (p. 20). Stating that 'global social responsibility needs an ethical basis commensurate in scope, that is, universal ethical principles rather than the parochial moral guidelines represented by codes', Christians and Nordenstreng list respect for human dignity based on sacredness of human life, truth, and nonviolence as three universal principles (p. 20). Ethicists, journalists, and scholars alike agree that any invention, evolution, or construction of global media and journalism ethics should be highly nuanced both in its epistemological approaches and in practical applications.

Christians, Rao, Ward, and Wasserman (2008), in their essay on global media ethics, propose a cross-disciplinary theoretical perspective. The essay does not presume to provide conclusive answers to theoretical questions about the relationship between the self and the other, the local and the global, or the universal and the particular, but it puts forward an argument about ways in which current disagreements about the nature, possibility, and desirability of a global media ethics could be addressed. 'Progress in developing a global media ethics is stymied by a number of wide-spread beliefs and presumptions,' write Christians et al. The authors contend that 'One issue is whether there *are* universal values in media ethics.' Their answer is a qualified 'yes'; they write:

> It appears there are universals. Even a cursory survey of many codes of journalism ethics would find agreement, at least on a denotative level, on such values as reporting the truth, freedom, and independence, minimizing harm, and accountability. Yet, a survey would also

find differences. Some media cultures emphasize more strongly that others such values as the promotion of social solidarity, not offending religious beliefs and not weakening public support for the military. Even where media systems agree on a value, such as 'freedom of press' or 'social responsibility', they may interpret and apply such principles in different ways.

(Callahan 2003)

In opening up these tensions, the authors describe several theoretical positions which might coalesce to form our current understanding of global media ethics. In their attempts to avoid errors of the past, Christians *et al.* propose an outline of a theory of ethics consisting of levels, 'the levels of presuppositions, principles, and precepts' (140), that interact dynamically in experience. Rooted in a holistic conception of theory in which basic values and ideas emerge from a 'common humanness in concrete contexts', Christians et al. see such values as 'context-influenced articulations of deep aspects of being human' (139). The most deeply embedded disagreements between factions (anti-foundationalist, poststructuralist, accounts of pluralism and multiculturalism), the authors argue, should not necessarily detract from the fact that they also come together at notable junctures and that most theories of ethics usually subscribe to a modicum of universalization and to some universal extension of nonviolence and sacredness of human life. Within such a conversation, Sen's interpretative use of *nyaya* can be most effectively used in global media ethics in two spheres: one, to seek relevance for global perspectives of justice and, two, to centralize poverty (and the question of class) as a depravation of justice.

'The world beyond a country's borders must come into the assessment of justice in a country for two distinct reasons', writes Sen. 'First, what happens in a country, and how its institutions operate, cannot but have effects, sometimes huge consequences, on the rest of the world' (2009, p. 347). He writes that each country's or a society's parochial belief might call for global examination and scrutiny; the world can establish common principles and question presumptions that lie behind particular ethical judgments. Sen's concept of *nyaya* makes justice not only a national process but also an international and global one. As applied to journalists, Sen's emphasis is on transnational considerations of justice, that media ethics can establish common principles of nonviolence and the sacredness of human life, and apply such principles to free media and its coverage of justice/injustice issues, such as crime and corruption.

The media's focus must remain, according to Sen's *nyaya* principle, on injustice. He writes of the importance of actual behavior (inter alia combining the operation of the principles of justice with the actual behavior of people) and to ground the assessment of injustice by combining social behavior with social institutions. 'What really happens to people', writes Sen, 'cannot but be a central concern of a theory of justice' (2009, p. 200). Only then *nyaya* will have the kind of applicability in guiding the choice of institutions in actual societies. For reasoned deliberations to take place in the media about *nyaya*, both vested personal interests and local parochialism must be questioned. Further, reasoned deliberation in the civil society and public sphere, such as the media, must be inclusive of multiple social trajectories which inform audiences, journalists, and other stakeholders alike. Reasoned deliberation, as advocated by Habermas, Rawls, and other egalitarian interpreters of reason as dialog between two 'rational and free' citizens, must be contextualized with a view that citizens do not enter reasoned deliberation in media without pre-existing power hierarchies and economic, cultural, and political affiliations.

Nyaya, for Sen, is ultimately a focus on human lives (which is different from ancient Indian philosophical traditions of *nyaya* overly focused on the *atman*) and a person's actual ability to do different things. One of the central issues of Sen's philosophy of *nyaya* is its connection to poverty. In rejecting previous claims of poverty as merely income based, Sen accounts for a poverty in 'capability deprivation', which he recognizes to be much more intense than what we can deduce from income data. Moving away from income-based approaches to poverty, Sen gives an example that even in high-income families, girls or women can be deprived of resource allocations (as seen in many parts of Africa and Asia). Thus, women in these families suffer from greater mortality, morbidity, undernourishment, and medical neglect that can be found simply on the basis of comparing incomes of different families. Understanding the nature and source of depravation and inequity is central to the removing of *anyaya*. If one identifies reducing the depravation of resources or poverty as a principle in global media ethics and juxtaposes it with nonviolence and sacredness of human lives, reasoned deliberation in the media would require a concerted effort to be cognizant of providing a space for discussions of not only class inequity, based on low income, but also the depravation of capability to live a flourishing life.

In this chapter, I have limited my discussions to Sen's formulation of a theory of *nyaya*, its use in journalism practices in the newly globalized, commercialized, and liberalized media in India, and to its possible theoretical relevance in developing a workable framework for global media ethics. As media worlds get increasingly rearranged, globalized, and interconnected, discussions of justice and injustice become imminent. Sen's analysis and use of *nyaya* can illuminate our understanding of justice in profound ways and can be a hugely constructive part in developing a theory of justice. *Nyaya* cannot be confined to a project dedicated to justice and injustice in nations that are already free and to the distribution of wealth in those that are already prosperous. The plea is a hope and expectation for the future of democracy and not forgetful of the harsh deeds that preceded it and made it possible. *Nyaya*, however, cannot become an intellectual 'standstill'; media scholars and journalists are obligated to achieve *nyaya*, and redress *anyaya*, in practice as much as in theory, but with continuous critical scrutiny.

References

Bhatt, S. C. 1996. *Satellite Invasion of India*. Delhi: Gyan Publishing House.
Callahan, Sidney. 2003. 'New Challenges of Globalization for Journalism', *Journal of Mass Media Ethics*, 18: 3–15.
Chatterjee, Satischandra. 1950. *The Nyaya Theory of Knowledge*. Calcutta: Das Gupta and Co.
Christians, Clifford and Nordenstreng, Kaarle. 2004. 'Social Responsibility Worldwide', *Journal of Mass Media Ethics*, 19: 3–28.
Christians, Clifford and Traber, Michael. (eds.) 1997. *Communication Ethics and Universal Values*. Thousand Oaks, California: Sage.
Christians, Clifford, Rao, Shakuntala, Ward, Stephen J. A., and Wasserman, Herman. 2008. 'Toward a Global Media Ethics: Theoretical Perspectives', *Ecquid Novi: African Journalism Studies*, 29: 135–172.
Coudry, Nick. 2006. *Listening Beyond the Echoes: Media, Ethics and Agency in an Uncertain World*. New York: Paradigm.
D'Almeida, A. 1973. *Nyaya Philosophy: Nature and the Validity of Knowledge*. Chennai: Pontifical Institute of Theology and Philosophy.
Guha Thakurta, Paranjoy. 2009. *Media Ethics: Truth, Fairness, and Objectivity*. Delhi: Oxford University Press.
Mattelart, Armand. 2002. 'An Archeology of the Global Era: Constructing a Belief', *Media, Culture and Society*, 24: 591–612.
Muhlmann, Geraldine. 2010. *Journalism for Democracy*. New York: Polity.
Natarajan, J. 2000. *History of India's Journalism*. Delhi: Sage.
Rao, Shakuntala. 2008. 'Accountability, Democracy and Globalization: A Study of Broadcast Journalism in India', *Asian Journal of Communication*, 18: 193–206.
Rao, Shakuntala. 2009. 'Glocalization of Indian Journalism', *Journalism Studies*, 10: 474–488.
Ravindranath, P. K. 2005. *Regional Journalism in India*. Delhi: Authors Press.
Saha, Sukharanjan. 1987. *Perspectives on Nyaya Logic and Epistemology*. Calcutta: K. P. Bagchi and Company.

Schudson, Michael. 2006. *Why Democracies Need an Unlovable Press*. New York: Polity.

Sen, Amartya. 1999. *Development as Freedom*. New York: Random House.

Sen, Amartya. 2009. *The Idea of Justice*. Cambridge: Harvard University Press.

Silverstone, Roger. 2007. *Media and Morality: On the Rise of the Mediapolis*. New York: Polity.

Sonwalkar, Prasun. 2002. 'Murdochization of the Indian Press: From By line to Bottom-line', *Media, Culture & Society*, 24: 821–834.

Thussu, Daya K. 1999. 'Privatizing the Airwaves: The Impact of Globalization on Broadcasting in India', *Media, Culture & Society*, 21: 121–131.

Ward, Stephen J. A. 2005. 'Philosophical Foundations for Global Journalism Ethics', *Journal of Mass Media Ethics*, 20: 3–21.

Ward, Stephen J. A. 2010. *Global Journalism Ethics*. Montreal: McGill University Press.

8

Justice as an Islamic Journalistic Value and Goal

Muhammad I. Ayish

Justice is a central component of Arab-Islamic morality,[1] often viewed as an indispensable condition for the institution and sustainability of the virtuous *Ummah* (community of believers). In broader abstract ways, justice in Islamic traditions epitomizes equilibrium in the Universe as created by God in the most perfect of ways. Through Islamic intellectual history, this comprehensive perspective of justice, with its physical and moral manifestations, has received profound attention in religious and philosophical traditions. In those traditions, justice derives much of its significance from its association with two overarching ethical concepts: fairness (*Qist*) and responsibility (*Masooliyya*). Fairness defines values like accuracy, balance, honesty, and respect, while responsibility embraces adherence to divine *Shari'a* (law) and 'bold advocacy of good and combat of evil'.[2] In this sense, it may not be adequate for the individual to be accurate, balanced, honest, respectful, and law-abiding; he/she should also be proactive in ensuring that those values are maintained and acted upon in the community.

From a normative ethical point of view, Muslim governments, institutions, groups, and individuals are expected to uphold the highest standards of justice in their relations with others. In this context, Muslims are encouraged to behave justly toward all. As noted in the Qur'an, just behavior is tied to an individual's very faith as a Muslim: 'Be just! For justice is nearest to piety.'[3] Acting justly in this life means that one is rewarded by similar justice from God in the Day of Judgment: 'Deal not unjustly and ye shall not be dealt with unjustly.'[4] According to this view, cultural and political leaders are held in high standards of fairness to their subjects, treating them as equal citizens. Justice as responsibility is also realized through individuals' *advocacy* of righteous causes. Any dysfunction of this dual system of justice (fairness and responsibility) at individual and institutional levels is bound to generate moral decadence and political and economic corruption, the prime causes of community disintegration and underdevelopment.

This chapter offers a normative perspective of justice as both a journalistic value (fairness) and a social goal (responsibility). I argue that justice, with its dual fairness and responsibility elements, has profound implications for how journalism is practiced in the region. The Islamic notion of justice suggests that journalists should uphold the highest levels of fairness in their news work by applying standards of accuracy, respect, and honesty. At a broader level, they are also expected to demonstrate responsibility toward their communities by advocating issues with redeeming social and moral values and exposing corrupt and faulty conducts. Journalists are expected to advocate the institution of just values and practices in their societies and hence should not turn a blind eye to corruption, deception, and oppression. This suggests, among other things, that the Arab-Islamic concept of justice intrinsically promotes an advocacy view of journalism that is practiced in the context of honesty, accuracy, respect, and adherence to *Shari'a* and collective community values. Through their investigative and reporting works, journalists are also seen as part of a broader system of justice and accountability in their societies.

For some, the fairness and responsibility features of justice (as a professional value and a social goal) may look rather contradictory in a normative Arab-Islamic perspective primarily because they involve both detachment from and commitment to community issues on the part of the journalist. But I believe that both complement one another, in the sense that they reflect a comprehensive sense of justice that precludes imbalanced and unfair representation of different actors in the public sphere. Fairness and responsibility also promote appropriate ethical ideas and practices in society. In this sense, we find the Islamic notion of justice in journalism operating in harmony with other ethical values like fairness, respect, equality, accountability, and accuracy. In the Arab world, media laws and codes of ethics incorporate much of justice-based values of fairness and responsibility. In recent years, the region's political turbulences taking place within the so-called Arab Spring have accentuated a greater drive toward a new journalism drawing on the Islamic value of justice.

Justice in global media ethics debates

Since justice is viewed as one of the basic universal ethical values shared by different cultures (Christians and Traber 1997), it is rather normal to see it defining global discussions of media ethics. In the diverse philosophical, cultural, and anthropological traditions around the world, the value of justice has been hailed as a powerful driver of human endeavors to foster equality, freedom, democracy, and dignity.[5] In Western intellectual traditions, the most fundamental principle of justice – one that has been widely accepted since it was first defined by Aristotle more than two thousand years ago – is the principle that 'equals should be treated equally and unequals unequally' (Velasquez et al. 2004). Bentham's and Mill's utilitarianism connected justice and utility when they argued that people's rights ought to be defended because of the benefit of protecting their security (Mill 2009, p. 226). For Mill (p. 231), justice based on utility is the 'chief part and incomparably the most sacred and binding part, of all morality'. Western intellectual traditions have also addressed the notion of distributive justice as an expression of egalitarianism, advocating the allocation of equal material goods to all members of society (Encyclopedia of Social Psychology 2007).

John Rawls' alternative distributive principle (1971), which he calls the 'Difference Principle', allows allocation that does not conform to strict equality so long as the inequality has the effect that the least advantaged in society are materially better off than they would be under strict equality. Rawls and Kelly (2001, p. 12) note that the distributive principle 'equates justice with fairness to members of society that grows out of a hypothetical "original position" in which no one knows his place in society, his class position or social status, nor does anyone know his fortune in the distribution of natural assets and abilities, his intelligence, strength, and the like, the principles of justice are chosen behind a veil of ignorance'.

In the communications context, a wide range of scholars (Wilkins and Christians 2001, Christians et al. 2005, Quinn 2007, Rao 2012) seem to be generally in full agreement on the centrality of justice in media ethics. It has been argued that media practitioners' commitment to ethical standards could not be fully realized without them possessing a solid sense of justice. The notion of particular and public interest (social) justice advanced by Quinn (2010, p. 272) provides an interesting perspective on how justice defines professional ethics in journalism. Particular justice guides journalists in their determination of whether individual actions are fairly conceived and acted upon, while social justice regards the fairness of institutional norms and rules and laws that affect society.

Bertrand (2002) argues that justice in journalism is part of a wider system of justice and accountability in which the media contribute to the institution of greater equity in society. According to the author, journalists, through their investigative reporting and inquisitive writings, serve as powerful tools for bolstering values of justice and accountability in tune with the workings of other justice-serving institutions. This notion of media as an instrument of a wider system of social justice is also espoused by Craft (2010), who believes media constitute a credible backup system for law-enforcement and legal institutions seeking to achieve justice in society. The same view is advocated by Borden (2010) when he argues that journalism is part of a justice system necessary for a democratic state. He elaborates that journalism is a crucial component of a checks-and-balances system to ensure that neither a single branch of government nor any other social institution, including big business, attains illegitimate power.

In significant ways, justice as a journalistic goal has been associated with the advocacy role of journalism. In its basic configuration, media advocacy is another facet of community advocacy where commonly recognized social and cultural values with enduring ethical implications are fostered in the public sphere. Media advocacy shifts the focus from the personal to the social, from the individual to the political, and from the behavior or practice to the policy or environment (Pooley et al. 2011). While traditional media approaches to community affairs try to fill the 'knowledge gap', media advocacy addresses the 'power gap' (Wallack 1994, p. 423). This suggests, among other things, a proactive press engagement in public life by addressing the critical issues impinging on community life. Christians et al. (2005, p. 86) ask whether the press has a legitimate advocacy function, or if it best serves democratic life as an intermediary, a conduit of information and varying opinions. In a similar vein, Pooley et al. (2011) sought to assign an activist role for media institutions in brining social justice to different community sectors by exposing corruption and combating inequities. Fink (1998, p. 18) sees nothing wrong with advocacy journalism, as it offers an exciting, rewarding, and meaningful social role. However, according to Fink (1998, p. 122), if advocacy is a professional's choice, he or she should consider two factors when dealing with advocacy: It is unethical and irresponsible to blur the distinction between advocacy journalism and the effort to practice the fair and objective reporting that is the core of most newspaper and television journalism today, and 'if advocacy is one's choice, openly put an advocate's label on and display it for all to see'. A more assertive statement on how justice permeates journalistic work is elaborated by Craig (2001, p. 22), who notes:

[W]hen reporters uncover corruption in a city police department, they are upholding justice as a value of journalism. When editors plan a series on inequities in availability of housing by race, they are making justice one of their goals. Whenever journalists do stories that point out unfairness in how people are treated, justice lies in the background even if it is not explicitly on the minds of editors and reporters.

But as much as advocacy journalism generates enthusiasm among those disenchanted with mainstream objectivity-based journalism, it continues to provoke misgivings among key journalism players. The Society of Professional Journalists Code of Ethics distinguishes between advocacy and news reporting. In the late 1970s, Gildea (1977) noted that the growing belief among some media that they must abandon neutrality was bound to undermine public confidence in society's major institutions, including, interestingly enough, the press itself. Gibson (2010: 45) notes that media advocacy's reliance on journalists working in commercial media radically constrains advocates' ability to reach policymakers and citizens in anything more than an episodic way. The debate on the relationship between objectivity and advocacy in journalism, in significant ways, seems to be ethically informed, drawing on our conceptions of notions of freedom and responsibility and the role of the professional journalist as a voice of public good in our societies. Proponents of both perspectives seem to base their arguments on a range of ethical values, foremost of which is justice. An objective journalist glorifies fairness as a derivative of justice to justify neutrality and detachment. Likewise, an advocacy journalist invokes social equality and fairness in dealing with community issues. This variation in conceptions of justice between the two streams would most likely continue to inspire future discussions in different cultures around the world.

Justice: An Islamic perspective

Muslim scholars and jurisprudence specialists (Kotb 1970, Barzangi et al. 1996, Souaiaia 2008) seem to be unanimous about conceiving justice as a central pillar of Islamic faith and morality. In the Qur'an, God says: 'Behold, God enjoins justice and good actions and generosity to our fellows',[6] and He commands us never to let hatred lead us into deviating from justice: 'Be just! That is closest to God consciousness... We sent Our Messengers with clear signs and sent down with them the Book and the Measure in order to establish justice among the people'.[7] The Qur'anic standards of justice transcend considerations of race, religion, color, and creed, as Muslims are commanded to be just to friends and foes alike, and to be just at all levels; as the Qur'an puts it: 'O you who believe! Stand out firmly for justice, as witnesses to Allah, even if it be against yourselves, your parents, and your relatives, or whether it is against the rich or the poor'.[8]

In the Prophet's *Hadith* (oral traditions that were preserved and documented after his death), the notion of justice also finds profound expressions in different contexts. The Prophet declared: 'There are seven categories of people whom God will shelter under His shade on the Day when there will be no shade except His. [One is] the just leader.' God spoke to His Messenger in this manner: 'My slaves, I have forbidden injustice for Myself and forbade it also for you. So avoid being unjust to one another.' The Prophet declared that blood relations should not obstruct the application of justice to deal with wrongdoing: 'if Fatima steals, I would get her hand cut off'.[9]

While Western philosophical and political traditions locate justice in the socio-economic conditions of the individual and society, the Muslim view of justice derives intrinsically from a rather metaphysical, physical, and social conception of the universe, society, and man. In his landmark book entitled *Social Justice in Islam*, Kotb (1970, p. 17) notes:

> We cannot study the nature of social justice in Islam unless we have first examined the general lines of Islamic theory on the subject of the universe, life, and mankind. For social justice is a branch of that great science to which all Islamic studies must run back... Islam has a universal theory which covers the universe, life and humanity, a theory in which are integrated all the different questions; in this Islam sums up all its beliefs, its laws and statutes, and its modes of worship and of work.

According to Kotb (1970, p. 24), Islam looks at Man as forming a unity whose spiritual desires cannot be separated from his bodily appetites and whose moral needs cannot be divorced from his material needs. He points out that Islam bases its definition of social justice on two major facts: the absolute, just, and coherent unity of existence; and the general, mutual responsibility of individuals and societies. The metaphysical nature of justice, defined by Khadduri (1984, p. 3) as 'Divine Justice', is enthroned in the Revelation and Divine Wisdom which the Prophet Muhammad communicated to his people. Revelation, transmitted in

God's words to His Prophet, is to be found in the Qur'an; while Divine Wisdom, granted to the Prophet through inspiration, was uttered in the Prophet's own words and promulgated as the *Sunna*, which subsequently came to be known as the *Hadith*, or the Prophet's traditions (p. 3). Khadduri argues that these two authoritative or textual sources provided the raw material on the basis of which scholars, through the use of a 'derivative source' of human reasoning called *ijtihad*, laid down the Law and the Creed, and the creative works of succeeding generations on justice. He points out that in Islamic theory God is the Sovereign of *Ummah* (Community of Believers). He is its ultimate Ruler and Legislator (Khadduri 1984, p. 7).

A semantic understanding of the Arabic word *adl* as the literal translation of justice would be helpful in comprehending the full meaning of this value in Arab-Islamic culture. Though the word *adl* has existed in Arabic since ancient times, it was the advent of Islam that conferred on it the rich social and religious meanings it has come to claim. In pre-Islamic times, the value of *adl*, which means straightforwardness, was eclipsed by competing values of honor, dignity, eloquence, gallantry, and blood relations (Ayish and Sadig 1997). Khadduri (1984, p. 6) notes that *adl* has come to be synonymous with other words like *qist* (lot), *qasd* (intention), *istiqama* (honesty), *wasat* (center), *hissa* (allocation), and *mizan* (balance). The antonym of *adl* (justice) is *jawr* (oppression) which has other synonyms like *zulum* (wrongdoing), *tughyan* (tyranny), *mayl* (inclination), and *inhiraf* (deviation). The notion of *adl* as right is equivalent to the notions of fairness and equitableness, which are perhaps more precisely expressed in the term *istiqama* or honesty.

Justice in Islam derives its significance from different contexts. At the psychological level, it is a value that should not be eclipsed by rival evils as noted in this Qur'anic verse: 'Let not the hatred of a people swerve you away from justice. Be just, for this is closest to righteousness'[10] and 'If you judge, judge between them with justice'.[11] It is also presented as synonymous with fairness among recipients of justice: God says: 'And approach not the property of the orphan except in the fairest way, until he [or she] attains the age of full strength, and give measurement and weight with justice' (6:152). It also denotes a sense of accuracy as noted in buying, selling, and, by extension, other business transactions. There is an entire chapter of the Qur'an, *Surah al-Mutaffifeen* (83), where fraudulent dealers are threatened with divine wrath. While pleading for fair and transparent economic transactions, it condemns, with all possible force, economic exploitation in the form of *riba* or *usury* and interest, which is regarded a major source of conflict and economic oppression in society by Islam. Referring to quality control and standardization of measure, it declares: 'Fill the measure when you measure, and weigh with a right balance, that is better and finest in the end' (17:35). Islam enjoins Muslims to be brave in upholding the standards of justice: 'O ye who believe! Stand out firmly for justice, as witnesses to Allah, even as against yourselves, or your parents, or your kin, and whether it is (against) rich or poor: for Allah can best protect both. Follow not the lusts (of your hearts), lest ye swerve, and if ye distort (justice) or decline to do justice, verily Allah is well-acquainted with all that ye do' (4:135).

Justice as a journalistic value and a social goal

It is clear that justice in Islamic traditions covers all facets of human interactions and relations, including communication. Ayish and Sadig (p. 117) note that the Arab-Islamic concept of justice suggests that communication, like action, is subject to the distribution of good and bad, rewards and penalties. Harboring ill suspicions, spying on others, leveling false charges against innocent women, backbiting, and lying are also seen as symptoms of an excessive abuse of the equilibrium in interpersonal and social relations in the community. Not only does the Islamic justice system seek to rectify those imbalances, it also generates temporal and religious rewards for those who adhere to its principles.

The motivation to seek and apply justice in normative Islamic ethics within the concept of *Taqwa* (piety) is yet another basis for developing an Islamic code of journalistic ethics. As Siddiqi (1999) noted, the concept of *Taqwa* goes beyond piety; it raises a person's individual, moral, spiritual, and psychological capacity to a level that the individual becomes immune from excessive material desires. It elevates a person to a higher level of self-awareness. *Taqwa* should be the underpinning element in the technical knowledge, managerial ability, scientific know-how, and communication skills of Muslim journalists. In debates (Christians 1985, Foster 2013) about codes of ethics in contemporary mass communication, the following question is often raised: Who should have the authority to enforce these codes of ethics – governments, media institutions, or individual journalists? The problem, according to Siddiqi (1999), is not the lack of a code; rather it is the lack of adherence to and implementation of a code. *Taqwa* combined with a true love of and commitment to God, consciousness of the life hereafter, and acceptance of the leadership of the Prophet Muhammad may provide the ultimate and definitive moral force to practice free and fair journalism.

In Islamic ethical theory, Muslims are expected to take the initiative in standing up against evil and advocating good with no fear. Mowlana (1989, p. 56) notes that the responsibility of a Muslim journalist is to destroy myths, adding that 'in our contemporary world these myths may include power, progress, science, development, modernization, democracy, achievement, and success. Personalities as they represent these must not be super-humanized and super-defined.' In doing so, journalists carry out their professional functions within a framework of social advocacy that turns them into participant actors in social issues and events, rather than as detached conduits. By taking such initiatives, Muslim journalists are contributing to the institution of justice in society.

In normative Muslim ethical thought, justice bears on journalists' works in two contexts: the professional and the social action context.

Justice in the professional context

This context describes day-to-day practices of journalistic work as manifested in news gathering, editing, and production. As gatekeepers, journalists are expected to uphold fairness as the defining epitome of justice in news. Fairness embraces allied values of honesty, respect, balance, and accuracy. In keeping those values in news selection, writing, and reporting, gatekeepers would be doing justice to governments, institutions, and individuals in society. While honesty suggests that journalists should not report lies or fake information, respect suggests that they should be considerate to others' dignity, privacy, and reputation. Balance suggests that whenever diverse views occur in news, they should be allocated equal space and time as long as what they express falls within nationally and culturally acknowledged parameters. Accuracy requires gatekeepers to report the exact facts in figures, labels, times, and spaces. Manipulation of facts to achieve certain objectives is strictly forbidden because it would contribute to offsetting social harmony and balance in society. The application of the four associate values is an expression of fairness in professional contexts.

Justice in the social action context

The social action context describes a broader sphere that goes beyond professional boundaries of the journalism profession. In this context, journalists are stretching their work practices beyond the reactive nature of newsroom work. They are rather proactive in taking initiatives by showing more inquisitive and investigative spirits. They are expected to be more daring in addressing social issues to unravel problems that embody serious facets of injustice. They are not expected to turn a blind eye to corruption or faulty practices that negatively bear on social harmony and integration. In some cases, an explicit media advocacy approach would be quite appropriate for empowering just practices and norms in society. This seems similar to Western advocacy journalism models, yet motivations are different in the Arab-Islamic model, where we see heavy emphasis on advocacy as a religious duty that has to be fulfilled. Hence, media would be harnessed not only to inform, educate, and entertain but also to promote sound ideas and combat evil ones. Like those working in law-enforcement agencies, educational institutions, and religious guidance apparatus, journalists always have something to offer toward the institution of social justice in their communities.

The social responsibility perspective is a critical foundation for the social action context of Arab journalism. As mentioned earlier, the social responsibility theory on which secular or Western media practices are based is rooted in pluralistic individualism; the Islamic principle of social responsibility is based on the concept of *amar bi al-Maruf wa nahi an al-munkar* or 'enjoining good and prohibiting evil'. This implies that it is the responsibility of journalists and media institutions to prepare individuals and society as a whole to accept Islamic principles and act upon them (Siddiqi 1999). In Arab-Islamic social traditions that promote community consensus and cohesion, media as social actors are expected to play a role in fostering cultural and national identity even if that takes on some paternalistic overtones.

Justice as a journalistic value in modern Arab journalism

The extent to which the notion of justice has trickled down into professional Arab journalistic values and practices varies from one country to another. But overall, it is clear that justice has been enshrined into most Arab world journalism's codes of ethics, yet less explicitly pronounced as a journalistic value by individual practitioners. Examples include codes of ethics adopted by Jordanian, Egyptian, Emirati, Iraqi, and Algerian Journalists Associations. Article (3) of the Jordanian Journalists Association expresses support for the application of justice in

society.[12] Article (4) of the Arab League Media Code of Ethics emphasizes the role of media in highlighting just issues in Arab societies.[13]
In Iraq, the new Journalists Association has called for basing its code of
ethics on values like transparency, honesty, and justice.[14] To understand
the permeation of justice into Arab journalism, we need to identify four
models of journalism that are manifested in different forms throughout the Arab-Muslim world. The first one is the government-controlled
model, where communicators' sense of justice is largely defined by government policies and orientations toward social and political issues.
In this case, journalistic justice expresses a state-defined (politicized)
sense of justice where a heavy government-dominated point of view
could not be overlooked. In this model, justice is terribly flawed not
only in how communicators perceive issues of fairness, balance, and
objectivity in their messages but also in how they handle issues bearing on the community. This model is common in all Arab countries
with state-owned and operated media institutions, such as newspapers,
radio stations and television channels. The second model describes non-
state media organizations which declare their public commitment to
the welfare of the community with what it takes to uphold principles
of justice, but in many cases their practice of justice is often compromised by flawed gate-keeping practices. The notion of self-censorship
seems to have a discouraging effect on how they approach pluralism and critical issues whose sound handling would help bring about
justice to the community. This model is typical of privately owned
media institutions with journalistic attitudes similar to those in state-
controlled media. The third view is modeled on Western notions of
media as a fourth estate playing a watchdog role with respect to government and community behavior. The investigative and inquisitive
nature of journalists in this category, however, may not always be understood on the basis of their sense of justice, as they tend to be driven
by pure political rather than professional motivations for their bold
journalistic ventures. But, all in all, communicators in this category
do have a stronger sense of justice and are more likely to translate it
into concrete journalistic practices. This model describes media institutions in countries like Lebanon and Kuwait, as well as media outlets in
diaspora.

The fourth model is termed as 'advocacy journalism', adopting a
rather proactive approach to social and political issues that define
the direction and substance of development in the community. Advocacy media are normally affiliated with specific political and social

movements and are expected to fulfill their duty as voices of the social causes championed by those movements. This model generally describes media outlets with less visible and more professional partisan or social movement affiliations operating in a rather free expression environment. Examples include media institutions in countries like Lebanon, Kuwait, Jordan, Egypt, and Morocco.

The 'Arab Spring' would most likely lead to an augmentation of the advocacy media model where journalists are expected to play a more proactive role in community issues. The rise of citizen journalism and online journalism has given good ammunition for this type of journalism, which is credited with contributing to the downfall of despotic and corrupt regimes and bringing about a more equitable and egalitarian system to the region. The fact that those media have come to be associated with Islamist movements would most likely give them more sustainability and would make justice one of their prime targets as Arab societies restructure their social, economic, and political systems in tune with the new transitions. More journalists are more likely to be inspired by Islamist views of justice and many of them take it as professional responsibility to bring about fair and just practices to their people.

The Arab media transitions taking place in the midst of the 'Arab Spring' developments are bound to strengthen the advocacy model of journalism in the region. The fact that emerging political parties in the region, like Egypt's *Freedom and Justice Party* and Morocco's and Turkey's *Justice and Development Parties*, have chosen to include 'Justice' as part of their names suggests this heavy drift toward this value in public life and the public sphere. In the emerging discourse, there is always an emphasis on the missing sense of justice in the region as the prime cause of the revolutions. Arab societies would most likely endeavor to build up and solidify their justice system apparatuses, including the judiciary and the media institutions (Pintak 2011). Drawing on the first broad cross-border survey of Arab journalists, first-person interviews with scores of reporters and editors, and his three decades' experience reporting from the Middle East, Pintak (2011) shows how Arab journalists see new roles and functions for them in the evolving political landscape. Based on his survey of Arab journalists, Pintak found that 75% of them see the main mission of Arab journalism to be driving political and social change. The contributions of social networks to the mobilization and coordination of Arab revolts have been viewed as yet another evidence of how citizen-empowered media could build up a more egalitarian and just society.

Conclusion

In Arab-Islamic traditions, no value, apart from belief in God and in His unity, has gained as much philosophical, theocratic, and political attention as has the notion of justice. The value of justice has been placed at the center of a comprehensive physical and moral system whose sustainability seems to be totally dependent on keeping up justice in religious and social interactions. Unlike its Western counterpart, the Muslim notion of justice is rooted in divine foundations that articulate its nature, contexts, and applications. It has been interchangeably used in connection with other values like equality, fairness, responsibility, balance, honesty, moderation, and divine revelation. Its meaning as equilibrium in physical and social features and relations makes it the driving force for social welfare and development. As such, the application of justice to real-life situations is not a matter of reacting to arising conditions but an issue of proactive initiatives that Muslims should undertake to keep that equilibrium in place.

While justice has been explicitly noted in almost all Arab journalism codes of ethics and media charters, it is difficult to ascertain how functional it is in driving day-to-day activities in the communications sphere. It is rather an abstract defining principle that lurks in the background of media institutions and practitioners' minds, but rarely does it seem to be brought to consciously bear on what journalists do. Since this chapter addresses justice as an Arab-Muslim journalistic value and goal from a normative perspective, the painful reality is that we find that while justice is visibly enshrined in Arab political and media discourse, its application in real-life situations remains precarious. Journalists undertake investigative reports perhaps more for professional or political purposes and less for keenness on applying the notion of justice in their work. Even when you mention advocacy journalism, you talk about partisan publications that are excellent in their investigative endeavors, but what they do falls within national or international power politics that demand certain issues to be exposed and others to be dumped. Journalists at the end of the day would have to answer to questions about how certain persons or organizations were covered in the frameworks of critical political, economic, or cultural settings that define how media would present them to the public. But in the aftermath of the 'Arab Spring', a whole range of journalistic conventions are bound to change. The introduction of online and social media technologies is empowering the rise of a new breed of journalists with new morality that emphasizes independence, integrity, honesty, and transparency.

The rising application of those normative values in daily journalism practices would certainly drive toward more ethical communication practices across the region.

Notes

1. Though Arab-Islamic morality has come to reflect more or less similar standards, both terms may not be used interchangeably. Pre-Islamic Arabian morality had drawn on tribal norms that gloried honor, eloquence, and dignity while Islam came with different norms that emphasize faith, justice, piety, fraternity, and others. These variations have been explained in detail in Ayish and Sadig (1997).
2. Holy Qur'an, Chapter (3) Verse (110).
3. Holy Qur'an, Chapter (5) Verse (2).
4. Holy Qur'an, Chapter (2) Verse (279).
5. This organic connection between justice, democracy, and development has defined the discourse of different United Nations programs around the world. For example, see the UN Development Program (UNDP) approach to international development at: http://www.undp.org/content/undp/en/home/ourwork/democraticgovernance/overview.html
6. Holy Qur'an, Chapter (16) Verse (90).
7. Holy Qur'an, Chapter (57) Verse (25).
8. Holy Qur'an, Chapter (4) Verse (135).
9. 'The Book Pertaining to Punishments Prescribed by Islam (*Kitab Al-Hudud*)' of Sahih Muslim.
10. Holy Qur'an, Chapter (5) Verse (8).
11. Holy Qur'an, Chapter (5) Verse (42).
12. http://www.jpa.jo/arabic/CodeOfEthics.aspx
13. http://ujcenter.net/index.php?option=com_content&view=article&id=69:2009-06-02-02-19-14&catid=32:2009-06-01-21-16-43&Itemid=47
14. http://www.ahewar.org/debat/show.art.asp?aid=208784

References

Ayish, Muhammad and Sadig, Haydar. 1997. 'The Arab-Islamic Heritage in Communication Ethics', in C. Christians and M. Traber (eds.), *Communication Ethics and Universal Values*, pp. 105–127. Thousand Oakes: Sage.
Barazangi, Nimat, Zaman, M. Raquibuz, and Afzal, Omar. (eds.) 1996. *Islamic Identity and the Struggle for Justice.* Gainesville: University Press of Florida.
Bertrand, Claude-Jean. 2002. *Media Ethics and Accountability Systems.* New Brunswick, NJ: Transaction Publishers.
Borden, Sandara. 2010. 'The Moral justification for Journalism', in C. Meyers (ed.), *Journalism Ethics: A Philosophical Approach*, pp. 53–68. Oxford: Oxford University Press.
Choueiri, Y. M. 1990. *Islamic Fundamentalism.* London: Pinter.
Christians, Cliff. 1985. 'Enforcing media codes', *Journal of Mass Media Ethics: Exploring Questions of Media Morality*, 1:1, 14–21.

Christians, Cliff and Traber, Michael. (eds.) 1997. *Communication Ethics and Universal Values.* Thousand Oakes: Sage.

Christians, Cliff, Rotzoll, Kim, Fackler, Mark, McKee, Kathy Brittain, and Woods, Robert. 2005. *Media Ethics: Cases and Moral Reasoning.* Boston: Person Education Inc.

Craft, Stephanie. 2010. 'Press Freedom and Responsibility', in C. Meyers (ed.), *Journalism Ethics: A Philosophical Approach*, pp. 39–52. Oxford: Oxford University Press.

Craig, David. 2009. 'Justice as a Journalistic Value and Goal', in L. Wilkins and C. Christians (eds.), *The Handbook of Mass Media Ethics*, pp. 203–216. New York: Routledge.

Encyclopedia of Social Psychology. 2007. 'Distributive Justice.' Sage Publications. September 15. Retrieved at: http://www.sage-erefernce.com/socialpsychology/Article_157.html

Fink, Conrad. 1998. *Media Ethics in the Newsroom and Beyond.* New York: McGraw-Hill.

Frost, Chris. 2013. Journalism Ethics and Regulation. New York: Routledge.

Gibson, Timothy. 2010. 'The Limits of Media Advocacy', *Communication, Culture and Critique*, No. (3), pp. 44–65. International Communication Association.

Gildea, Robert. 1977. 'Doubting Thomas Our Patron Saint', *Public Relations Quarterly*, 22(1): 25–28.

Khadduri, Majid. 1984. *The Islamic Conception of Justice.* Baltimore: The Johns Hopkins University Press.

Kotb, Sayed. 1970. *Social Justice in Islam.* New York: Octagon Books.

Mill, John Stuart. 2009. *Utilitariansim.* Adelaide: University of Adelaide Press.

Mowlana, Hamid. 1989. 'Communication, Ethics, and Islamic Tradition', in T. W. Cooper (ed.), *Communication Ethics and Global Change*, pp. 147–158. White Plains, NY: Longman.

Pintak, Lawrance. 2011. *The New Arab Journalist: Mission and Identity in a Time of Turmoil.* Cairo: Library of Middle East Studies.

Pooley, Jefferson, Taub-Pervizpour, Lora, and Curry Jansen, Sue. 2011. *Media and Social Justice.* New York: Palgrave Macmillan.

Quinn, Aaron. 2007. 'Moral Virtues for Journalists', *Journal of Mass Media Ethics*, 22 (2&3): 168–186.

Quinn, Aaron. 2010. 'Respecting Sources' Confidentiality: Critical but Not Absolute', in C. Meyers (ed.), *Journalism Ethics: A Philosophical Approach*, pp. 271–282. Oxford: Oxford University Press.

Ralws, John. 1971. *A Theory of Justice.* Cambridge: Harvard University Press.

Rao, Shakuntala. 2012. *Third Global Media Ethics Roundtable: A Meeting of Minds.* Center for Journalism Ethics. Madison: School of Journalism and Mass Communication, University of Wisconsin.

Rawls, John and Kelly, Erin. 2001. *Justice as Fairness: A Restatement.* Harvard President and Fellows College. Cambridge, MA: Harvard University Press.

Siddiqi, Mohammad. 1999. Ethics and Responsibility in Journalism: An Islamic Perspective. World Association for Christian Communication. Retrieved at: http://waccglobal.org/en/9991-children-and-media/845-Ethics-and-responsibility-in-journalism-An-Islamic-perspective-.html

Souaiaia, Ahmed. 2008. *Contesting Justice: Women, Islam, Law, and Society.* State University of New York Press.

Velasquez, Manuel, Andre, Claire, Shanks, Thomas, and Meyer, Michael. 2004. 'The Common Good. Markkula Center for Applied Ethics', Santa Clara University Retrieved at: www.scu.edu/ethics/practicing/decision/commongood.html
Wallack, Lawrance. 1994. 'Media Advocacy: A Strategy for Empowering People and Communities', *Journal of Public Health Policy,* 15(4): 420–536.
Wilkins, Lee and Christians, Cliff. (eds.) 2008. *The Handbook of Mass Media Ethics.* New York: Routledge.

9
Rammohun Roy's Idea of 'Public Good' in the Early Days of Journalism Ethics in India

Prasun Sonwalkar

> 'But to no individuals is the Indian Press under greater obligation than to the lamented Rammohun Roy and the munificent Dwarkanaut Tagore'.
>
> R. Montgomery Martin (1834, p. 254)

Introduction

The main purpose of this chapter is to provide a historical context and reference point against which the development of journalism ethics in India in a global context can be framed. At a time of democratic deficit due to 'paid news' seriously narrowing the range of facts and opinions available to citizens to enable them to make informed choices (Guha Thakurta 2011), the reference point is important if only to assess – or lament – the state of journalism ethics in contemporary India. The effort is more to set out the context in which ethical considerations engaged the first Indians who ventured into modern journalism, than to build or explore theory. The chapter is focused on a point in time when the first printed journals – in English and 'native' languages – came into existence and marked a significant height in India's ancient tradition of argument and debate. Several events and issues of the period between the late 18th and early 19th centuries sowed the seeds of political activism, prose and literature in Indian languages, social and religious reform, and the conceptual beginnings of an imagined nation. After 1780, when the first journal was published by James Augustus Hicky, print journalism soon outlined the contours of a reading public, a colonial public sphere, and became a forum of debate between the colonial rulers and the colonized, with Calcutta as the 'contact zone', to use Pratt's term, to refer to social spaces 'where cultures meet, clash, and grapple with each other, often in contexts of highly asymmetrical relations of power, such as colonialism, slavery, or their aftermaths as they are lived out in many parts of the world today' (1991, p. 1).

Throughout recorded history, India has been part of global narratives of progress, practices, and the flow of ideas, absorbing the useful while retaining its distinct worldview. For our purpose (as this chapter will show), this is also reflected in the parallelism of structures, ethics, and practices of journalism in India in the colonial context, with what was then a developing Anglo-American model of journalism in the West. Indians constructively adopted and adapted the Western technology of print on their own terms, along with its ideas, ideology, and idealism of journalism, while maintaining continuities with their own ways of social communication and engaging in selective responses to Western influence. More recent examples of the instrumental duality of absorption and rejection include the 'Murdochization' of Indian journalism since the early 1990s (Sonwalkar 2002) – the enthusiastic adoption in India of the commercial-to-the-exclusion-of-editorial approach espoused by Rupert Murdoch, but at the same time largely rejecting, for example, Western tabloid-style intrusion into the private lives of public personalities. This duality is reflected in the notion of 'glocalization' (Robertson 1992, pp. 173–174, Wasserman and Rao 2008) and Gandhi's famous quote: 'I do not want my house to be walled in on all sides and my windows to be stuffed. I want the cultures of all the lands to be blown about my house as freely as possible. But I refuse to be blown off my feet by any.'

In the period under focus, the matrix of local–global, 'us'–'them', tradition–modernity, colonial–native, print–oral communication, Western influence–local resistance was remarkably represented in the personality of Rammohun Roy (1772–1833), who is less known for his contribution to Indian journalism than for his reformist initiatives in the realm of religion, education, politics, and social campaigns (in particular, his campaign for the abolition of 'sati'). Considered in hagiographic and nationalistic accounts as the 'founder of modern India', most of his reformist exertions and debates were conducted through the technology of print, in the form of pamphlets, translations, tracts, and journals. Roy – easily one of the foremost examples of an 'argumentative Indian' (Sen 2005) – engaged in lengthy debates with Baptist missionaries, who used print on an industrial scale in Serampore (near Calcutta), printing some of the first journals and religious texts in various Indian languages from the early 19th century. At a time when editorial content was physically carried and circulated over days and months through ships (to and from London) and manual couriers within India, Roy demonstrated a remarkably acute understanding of global events and wrote feelingly about the Irish and the Italian and Spanish revolutionaries of the 1810s. As Bayly noted in a synthesis of the emergence of the modern world, Roy 'made in two decades an astonishing leap from the intellectual status of a late-Mughal state intellectual to that of the first Indian liberal' (2004, p. 292). He further added:

> By the late 1820s Bengalis in the new city of Calcutta, with Raja Ram Mohun Roy at their head, began to discover what they call the 'Hindu race' and, a little later, 'India' itself. They began to speculate that this race of culture had 'rights' and needed representation, pointing to both the Hindu past and to the European present. Newspapers, which fed on the events of the world crisis, made them aware of the post-revolutionary struggles of the Irish and the Genoese. If there were bodies of people called Irish or Genoese who had rights as peoples, then surely there must be 'rights' for Indians as well. (p. 114)

Roy, who launched, inspired, or was closely associated with at least five journals in English, Bengali, and Persian in the early 19th century, was the first public figure to systematically exploit print journalism to pursue political and reformist objectives within an ethical context; his example was later followed by Mahatma Gandhi, Jawaharlal Nehru, and Bal Gangadhar Tilak, who launched journals and used them to counter colonial perspectives until India achieved freedom in 1947. Roy not only led debates through his journals on issues of the day but also collaborated with British editors such as James Silk Buckingham to push the colonial envelope on press freedom to achieve larger political and social goals for Indians.

The focus here is not so much on Roy's pamphlets and tracts on religion, but his engagement with journals and his role in leading the ethical-political opposition to restrictions on the press imposed by the East-India Company (EIC). Of particular salience are the reasons he set out to launch his journals, as also his reasons to close one of his journals in protest against restrictions imposed by the colonial rulers. Roy drafted two significant 'memorials' addressed to the Supreme Court in Calcutta and to the King in London to protest against restrictions on press freedom and to fight for justice. His opposition to the colonial rulers was marked by civil and courteous overtones – he sought change through polite engagement rather than blind opposition – but at the same time, armed with wide knowledge, reason, and argument, he doggedly defended his position in debates of the day. As Roy's actions at the time suggest, themes such as justice, ethics, and globalization were as much rooted in what Bayly calls the 'Indo-Muslim ecumene' (1996, p. 86) as were introduced by ideas brought to India by the colonial-era soldier, trader, and missionary.

The context and origins of print journalism

A unique set of conditions prevailed in India and the West when the first journal was printed in Calcutta on January 29, 1780, by Hicky, called *Hicky's Bengal Gazette Or Calcutta General Advertiser*, which described itself as 'A Weekly Political and Commercial Paper, Open to All Parties but Influenced by None'. The close of the 18th century was a period of cataclysmic change: American and French Revolutions had a profound influence not only on rulers in England but also on officials of the EIC. Radical politics began to emerge in England from the 1750s, which was strongly resisted by the forces of status quo. The same fears gripped the early officers of the expansionist EIC as the company established itself in Calcutta and slowly spread its influence across India.

In mid-18th-century Mughal India, slowly but surely, the old was giving way to the new in complex ways. The Mughal Empire was losing its influence, while the EIC gained political power and influence after the Battle of Plassey (1757), Battle of Buxar (1764), and the Treaty of Allahabad (1765), in which the Mughal Emperor formally acknowledged British dominance in the region by granting EIC the 'diwani', or the right to collect revenue, from Bengal, Bihar, and Orissa. The Supreme Court was founded in Calcutta in 1774. The EIC ceased to be merely a trading company and transformed into a powerful imperial agency with an army of its own, exercising control over vast territories and millions of people.

It is important to note that at this point in history, the press in England was tethered to the government, with 'taxes on knowledge'; it was yet to achieve the status of an institution that holds those in power to account. It was only in the mid-19th century that the press acquired its watchdog orientation, when, free from political shackles due to revenue gained by advertising, newspapers in England began to see themselves as providing a platform on which citizenship, accountability, and democracy could be built. Such ideas were considered subversive in the colonial situation in India in the 1780s. However, by 1799, when British entrepreneurs and agency houses came together to launch more English journals in Calcutta, the EIC was forced to deal with issues of press freedom. Several English-language journals followed Hicky's journal, as members of the small British community in Calcutta sought to recreate the cultural conditions in England: '[As] the German demands his national beverages wherever he settles, so the Briton insists on his newspaper' (Mills 1924, p. 103).

Calcutta became the setting for the origins of Indian journalism and the crucible of the first sustained cultural encounter between Indian intellectuals and the West. In the late 18th century (1780s), the white population in the town was less than 1,000; in the 1837 census, 3,138 'English' were returned, with soldiers forming the main element of the community. A part of Calcutta came to be known as the 'white town', where the British based themselves and sought to recreate British cultural life through news, goods, music, theater and personnel that arrived and left for England by sea. As Marshall (2000, pp. 308–309) noted, the 'vast majority of the British were not interested in any exchange of ideas with the Indians. They did not expect to give anything, still less to receive. They were solely concerned with sustaining British cultural life for themselves with as few concessions as possible to an alien environment.'

Yet, members of the Indian intelligentsia, such as Roy living in Calcutta, responded in creative ways to aspects of European culture that became available to them. Some members of the British community, on their own, developed cultural contacts with the local population, notably Sir William Jones, Nathaneil Halhed, Charles Wilkins, and for evangelical reasons, the Baptist missionaries in nearby Serampore. Indian scholars employed at the Fort William College also brought them in close contact with the British. As EIC's presence spread and grew in its influence, Calcutta became the center of governance, attracting 'unofficial' Britons seeking to make a fortune, thus setting the scene for discursive interactions with the local population at various levels, including in the field of journalism (such as it was then). Indian intellectuals such as Roy were quick to absorb new ideas from the West. At the time, as Raichaudhuri noted, 'The excitement over the literature, history and philosophy of Europe as well as the less familiar scientific knowledge was deep and abiding' (1988, p. 3).

At the heart of this 'excitement' was the technology of print, which enabled the flow of ideas and news from the metropole to the colonial periphery, vice versa, and slowly beyond Calcutta and the other two presidencies of Madras and Bombay. The printing press first arrived in India in Goa with Portuguese missionaries in the mid-16th century. Several religious texts were later printed in Konkani, Tamil, and other Indian languages, but it was not until the late 18th century that the first English-language journals were launched in Calcutta, followed by journals in Bengali, Persian, and Hindi in Calcutta, and in other Indian languages in Madras and Bombay. In the last two decades of the 18th century, 'Calcutta rapidly developed into the largest centre of printing in the sub-continent...appropriate to its paramount importance to the British as an administrative, commercial and social base' (Shaw 1981, p. ix). The first attempt to launch a journal was made by William Bolts in 1768, when he put up a notice in the Council Hall in Calcutta, but it did not amount to much as the colonial administration soon deported him to England. It was 18 years after Bolts' initiative that Hicky arrived on the scene and launched what was to become the first printed journal in the history of Indian journalism.

Hicky catered to the small British community, which was soon able to sustain more English journals, some of them launched with the support of the EIC. As Marshall noted, 'White Calcutta sustained a remarkable number of newspapers and journals in English. Between 1780 and 1800, 24 weekly or monthly magazines came into existence...The total circulation of English-language publications was put at 3000...These are astonishing figures for so small a community' (2000, p. 324). It was the era of 'journalist as publicist', as editors – in England and in colonial India – stamped their own personalities on their journals, often entering into scurrilous attacks against rival editors and officials of the EIC. Hicky bitterly attacked Governor-General Warren Hastings, Chief Justice of the Supreme Court Sir Elijah Impey, and others in the British community in Calcutta.

The English journals were mainly non-political in character, sustained by advertising and had the British community as its audience. Besides some criticism of the EIC by mostly anonymous letter writers to the editor, the journals published orders of the colonial government, Indian news, personal news, notes on fashion, extracts from papers published in England, parliamentary reports, poems, newsletters, and reports from parts of Europe. Editorials and other content would mainly interest the British community.

If Hicky's journal is better known historically for publication of scandals, scurrilous personal attacks, and risqué advertisements selling sex and sin, he was also the first to fight against the colonial government, then almost single-handed, to defend the liberty of the press. His words deserve a place in the history of Indian journalism: 'Mr Hicky considers the Liberty of the Press to be essential to the very existence of an Englishman and a free G-t. The *subject* should have full liberty to declare his principles, and opinions, and every act which tends to *coerce* that liberty is *tyrannical* and injurious to the COMMUNITY' (Barns 1940, p. 49; italics, capitals in original; in the days of letter press, 'G-t' meant 'Government'). Hicky was soon hounded by Hastings and Impey, fined, imprisoned, and his journal closed in March 1782. He died in penury in 1802. He was the first of several editors of English journals to invite the wrath of EIC officials, who were wary of the effects of the ideas spawned by the French Revolution in India, and were highly sensitized to any threats to the existing order. By 1800, some journals closed for want of advertising and subscription, while others closed when British editors were deported to England after publishing material that was considered unacceptable by the EIC.

Editors who attracted EIC's ire and found themselves on ships back to England included William Duane, editor of *Bengal Journal*, removed as editor and almost deported in 1791, and finally deported as editor of *Indian World* in 1794; Charles Maclean, editor of *Bengal Hurkaru*, deported in 1798; James Silk Buckingham, editor of *Calcutta Journal*, deported in 1823; and C.J. Fair, editor of the *Bombay Gazette*, also deported in 1823. The question of freedom of the press first exercised colonial authorities at the time of Richard Wellesley's governorship (1798–1805), when EIC interpreted any criticism in journals as lurking Jacobinism. In 1799, Wellesley introduced regulations for the press, which stipulated that no newspaper be published until the proofs of the whole paper, including advertisements, were submitted to the colonial government and approved; violation invited deportation. Until the mid-1810s, the regulations applied only to the English journals, because until 1818, there were no journals in Indian languages.

The year 1818 witnessed developments that catalyzed the growth of journalism in an expanding colonial India. As noted above, deportation remained a key instrument to discipline British editors, but the measure could not be applied to editors who were Indians or to Europeans born in India. To remove the anomaly, the Marquess of Hastings, who was governor-general from 1813 to 1823, removed the 1799 censorship and issued a new set of rules in 1818. In a circular to all publishers, he set out guidelines with a view to prevent the publication of topics considered dangerous or objectionable, or face deportation. But his new rules did not possess the force of law as they were not passed into a 'Regulation' in a legal manner, which meant that in practice there were no legal restrictions on the press. The Marquess of Hastings was soon hailed in Calcutta as a liberator of the press.

In the same year, the first journals in an Indian language – Bengali – were launched; they were the precursors of several Indian language journals in other parts of India. There is a dispute about which was published first, the *Bangal Gejeti* edited by Harachandra Roy with the assistance of Gangakishore Bhattacharya, or *Samachar Darpan*, launched by the Baptist missionaries at Serampore – both were launched in May 1818 (some scholars claim that *Bangal Gejeti* was launched in 1816). The missionaries had earlier launched the monthly *Digdarsan* in April 1818, but due to the missionary context, nationalist historians credit *Bangal Gejeti* as the first journal in an Indian language, but it did not last for more than a year (none of its issues are known to exist).

The year 1818 also saw the launch of Buckingham's *Calcutta Journal*, on October 2, a biweekly of eight quarto pages, which was to come into frequent conflict with EIC and also encouraged the growth of the 'native' press by often publishing extracts from the Indian language journals and commenting favorably on their growth. A Whig, Buckingham propagated liberal ideas and views through his journal that almost reached the record circulation figure of 1,000 copies. As the editor, he wrote, he conceived his duty to be 'to admonish Governors of their duties, to warn them furiously of their faults, and to tell disagreeable truths'. Setting himself up as a champion of free press, Buckingham saw a free press as an important check against misgovernment, especially in Bengal, where there was no legislature to curb executive authority.

Buckingham was a friend and ally of Rammohun Roy. It is clear from the contents of *Calcutta Journal* and other records that the two collaborated to push for greater press freedom as well as for Roy's reformist campaigns. Their collaboration continued even after Buckingham was deported to England in 1823 (by acting Governor-General John Adam), and when Roy travelled to England in 1831 (Roy died in Bristol on September 27, 1833). Buckingham was central to the story of Roy's tryst with journalism, often commenting on the latter's scholarship and publishing extracts from his Bengali and Persian journals. Buckingham termed the press as 'this powerful Engine for spreading light and civilization'. It was against the background of Marquess of Hastings' light-touch approach toward the press that Roy launched journals and used print journalism to further his reformist objectives. In this, he was aided by a group of associates and followers that included the entrepreneur

Dwarkanath Tagore (1796–1846), who supported his campaigns and provided funds for journals with which Roy was associated. By the beginning of the 19th century, a 'multifarious culture of the print medium' had come into existence in India: 'It was the first fully formed print culture to appear outside Europe and North America and it was distinguished by its size, productivity, and multilingual and multinational constitution, as well as its large array of Asian languages and its inclusion of numerous non-Western investors and producers among its participants' (Dharwadker 1997, p. 112).

After a brief biography, the next section focuses on Roy's reasons and objectives for launching and closing his journals. His writings underlined idioms of improvement, education, progress, and the 'public good'. The contents of his journals symbolized the contrast in ethics that underpinned content in the English-language journals and in those launched by Indians, whose tone was distinctly polite toward the colonial rulers (until Indian opinion hardened against the colonial rulers in 1857). In contrast, the English journals' content mainly focused on amusement and entertainment and included scurrilous attacks against rival editors and other members of the British community. Their audience was the British community, and they neither represented nor defended the interests of the Indians. The focus in the Indian journals during this period was on disseminating useful knowledge, information, and discussing problems of public interest with a view to instructing or educating the people. There were also occasional examples of attacks against rival editors; for example, Bhabani Charan Bandopadhyay, who was closely associated with the first issues of Roy's *Sambad Kaumidi*, but left him to launch the rival *Samachar Chandrika* on March 5, 1822, used satire to ridicule Roy. The situation later became more complex as Indians launched journals in English; the first of these was the *Bengal Herald* (1829), which was supported by Roy and Tagore, among others.

Rammohun Roy and his journalism

In modern India's iconography, Roy has an exalted status as the 'founder of modern India' or as the 'father of modern India'. His life and work have been the focus of much academic research and analysis. The facts of his life have been the subject of some debate, particularly the date of birth, since no records were kept at the time. Roy's year of birth has been variously mentioned as 1772, 1774 or 1780; the date generally accepted, and for which the evidence is the strongest, is May 22, 1772. The second of three sons of Ramakanta Roy, he was born in Radhanagar, Burdwan district, and was married more than once in childhood. There are stories about his being sent to Patna for education in Arabic and to Calcutta or Varanasi for Sanskrit. Not much is known of his whereabouts until 1796, when he was recorded as having managed his father's property. In the same year, Ramakanta Roy divided his property between his three sons, and Rammohun's share included a house in Jorasanko in Calcutta. Between 1797 and 1803, when his father died, he acquired a fortune as a financier in Calcutta, lending money, dealing in 'Company paper' (EIC stock), and buying land.

It was while working for EIC between 1803 and 1814 that he came in close contact with the British and Western ideas. During this period, he worked for John Digby, a covenanted servant of the EIC in Rangpur, and used the association to learn English. Digby later commented that Roy began to take a keen interest in European politics, especially in the course of the French Revolution. Until Roy's retirement from EIC in 1814, Roy would avidly read journals that arrived from England in Digby's office. After settling down in the then rapidly growing Calcutta, he came in contact with several people who were influenced by Western ideas, and founded the Atmiya Sabha in 1815, which held weekly debates and meetings to propagate monotheistic doctrines of the Hindu scriptures. Members of this group later joined Roy's ventures in journalism; for example, Harachandra Roy and Gangakishore Bhattacharya, who launched *Bangal Gejeti*, which several scholars consider to be the first Indian journal; that is, one that was not associated with the British or the Baptist missionaries. For some time, Roy contributed to journals launched by the missionaries, but soon turned away when there was reluctance to publish his responses to attacks on Hinduism. Roy fed various presses operating in Calcutta at the time, writing and translating extensively on various subjects.

In the relatively liberal climate for the press in 1818, Roy ventured into journalism and worked closely with Buckingham. There are suggestions that for some time Roy was a partner in Buckingham's *Calcutta Journal*, and that Buckingham had more than just goodwill for Roy's Persian journal *Mirat-ul-Akhbar*, launched in 1822. Buckingham often published extracts from Roy's journals and citing Roy's scholarship and erudition commented in glowing terms about the growth of the 'native' press. Most contemporary knowledge about the contents of Roy's Bengali and Persian journals is based on their translations published in *Calcutta Journal*, whose copies are available in hard copy and digital form in Britain and India. An interesting aspect of the collaboration between the two is that a considerable portion of contents translated into English from Roy's journals was done by Roy himself.

From 1815 to 1830, Roy lived in Calcutta and was closely associated with the launch of at least five journals: *Bengal Gejeti* (1818), *The Brahmunical Magazine* (1821), *Sambad Kaumidi* (1821), *Mirat-ul-Akhbar* (1822), and *Bengal Herald* (1829). It is important to note here that Roy was not the only person then who ventured into journalism. Other Indians also saw business and ideological opportunities in publishing a journal. For example, Bhabani Charan Bandopadhyaya, who edited and managed the first 13 issues of Roy's *Sambad Kaumidi*, fell out with Roy over his ideas to reform Hinduism and set up the rival journal *Samachar Chandrika*, which succeeded in weaning away many subscribers of *Sambad Kaumidi*. None of Roy's journals lasted long, but during their existence they became the focal point of debates and information about issues and events that concerned the EIC and the Indians. At a time of low literacy and a printed journal being seen as a novelty, Roy wrote about the benefits Indians could gain from developing the habit of reading journals.

The ethical compass from which Roy launched his journals is evident from the contents of the first issues of *Sambad Kaumidi* (Bengali) and *Mirat-ul-Akhbar* (Persian). On December 20, 1821, the *Calcutta Journal* published an editorial, titled 'Establishment of a Native Newspaper, edited by a Learned Hindoo', followed by a copy of the 'Prospectus' and an 'Address to the Bengal Public'. The 'Address', written by Roy, set out the scope and objectives of the new journal, *Sambad Kaumidi*, thus (worth quoting in full):

For the information of the Literati, under the immediate Province of Bengal, the Conductors of the newly established Bengally Newspaper, entitled *Sungbaud Cowmuddee*, or 'The Moon of Intelligence' respectfully beg leave to state in a brief manner that the object of that Publication is the Public Good. The subjects to be discussed will have that object for a *Guiding-Star*. Any Essay bearing upon this primary object will always meet with ready attention. As to minor points, the Prospectus, already published, will afford every information that can be desired; and as a Newspaper conducted *exclusively* by Natives, in the Native Languages, *is a novelty at least*, if not a *desideratum*, it will of course ever be the study of its Conductors to render their labours as interesting as possible; for which purpose they hereby solicit the hearty co-operation of the *Literati* and *well-wishers of the Cause* to contribute their aid in bringing this Publication to the highest pitch of perfection which it is capable of attaining. Nothing need be apprehended on this subject, when the state of the Press in India is considered: that it was *hitherto shackled*, and that owing to the liberal and comprehensive mind of our present enlightened and magnanimous Ruler, the Most Noble the Marquess of Hastings, these shackles have been removed, and the Press declared Free; and when it is further considered, that many celebrated publications (which are a continual source of delight and instruction to Europeans in this country), first appeared in the *humble* though *useful* channel of a periodical Newspaper, we need not apprehend but that by due exertions we shall also be able to rescue our names from oblivion, and eventually be held up to future generations as examples for imitation, obtaining by such notice the need of praise to which all noble minds are ever alive, and which is never withheld from superior merit. It will readily occur from what has been just stated, that is our intention hereafter to give further currency to the Articles inserted in this Paper, by translating the most interesting parts in the different languages of the East, particularly Persian and Hindoostanee; but as this will entail considerable expense, the accomplishment of it will of course depend upon the encouragement which we may be able to obtain. The foregoing being an outline of what we are desirous of performing, our countrymen will readily conclude that although the Paper in question be conducted by us, and may consequently be considered our property, yet *virtually* it is the 'Paper of the Public,' since in it they can at all times have inserted, anything that *tends to the public good*, and by a respectful expression of their grievances, be enabled to get them redressed, if our Countrymen have not already been able to affect that desirable object by publishing them in English.

(italics in original; emphasis added)

According to Banerji (1931, p. 409), *Sambad Kaumidi*, with its focus on the 'public good', was 'virtually the first Bengali newspaper worth the name, published from Calcutta'. Some of the contents of the first issues of the journal were summarized in *Calcutta Journal*:

1. An appeal to the Government for the establishment of a seminary for the gratuitous instruction of the children of poor though respectable Hindoos.
2. A brief address to the natives, enumerating the advantages of reading newspapers.
3. An appeal to the magistrates of the Calcutta police, to resort to rigours measures for relieving the Hindoo inhabitants of the

metropolis from the serious grievances of Christian gentlemen driving their buggies amongst them, and cutting and lashing them with whips, without distinction of sex or age, whilst they quietly assemble in immense numbers to witness the images of their deities pass in the Chitpore road, when many of them, through terror and consternation, caused by the lashing inflicted on the spectators, fall down into drains, while others are trampled under foot by the crowd.

4. An interesting and satirical account of the rich natives, at whose death and mourning ceremonies considerable sums of money are expended, but who during their lives, give strict injunctions to door-keepers of their mansions not to admit anyone in who might possibly want anything.

5. A correspondent brings to the notice of the public the serious evils which result from the present practice of the poor Hindoos throwing the bodies of their deceased relations into the river Ganges, from want of resources to burn them, and under a firm conviction of the unbounded liberality of the richer class Hindoos, evinced by the expenditure of large sums of money in the celebration of the ceremonies of their parents, and in other numerous charitable acts, strongly appeals to their humanity and benevolence to establish a fund, by subscription, for the purpose of enabling the poor to defray the necessary expenses of the burning their deceased relations.

Roy wrote extensively to oppose the practice of 'sati', which brought him into conflict with the dominating conservative sections of the Hindu community. His critics already had the rival journal, *Samachar Chandrika*, which lured away most of Roy's subscribers, resulting in Roy closing *Sambad Kaumidi* for want of support. The *Calcutta Journal* lamented its demise on February 14, 1823, thus: 'The Paper which was considered so fraught with danger, and likely to explode over all India like a spark thrown into a barrel of gunpowder, has long since fallen to the ground for want of support; chiefly we understand because it offended the Native community, by opposing their customs, and particularly the Burning of Hindu Widows'.

Next, Roy launched the *Mirat-ul-Akhbar* in Persian on April 12, 1822, and went further in setting out its ethical framework. Persian was then the language of the Indian elites, and the *akhbarat* (news-letters) tradition initiated during the Mughal Empire was still in practice. An extract from Roy's 'Prospectus' for this journal (also reproduced in *Calcutta Journal*) is revealing in its advancement of journalism ethics from the goals mentioned while launching *Sambad Kaumidi*, particularly in its stress on 'regard for truth' and to guard against anything hurtful to any individual:

> [But] as the English language is not understood in all parts of India, those unacquainted with it must either have recourse to others in their enquiries after information, or remain totally uninformed. On this account, I the humblest of the human race am desirous of publishing Weekly Newspaper, written in the Persian language which is understood by all the respectable part of the Native Community, and am ready to distribute it to all who may be so inclined. I solemnly protest that it is not my object to make this Paper the channel of exaggerated praise to the great, or to my own friends, that I may hereby meet with favor and promotion; nor is it my intention in this my Editorial capacity to permit unmerited claim or reproach to be cast upon others. On the contrary, I shall have a due regard for truth and for the rank of persons in authority, and in composing every sentence, keeping in view the saying of the Poet, that – 'The wounds of the spear may be healed, but a wound inflicted by the tongue is incurable' – I shall guard against any expression that might tend to hurt the feelings of any individual. In short, in taking upon myself to edit this Paper, my only object is that I may lay before the Public such articles of Intelligence as may increase their experience, and tend to their social improvement; and that to the extent of my abilities, I may communicate to the Rulers a knowledge of the real situation of their subjects, and make the subjects acquainted with the established laws and customs of their Rulers: that the Rulers may the more readily find an opportunity of granting relief to the people; and the people may be put in possession of the means of obtaining protection and redress from their Rulers.

(emphasis added)

Mirat-ul-Akhbar was more theoretical and international in scope. Its contents included accounts of military events in the Ottoman Empire and the history and turmoil in Ireland at the time. There were 'editorials on the function and forms of government – constitutional monarchy got the nod as the ideal – and on the need for more checks against abuses of magisterial authority' (Zastoupil 2010, p. 100). By this time, Roy was already using international events as examples to push for reform for Indians. In a lengthy article titled 'Ireland: The Causes of its Distress and Discontents', Roy wrote that Ireland had been fighting off the unjust rule of the kings of England for a thousand years. Its peasants were impoverished, yet non-resident Anglo-Irish landlords remitted huge sums of cash regularly to England. As Bayly noted, 'It is again difficult to believe that this articulate concern with Ireland was not, and was not perceived to be, a veiled attack on the Company's rule in India' (2007, p. 39).

The freedom enjoyed by the press after 1818 proved to be short-lived as Buckingham's *Calcutta Journal* and other journals, including the ones launched in Indian languages, were perceived by EIC officials as being offensive and mischievous. In a lengthy minute to the Governor-General's Council on October 10, 1822, Chief Secretary W.B. Bayley named *Mirat-ul-Akhbar* (and the Persian *Jam-i-Jahan Numa*) as errant journals and mentioned examples of Roy's writings that were considered offensive. EIC's patience was already being tested by the irrepressible Buckingham, who was given several warnings by the administration, but refused to tone down his writings. On October 17, 1822, the Marquess of Hastings wrote to the Home authorities for powers to enable the Indian government to exercise more efficient control over the press than it could then legally do. On the subject of controls over the press, there was similarity of thought between the EIC officials in London and Calcutta.

The Marquess of Hastings sailed for England on January 9, 1823. He was succeeded as the acting Governor-General by John Adam, whose first act on assuming the office was to deport Buckingham to England, which led to the closure of *Calcutta Journal*. Secondly, Adam promulgated a rigorous Press Ordinance on March 14, 1823, which made it mandatory for editors and publishers to secure licenses for their journals. To secure the licenses, they had to submit an affidavit to the chief secretary. For any offence of discussing any of the subjects prohibited by law, the editor or publisher was liable to lose the license. Adam's Press Ordinance was strongly opposed by Rammohun Roy and his associates (including Dwarkanath Tagore) in the form of two Memorials, first addressed to the Supreme Court, where it was rejected, and another, more sophisticated in its arguments, to the King in Privy Council. Sophia Dobson Collett, whose 1900 book, *The life and letters of Raja Rammohun Roy*, is one of the key works on Roy, wrote of the Memorial to the Supreme Court: 'It may be regarded as the *Aeropagitica of Indian history*' (1900, p. 180; italics in original).

The 'daring act' of Roy and his associates to oppose the Press Ordinance through the Memorials, according to Majumdar (1965, p. 233), 'marks the beginning of a new type of political activity which was destined to be a special characteristic of India for nearly a century'. The protest was seen as the beginning of a long campaign of constitutional agitation for political rights. The Memorial to the King drew on history and the benefits of a free press and noted that '[A] free press has never yet caused a revolution in any part of the world because, while men can easily represent the grievances arising from the conduct of the local authorities to the supreme Government, and thus get them redressed, the grounds of discontent that excite revolution are removed; whereas, where no freedom of the Press existed, and grievances consequently remained unrepresented and unredressed, innumerable revolutions have taken place in all parts of the globe, or if prevented by the armed forces of the Government, the people continued ready for insurrection' (Collett 1900, p. 407). The Memorial also recalled that the Baptist missionaries' publication, *Friend of India*, had noted in December 1822 that the native press had not abused liberty of the press 'in the least degree'.

The Memorials were much appreciated in England, but failed to change policy. Roy decided to close *Mirat-ul-Akhbar* in protest against the Press Ordinance (and also due to some financial problems). In the last issue of the journal, he stated his reasons for not being able to comply with the new regulations, and added: 'I...here prefer silence to speaking out'. He also cited a Persian couplet:

> *Guda-e goshah nashenee to Khafiza makharosh*
> *Roo mooz maslabat-i khesh khoosrowan danand*

> (Thou O Hafiz, art a poor retired man, be silent,
> Princes know the secrets of their own Policy)

Roy's only known journalistic venture after closing *Mirat-ul-Akhbar* was the *Bengal Herald*, the first English-language journal launched by Indians. It was supported by Roy and five others, including Dwarkanath Tagore and R. Montgomery Martin. According to Chanda (1987, p. 116), '*The Bengal Herald* occupies an important place in the history of the English Press in Bengal. For, it was the first regular venture of the natives in the field of English journalism. Officially R.M. Martin had the editorial responsibility. But in the columns...we mostly get reflection of the views of Rammohun Roy'.

The influence of Roy and other Indians who launched journals in the early 19th century was discernible in the ethical framework that guided their successors; for example, on September 16, 1841, the *Friend of India* reported a resolution adopted by Indian editors:

We learn... that a meeting of the Editors of Native newspapers, and other influential members of the Hindoo community, was held on Sunday last, to consider the best means of improving the tone and of raising the character of the Native Press. One of the resolutions passed was, that the editors should no longer indulge in personal invective and gross abuse, but cordially co-operate with each other in advocating the best interests of the country.

Conclusion

During the period under focus – an era of mass illiteracy – the impact of the press was limited to the elites among the British and the Indians. Yet, it soon achieved the status of a forum in which current issues were highlighted and debated and provided ideas for future political campaigns. It was remarkable that soon after the first journal was printed in 1780, issues of press freedom engaged the elites, grouping together British and Indian liberals who presented increasingly sophisticated arguments in its favor. In this process, Rammohun Roy was one of the key players. Revisionist historians such as R.C. Majumdar have sought to debunk the 'Rammohun myth' (1972, pp. 19–51), but in the area of journalism, Roy was clearly the first major public figure to foresee the potential of journalism for the 'public good' and to use it to the extent he could in colonial circumstances to drive his reformist objectives. The colonial context and the opposition it engendered made politics a central theme of journalism, which continues today, despite contemporary efforts to 'dumb down' news content in pursuit of profits. Roy engaged with Western ideas in order to bring about change in Indian society and brought late-Mughal courtesies and politeness to his journalism. In the process, by focusing on 'truth' and seeking not to hurt any individual through his writings, he continued India's ancient tradition of reasoned argument and debate through his journalism, which stood in some contrast to the amusement-oriented journalism in journals at the time, owned and edited by the British.

The larger point that emerges from Roy's intervention in early Indian journalism is that contrary to the implied claims of West-to-Rest diffusionism in media history, the evolution of journalism and media ethics in what used to be called the Third World – and in India in particular – was a complex process (for example, in a seminal analysis of the development of media professionalism in the Third World, Golding (1977, p. 291) began with this claim: 'Mass media in Africa, Latin

America and Asia have developed, almost invariably, as derivatives of those in the advanced industrialized countries'). In India, British rule did not mean a 'switch-off' of earlier oral-based repertoire of social communication and communal reading practices, but that from the late 18th century, and print journalism revitalized and reinvented the existing forms of social communication. As Bayly noted in his influential study of the British Empire and the then prevailing information order in India, 'Print in itself did not create an information revolution. Rather, it speeded up the velocity and range of communication among existing communities of knowledge' (1996, p. 243).

Roy's idea of ethics and 'public good' implied a focus on education and instruction to raise the level of awareness of Indians at the time. Since then the idea has undergone several changes, particularly during the freedom struggle, when 'public good' primarily meant opposition to British rule. The changes prompted further legislation to control and suppress the growing nationalist press. By 1870, the influence of Indian-language newspapers had grown, so that they were perceived as a threat by the colonial government, leading to the enactment of the repressive Vernacular Press Act of 1878. But despite the constraints, the press continued to grow, and within a century of the publication of Hicky's *Bengal Gazette*, more than 140 newspapers in Indian languages were being published, representing and providing a forum for a new sense of nationalism. Most nationalist leaders were activists and involved in campaigning journalism, including Gandhi, who realized the importance of the written word and used Gujarati, his mother tongue, as well as English, to spread the message of freedom. By 1941, about 4,000 newspapers and magazines were in print in 17 languages, all anticipating and seeking to hasten the end of colonial rule.

In 21st-century India, the idea of 'public good' has undergone further redefinition and narrowing (as 'personal good'?). Politics, however, continues to be the default setting of Indian journalism despite rapacious and unethical commercial practices by owners of news organizations and practitioners. As political communication becomes more professionalized, American-style branding and 'advertorial' practices lend new colors to a journalism that grew out of the British model of journalism in the late 18th century.

References

Banerji, B. N. (1931) 'Rammohun Roy as a Journalist', *The Modern Review*, April 1931.
Barns, M. (1940) *The Indian Press: A History of the Growth of Public Opinion in India.* London: Allan & Unwin.

Bayly, C. A. (1996) *Empire & Information: Intelligence Gathering and Social Communication in India, 1780–1870*. Cambridge: Cambridge University Press.

Bayly, C. A. (2004) *The Birth of the Modern World: 1780–1914*. Oxford: Blackwell.

Bayly, C. A. (2007) 'Rammohan Roy and the Advent of Constitutional Liberalism in India, 1800–30', *Modern Intellectual History*, 4(1): 25–41.

Dharwadker, V. (1997) 'Print Culture and Literary Markets in Colonial India', in J. Master et al. (eds.), *Language Machines: Technologies of Literary and Cultural Production*. pp. 108–133. London: Routledge.

Golding, P. (1977) 'Media Professionalism in the Third World: The Transfer of an Ideology', in J. Curran et al. (eds.), *Mass Communication and Society*. pp. 291–308. London: Edward Arnold.

Guha Thakurta, P. (2011) 'Manufacturing "News" ', *Economic and Political Weekly*, XLVI(14), 2 April.

Majumdar, R. C. (1965) *British Paramountcy and Indian Renaissance*. Part II. Bombay: Bharatiya Vidya Bhavan.

Majumdar, R. C. (1972) '*On Rammohan Roy*', Dr Bemanbehari Majumdar Memorial Lecture. Calcutta: Asiatic Society.

Marshall, P. J. (2000) 'The White Town of Calcutta Under the Rule of the East India Company', *Modern Asian Studies*, 34 (2): 307–331.

Martin, R. M. (1834) *History of the British Colonies*. London: Cochrane and M'Crone.

Mills, J. S. (1924) *The Press and Communications of the Empire*. London: W. Collins Sons & Co.

Pratt, M. L. (1991) 'Arts of the Contact Zone', *Profession,* 91: 33–40; New York: MLA.

Raichaudhuri, T. (1988) *Europe Reconsidered: Perceptions of the West in Nineteenth-Century Bengal*. New Delhi: Oxford University Press.

Robertson, R. (1992) *Globalization: Social Theory and Global Culture*. London: Sage.

Shaw, G. (1981) *Printing in Calcutta to 1800*. London: The Bibliographical Society.

Sen, A. (2005) *The Argumentative Indian*. London: Allen Lane.

Sonwalkar, P. (2002) 'Murdochization of the Indian Press: From by-Line to Bottom-Line', *Media Culture & Society*, 24(6): 821–834.

Wasserman, H. and Rao, S. (2008) 'The Glocalisation of Journalism Ethics', *Journalism: Theory, Practice and Criticism*, 9(2): 163–181.

Zastoupil, L. (2010) *Rammohun Roy and the Making of Victorian Britain*. Basingstoke: Palgrave Macmillan.

10

The Chief and the Channels: How Satellite Television Sparked a Social Movement for the 'Rule of Law' that Is Restructuring Political Power in Pakistan

Shahan Mufti

It started with a single photograph of Pakistani government security forces making an arrest in Islamabad on March 13, 2007. The photograph, a miscellany of limbs and heads, captures perfectly the commotion that would have ensued outside the building of the Supreme Court of Pakistan that afternoon. A hand clutches a head that is half obscured by someone else's shoulder, pulling it down by the hair and forcing it through an open rear door of an official-looking car. Just enough of the eyes are visible in the photograph to suggest that the person being arrested is Iftikhar Muhammad Chaudhry, the Chief Justice of Pakistan. The photograph appeared the following day in the pages of the *Nawa-e-Waqt*, one of the largest Urdu daily newspapers in Pakistan, and *The Nation*, its sister English publication. The caption in *The Nation* read: 'ISLAMABAD: Police "requesting" suspended Chief Justice Iftikhar Mohammad Chaudhry to sit in the police car after he refused to do so'.[1]

The arrest of the Chief Justice was made on the instructions of Pakistan's military ruler Pervez Musharraf. It was a potentially explosive image showing how a military ruler was trampling over the judiciary of the country. Yet the newspaper chose a clever but subdued caption. It was vintage Pakistani print journalism – biting yet watchful. Pakistani journalists have experienced it all in the six decades that the country has existed as an independent nation-state. Pakistan has been through periods of imperfect democratic rule, several periods of military rule, civil wars, and global and international conflicts. Pakistani journalism has also been repeatedly been caught in the middle of complex struggles between the country's executive, judicial, and legislative branches and the powerful military.

The news media had been in the eye of the storm many times, and as a result, it is mature beyond its years. While media business owners and journalists have always been aware of the many invisible 'red lines' that surround the business of reporting news, which have been drawn by the many powerful elites in the country that wish to control it, over the decades it has also demonstrated an obstinate will to push those lines, however slightly, any chance they get.[2] In the spring of 2007, as Pakistan's military ruler Pervez Musharraf butted heads with the Chief Justice of Pakistan, the news media was there as always. The photographers were dutifully on the scene to document the events and capture the perfect moment, the reporters wrote up their stories, and the editors churned out the provocative captions.

But Pakistan was no longer informed by print journalism alone. In the five years leading up to this event, the country had welcomed a feisty newcomer in the world of news: independent satellite television. Pakistan's first satellite news stations had started telecasting in 2002, a few years after Pervez Musharraf came to power in a military coup. Ever since, television had become a powerful social force, especially in urban Pakistan, where television sets are plentiful. By 2007, Pakistan had nearly one dozen private channels dedicated to news and dozens of others for entertainment, music, fashion, and sports. For the TV news channels, the arrest of the Chief Justice of Pakistan was the first taste of a major political crisis. Since there was no precedent, no set rules on how to cover such a clash of institutions, and no self-regulating code of conduct for TV news, the journalists and media owners decided to write the standards as they went along. What would result in the course of the following few years was a momentous dialog between the military, civilian political forces, and the judiciary, with private TV news channels at the center of it all. Through all this, TV would forever reconfigure political power in Pakistan.

An old institutional imbalance

The relationship between the judiciary and the military and civilian political leaders in Pakistan has historically always been very lopsided. While the country's most important legal documents, the constitution and the Objectives Resolution, which formed the basis of the constitution, both guarantee the independence of the judiciary, in reality the courts were always the weakest of the state's institutions.[3] At times, the judiciary has been subservient to the military, and at other times it has done the bidding of civilian forces that controlled the executive and legislative branches. For example, the 'Doctrine of Necessity', first used by the courts to justify the dissolution of an elected government in Pakistan in 1954, was invoked repeatedly by later military dictators to legalize and legitimize their own rules. Civilian rulers, meanwhile, strong-armed and manipulated the courts on many occasions. In one instance, a ruling government ordered mobs to attack the Supreme Court building and harass judges. At other times, there have been accusations of the country's top judges accepting bribes by civilian rulers to pass favorable rulings. All rulers, military and civilians, have sought to stack the courts with loyalists. The courts have resisted at times, but had mostly proved to be either easily corruptible or spineless in the face of more forceful institutions.[4]

The military's stranglehold on Pakistani politics, in particular, has always been enabled by the judiciary's compliance. Like all of his military predecessors, General Musharraf ruled Pakistan on the shoulders of the country's highest court, which legalized his coup on the basis of the 'Doctrine of Necessity'. Musharraf initially enjoyed widespread popularity, at least in Pakistani cities. The economic growth spurred by American aid in the aftermath of the war in Afghanistan, which began in 2001, translated into stunningly economic growth rates, some of the fastest in Asia and in the world at the time. This growth also led to lower rates of unemployment and growth of a mobile middle class.[5] The economic growth was only one of the aspects of the military ruler's larger plan for Pakistan. Musharraf's program of 'Enlightened Moderation' was a grand socio-economic and political vision geared to create a more prosperous and open society. Musharraf wished to make the Islamic Republic of Pakistan a model for other Muslim countries to follow.[6] The liberalization of news media and in particular satellite television was an important element of Enlightened Moderation.

The first licenses for private satellite television channels were issued, a few years after the general came to power, to a handful of businesses and media moguls. The news and entertainment channels that started to blossom in the following years became the most visible representations of Musharraf's Enlightened Moderation campaign. Musharraf's emphasis on 'open society' was applauded internationally as well as in important and influential domestic populations.[7] And while the Musharraf regime was stable and popular, the new private TV outlets seemed only to cement his reputation as a progressive and benevolent leader. But what would happen when something went wrong? What if Musharraf's hold on power was threatened? These important questions would get answered when Musharraf took on the country's judiciary in 2007.

The military and judiciary faceoff

The trouble between the military ruler, President Musharraf, and the Chief Justice of the Supreme Court, Iftikhar Chaudhry, began brewing soon after Musharraf appointed Chaudhry as the country's top judge in 2005. As has been the story of so many leaders in Pakistan, Musharraf's handpicked choice would prove to be his biggest tormentor. In early 2006, Chaudhry suddenly stepped into the middle of the privatization of the Pakistan Steel Mills, the largest and most productive state-owned corporation in Pakistan. Factory workers and union members at the corporation had filed a lawsuit complaining that the Steel Mills had been badly undervalued in the sale, and Chaudhry decided to launch an investigation into the matter.[8] In August of that year, the Supreme Court issued a judgment reversing the sale and declaring it null and void, while suggesting that cronyism and corruption were responsible for the shape of the deal. It was the first time Chaudhry stepped into the middle of the government's affairs, and the scandal about the major privatization scheme caused deep embarrassment to Musharraf.

It did not stop there. The following year, in 2007, Chaudhry called out the military on its heavy-handed tactics in the War on Terror being fought along the western border with Afghanistan.[9] Pakistan had become a crucial ally of the United States in the war against Afghanistan by offering airspace, highway networks, and intelligence cooperation. But the military had also used this time to crack down on a festering nationalist separatist movement in the southern province of Baluchistan.[10] Musharraf had ordered the Pakistani army to embark on a fresh offensive against Balochi separatists, and in the process of the crackdown the military abducted and secretly held many dozens of Balochi men and women in custody. In October 2007, the Supreme Court, led by Iftikhar Chaudhry, summoned the heads of the country's powerful military intelligence agency, the Inter-Services Intelligence (ISI), to explain their role in forcibly 'disappearing' hundreds of people in Pakistan. Now the judge also seemed ready to embarrass the military by checking its supreme power.

Perhaps most importantly, Musharraf would have felt threatened by the Chief Justice for more personal reasons. In February 2007, Chaudhry had told trainee military officers in a public address that in his opinion President Musharraf could not legally continue to carry the office of army chief, if he chose to run for the office of president once again in scheduled elections. In saying this, Chaudhry was echoing what Musharraf's growing political opposition had been arguing as well.[11] Ordinarily, a military dictator in Pakistan would have been able to count on a Supreme Court Chief Justice to toe the line in case that such a matter of opposing a military ruler had gone to the courts. Musharraf was no ordinary military ruler, after all. He was powerful and ruled with full support of the United States. Still, Musharraf felt he could not take any chances with Chaudhry and so he made his move.

On March 13, 2007, Musharraf called the Chief Justice of Pakistan to his military headquarters and confronted him with a list of allegations of misconduct that suggested that the top judge was using his office for personal gain. As the prime minister and six uniformed military officers watched, Musharraf strongly encouraged Chaudhry to resign from his position. Faced with this situation, the Chief Justice did what no sitting judge had ever done in such a situation before: he said 'no'. Musharraf moved ahead anyway, and in his capacity as president, declared the Chief Justice as 'non-functional'.[12] It was the first time in the history of the country that an executive ruler had to resort to firing the country's top judge.

The photograph of the security officials pulling the country's highest legal authority by the hair and dragging him into the back of the car in the aftermath of this meeting captured the lengths to which Musharraf was going to retain power. It also showed the brutal manner in which he was suppressing the judicial activism of Iftikhar Chaudhry, who had become increasingly popular for his anti-corruption campaign and his populist stance on issues of social justice. At worst, the photo illustrated the disdain that Musharraf had for the law of the land. But which military ruler in Pakistan had not ruled the country by fiat? Was Musharraf's act truly grave enough to spark a revolutionary movement? Arguably, it all might have passed over as just another moment in Pakistani history when a ruler brutalized the judiciary. Musharraf's firing of the Chief Justice might just have been listed with many other occasions when judges were forced out of office or plied by iron fists. Had the photograph of the arrest stayed on the front page of a large newspaper with reported circulation of a few hundred thousand, it might have all been forgotten fairly soon. But the photograph did not stay on paper for very long. It was soon picked up by the private news channels, and on the TV screen the photo became a lightning rod for a social movement.

A history of television in Pakistan

Television had always been an important medium in Pakistan. In October 1998, for example, when Pervez Musharraf's loyal generals launched a coup against the elected government of Prime Minister Nawaz Sharif, the first location that the army's 111 Brigade took over in the capital was the headquarters of Pakistani Television (PTV). PTV was the state-owned Pakistani television station and the largest of a handful of television channels on-air. Once inside, the military officers were heard shouting, 'Take it off! Take it off' and the transmission of PTV abruptly went off-air. More than five hours later when the PTV broadcast came back on-air, the country was under a new ruler, General Pervez Musharraf. He came on-air after midnight to address the nation and announced that the 'armed forces have moved in as a last resort' to save the country from 'further destabilization'.[13] It was all that easy. PTV was the singular path into the national imagination. Whoever controlled PTV, it seemed, controlled reality in the country.

PTV began its transmission in 1964 after the NEC Corporation of Japan built a broadcasting facility for the state in Lahore during the rule of Pakistan's first military ruler General Ayub Khan. The Japanese gave the gift of TV, and the young state began to use it as a tool for 'educating the people of Pakistan'. Studio C at the Pakistan Broadcasting Corporation began transmission with three cameras, one audio tape recorder, one 35mm and one 16mm telecine, and one opaque projector.[14] Recording technology had not arrived for another few years, and so in these early days all transmission was live. Based in Lahore, the cultural capital of Pakistan, popular for its roadside food, historic architecture, and performing arts and culture, PTV became, among other things, a forum for the literary tradition and the arts of Muslim South Asia to come back to life. Soap operas like 'Khuda ki Basti' (God's Country) and other classics of Urdu literature were translated into celluloid and consumed afresh by those fortunate enough to have a television set. Pakistanis began enjoying the fete of their favorite cricket and hockey teams playing around the world. The founding fathers of the country made a comeback too. Their faces and speeches adorned television screens all over the country.[15]

With each passing regime, PTV molded itself to the particular ruler's tastes and his or her aspirations for the nation. Zia ul Haq, as one example, made it mandatory for all women news announcers to cover their heads with *dupatta* head scarfs, as an expression of conservative Islamic values. But under the rule of Benazir Bhutto, they were once again taken off. In 1990, with the return of civilian rule after a decade of military rule, Pakistan's first private television station, the Shalimar Television Network, began telecasting on the terrestrial network. For the first time, Pakistanis had a choice on television other than the state-controlled broadcast of PTV. The new channel carried mostly English programming and was aimed at urban elites. During the daytime the new channel broadcast CNN international. This was the first exposure Pakistanis had to news on television other than state-controlled news and it was no ordinary change. It was on this private news channel that the Pakistanis watched with the rest of the world the end of the Cold War and America's first war in Iraq as Operation Desert Storm began.

With this initial exposure, many urban Pakistanis were encouraged to install dish antennas on their rooftops to obtain transmission of other international channels being broadcast via satellite. The private media boom had begun in neighboring India in 1992, with the launch of Zee TV. India's first satellite television channel swept the entire region, and gained popularity among many Pakistanis who owned satellite dishes. Pakistani businessmen and print media moguls, seeing an opportunity, lobbied the democratic governments of Benazir Bhutto and Nawaz Sharif to open up the airwaves to Pakistani private satellite channels. But the democratic governments were not interested in introducing locally produced content. Other than the introduction of Shalimar Television Network, which was only partly privately owned, television as a news medium remained stifled throughout the 'democratic' 1990s.

General Musharraf, meanwhile, came to power on the heels of Pakistan's war with India in the Kargil region of Kashmir, in the summer of 1999. The conflict was deeply embarrassing for Pakistan. The world witnessed the stark contrast between the news reports flowing freely out of Indian news channels and the virtual silence from Pakistan. While Indian news reporters reported from the frontlines of the battle, Pakistan's own Prime Minister feigned ignorance of any war occurring in the Himalayan highlands. In the end, Pakistan was forced by American and international pressure to withdraw from their advantageous military positions in the mountains of Kashmir.[16] For many observers the difference between India and Pakistan's international influence was the news media. The experience was defining for Musharraf, who might have felt that Pakistan, besides losing military advantage, was also losing the information and cultural war to India. When he came to power, like any good Pakistani general, Musharraf decided his country would compete with India in this realm too.[17]

Challenges of ethics and regulation of private television

The Pakistan Electronic Media Regulatory Authority, commonly known as PEMRA, was established on the orders of General Musharraf in 2002 as the first step, before the first satellite channel took to the airwaves. The agency was made responsible for issuing licenses to new private FM radio and television channels, and also for regulating them by deciding what qualified as acceptable content. It was fairly liberal at first and it encouraged an 'electronic media boom', even if it was turning out a bit unruly at times.[18] GEO-TV, owned by the Jang Group of Newspapers, one of the oldest news groups in the country, went on air the same year and became the first Pakistani satellite channel. It was mainly a news channel and other new and entertainment channels began mushrooming after that.

Prohibitive local fees forced some operations like GEO to set up their broadcasting facilities and headquarters in the nearby tax free zones of Dubai. While they were essentially Pakistani channels broadcasting and reporting on the country, they did so from a few hundred miles outside its borders in the United Arab Emirates.[19] 'Infotainment' became a winning formula, and GEO and a few other news outlets, like ARY-TV and AAJ-TV, emerged as serious competitors for state-run PTV, especially in the large cities. Cable lines, carrying satellite television signals, soon started creeping into the more remote rural areas. In a few years GEO had grown to five 24-hour channels dedicated to different tastes like entertainment, sports, news, and the youth, and an English-language news channel watched by millions of Pakistanis living as expatriates in the West.

'Eyewitness news' style programming became popular on these new satellite channels. Shows like *Ham Awam* (With the People) and *Zara Sochiye* (Think a Little) on GEO TV brought on issues of social justice to the television screen in hard-hitting fashion. Not only did the problems of the many disenfranchised Pakistanis make for compelling television, which pleased advertisers, it also gave many people suffering from extreme poverty, who had historically had little influence in Pakistan, a new recourse to have their problems addressed. By examining basic issues like clean drinking water, access to justice, and police corruption, GEO found a formula for television that sold well, and it was a formula that other news channels copied.

For the first time in Pakistan, as the television business became about ratings rather than a grander educational and nation-building project, social justice issues gripped the public imagination.[20] By allowing for a private news channels to flourish, Musharraf had not only given up the state's monopoly on information; he had also given up the state's monopoly on the national conversation. For the first time, Pakistanis began seeing images that were not controlled and approved by the highest governmental authorities. It was a bold step. Television personalities, especially news anchors, were becoming recognizable and powerful public figures. They were inside people's homes at dinnertime, which was a place that had previously been held only by revered leaders and artists. News channels were all of a sudden competing with politicians for people's ears, hearts and minds on political matters, and they were perceived as the voice of the millions of voiceless, many of them demanding greater justice in society.

When Pervez Musharraf fired the Chief Justice and the photograph of the arrest spread like wildfire across Pakistani television screens in 2007, these vague notions of social justice finally found a concrete embodiment in Iftikhar Chaudhry. The Chief Justice, a populist judge who was increasingly seen as a protector of people's rights, was lovingly referred to as 'Chief' by many of his supporters, and his removal sparked a general outrage and demands for his restoration. The largely non-violent social movement became one of the largest in Pakistan's history. While the lawyers took to the streets in support of the country's top judge with demands that the 'Chief' be restored to his rightful place, the television cameras and satellite vans followed them wherever they went. The lawyers community, the men wearing black suits and ties and the women with white scarves and jackets, were the last people Pakistanis would have expected to become national heroes. But they suddenly became the star attraction on private TV news channels, the standards of bravery for stance against a military ruler.

Young, inexperienced, and lacking any self-regulating code of conduct, it was unrealistic to expect the TV news journalists to remain neutral and objective observers of the crisis. Soon they were sucked into the power play. As the judiciary's battle with the government spilled on to the streets of Pakistan's major cities, the journalists were swept away with it. Very early on, there were signs of the channels' cheerleading for the 'Chief'. They were hard to ignore in media coverage as the Chief Justice was lionized for his stance against Musharraf.[21] The young journalists working for the news channels found special camaraderie with the lawyers marching in the streets. If there was any hope of objective reporting, it was lost a few days into the protesting, when on March 16th government security forces attacked GEO's offices after the channel crossed an invisible boundary by deciding to broadcast live coverage of a defiant public rally by the Chief's supporters. Security forces broke into the GEO building shattering windows with batons, firing tear gas, and roughing up the men and women inside, demanding that the live coverage stop.

That day Pakistanis sat glued to their television sets, mesmerized by scenes of the kind they had never witnessed before. Hamid Mir, GEO's Islamabad bureau chief and the most widely recognized face on television, led a live on-air battle against the police. Locking himself in the newsroom in the basement he gave a minute-by-minute account of what unfolded. 'They're attacking us with tear gas now', he yelled at one point, as shaky, raw footage of the clash was beamed over satellite. It was a moment when the news media themselves became deeply caught up in the power struggle in Pakistan. But that wasn't all. A few hours later it became clear that the media were also a defining force. Hours later Mir, wearing a sober blue suit, was back on the air for his weeknight primetime show. He announced he had a special guest for the night. A more serious gaze replaced Mir's trademark playful spark as a phone line crackled through to President General Pervez Musharraf. 'I would like to apologize', the country's military ruler said a few minutes into the interview. 'This should never have happened. Freedom of speech, freedom of expression and the freedom of media, this is my mandate', he said. 'I strongly condemn any violation of this.'[22]

The pugnacious general's decision to soften his stance and apologize live on air to television's biggest personality surprised many, but it signaled that the channels were now a force to be reckoned with when it came to public opinion. In the days and weeks that followed, the television channels became even more supportive of the Chief Justice's cause and the Iftikhar Chaudhry was restored to his position a few months later when the remaining judges in the Supreme Court declared his removal by Musharraf illegal. The television news channels beamed live pictures of the Chief Justice being reinstated that summer. At a flag raising ceremony at the Chief Justice's home on July 20, 2007, there was a group of political and civil activists and lawyers who gathered to do the honor of raising the Pakistani flag at his official residence and they were joined by four journalists representing the news media, three of whom were satellite television news anchors. The Chief Justice later specifically and publicly thanked the 'media fraternity', without which he said the rebirth of the judiciary would have been impossible.[23]

In reality, Musharraf had only backed down; he had not given in. This series of events in the spring of 2007 seemed to have only strengthened his resolve to cut down the growing power of the judiciary. A few months later, in November of 2007, as the courts were preparing to rule on Musharraf's eligibility to rule as president while remaining the chief of the army, Musharraf declared a state of emergency in the country. This time he acted more decisively against all of his opposition. Not only did he order the arrests of all major political leaders and many dozens of civil society activists, he also sacked the entire judicial bench of the Supreme Court. Most fatefully, for the first time ever, he also decided to pull all satellite news channels off the air. In one fell swoop he attempted to secure his future as the indefinite ruler of Pakistan.

It was a miscalculation. This time, the lawyers, rights activists, and journalists were joined by political workers who came out under the banners of their respective political parties along with masses of ordinary people to lend muscle to the anti-Musharraf movement. Faced with public outrage Musharraf quickly restored the broadcast of the news channels. Still, Iftikhar Chaudhry remained under house arrest. The judge became the symbol of a truly widespread social movement against the military ruler. In its first phase, the movement to restore the 'Chief' had been a niche movement of lawyers and journalists, which people all over Pakistan had watched with great enthusiasm on live television. But now, for the second phase of the movement, people came out to join in the action. 'Rule of Law' became that slogan of the street movement.

Over the years as the country's top judge, Iftikhar Chaudhry had cultivated a reputation as a fair-minded man who looked out for the needs of the poor, voiceless, and the defenseless. And while he did not always have a political organization behind him, he had found an even more effective partner in his battle with a military ruler: an untamed television news media. In the months that followed, the channels kept up their relentless campaign by providing a platform for all kinds of opposition to voice dissent and organize on the air. Finally, less than a year after Musharraf had sacked the entire Supreme Court, the military ruler was finally forced to hold new elections and allow opposition parties to come into power. Soon after, Musharraf resigned as president and left the country. But overthrowing the dictator was not the end of the movement that had been started by the judiciary and galvanized by the TV channels. It would go on. It might have been the end of military rule, but the Chief Justice remained deposed. And it became clear that elected civilian rulers were equally jittery at the thought of a powerful and activist judiciary and a free media.

The civilian government learns the new rules of the game

In May 2011 Hussain Haqqani, an on-and-off Pakistani politician and professor at Boston University, wrote an op-ed in the *New York Times* on the first anniversary of Osama bin Laden's killing by American special forces inside Pakistan. Haqqani used the occasion to lambast the Pakistani Supreme Court in the pages of America's paper of record. 'Over the last four years, the Court has spent most of its energy trying to dislodge the government by insisting on reopening cases of alleged corruption from the 1990s.' Instead, he argued the courts should be helping the government try terrorists and domestic militant outfits. 'Meanwhile,' Haqqani argued, 'Pakistan's raucous media, whose hard-won freedom is crucial for the success of democracy, has done little to help generate support for eliminating extremism and fighting terrorism. The Supreme Court, conservative opposition parties and the news media insist that confronting alleged incompetence and corruption in the current government is more important than turning Pakistan away from Islamist radicalism.'[24]

Iftikhar Chaudhry had been reinstated to his position in 2009 by the new government and since then the judiciary had become a more established force in the Pakistani state structure. Haqqani's was not exactly a dispassionate view since he had been a recent victim of the more activist and bloated judiciary. Only a few months earlier, in what had become a recognizable partnership, the Pakistani media and Supreme Court had skewered him in a controversy that became known as 'memo-gate'. At the center of the memo-gate scandal was a letter allegedly written by a Pakistani government interlocutor and received by American Admiral Mike Mullen a few weeks after the American military raid in Abbotabad, Pakistan, that killed Osama bin Laden. The letter had asked for America's help in cutting down the power of the Pakistani military and intelligence services. The existence of this secretive memo was revealed in the news media in October 2011, when a Pakistani-American businessman named Mansur Ijaz wrote an op-ed in the British paper *Financial Times* explaining his role in delivering the letter to top American military officials. In his op-ed Ijaz explained he had delivered it on behalf of 'a senior Pakistani diplomat' and the letter included offers by the Pakistani civilian leadership to 'eliminate Section S of the ISI' which was charged with maintaining relations with the Taliban.[25]

This time a foreign newspaper had provided the Pakistani TV news channels with the fodder for a spicy political scandal. Like before, the channels picked up a piece of news from print and made it their own.

The following few weeks became one of the most tense times in Pakistan civil–military relations since Musharraf's departure from the political stage in 2008. In getting transposed from the pages of a foreign newspaper to the Pakistani television screen, the debate changed from one about the role of the ISI in supporting militants into a media-led investigation into the identity of the person responsible for drafting the memo to the Americans. The larger question was whether the writing of the memo constituted 'treason' because it asked Americans to interfere in domestic matters.[26]

The news channels quickly settled on the name of Hussain Haqqani, as the 'diplomat' mentioned in the businessman's op-ed and a discussion his close ties to the President Asif Zardari soon followed. This chatter of 'treason' on Pakistani TV channels was leading right to the top levels of government. As tension mounted in the weeks following, on December 1st, 2011, the Supreme Court heard the first of the petitions about 'memo-gate' and ordered all parties to submit replies explaining their positions, including the President of Pakistan and the military's top brass. The Government tried to resist the court's powers at first, by arguing that the Supreme Court was overstepping its jurisdiction, but eventually went along with it.[27] The episode marked another stage in the rise of the judiciary, thanks, in no small part, to satellite television's relentless focus on the 'memo-gate' issue.

Since the restoration of the Chief Justice in 2009, and since the elected government led by Pakistan People's Party had come to replace Musharraf, this had become a well-established formula: TV channels would report hearsay and thinly sourced reports as news; depending on their severity, scale, and content the Chief Justice of Pakistan would either decide to hear a related petition filed in the court or even take notice of the report and launch an investigation at his own behest. The Chief Justice had followed up in this fashion on media reports that ranged from news of missing babies from hospitals to a mob lynching, financial irregularities in government ministries, and of course wrongdoing by politicians.[28] Anything reported by the TV channels that fit into the larger umbrella of social justice the Chief Justice seemed eager to hear.

But some of the investigations, like the one into Haqqani's role in drafting the infamous memo, also had major implications for Pakistan's external relations, especially with the United States. In a similar case, the Chief Justice had also ordered an investigation into the legality and function of the military supply route for American forces that ran through Pakistan.[29] All this was a way to turn the spotlight on the policies of the new Pakistani government, which in the mind of the Chief Justice and his many supporters on TV channels was still unduly siding with America, and not sufficiently attentive to the desires and betterment of the people of Pakistan.

It was clear that what the Supreme Court had started with Musharraf was continuing with the democratic government. It wasn't completely surprising that the Chief Justice decided to take on Pakistan's entrenched political elites with the same vigor as he had taken on a military ruler. In almost every way, from supporting *jihadis* to cronyism and corruption, Pakistan's civilian political elite are perceived by Pakistanis to be worse than military rulers in the country.[30] Haqqani argued in his *New York Times* op-ed that this insistence by the courts on rooting out corruption was distracting from more important matters. 'The media and judiciary have helped redirect attention away from the threat of jihadist ideology,' he said. In other words, the courts needed to direct less attention to corruption and social justice issues and more to terrorism.

It was a fair view but one that a diminishing number of Pakistanis were supporting. And so the Chief Justice continued his targeting of the sitting government. A few months after memo-gate, the Supreme Court ruled that the Prime Minister was also ineligible to rule after his refusal to open criminal charges against his party boss, President Zardari. He was forced to resign. A slew of other lawmakers from the ruling party also lost their posts after a decision by the Supreme Court that ruled that people holding multiple nationalities are ineligible for holding public office in Pakistan. While many continued to support the Chief Justice, others argued that the judiciary was routinely overstepping its institutional bounds and was now a real hurdle in the way of functioning democracy.[31] One thing that no one could deny though was the fact that the judiciary, which was not too long ago the weakest and least respected institution in Pakistan, had become a major and central power broker and one of the most popular, trusted, and respected institution in the country.

The evolution continues

Has the judiciary, backed by its cheerleaders on private television, become unstoppable? Has the Chief Justice become, over a decade of political tumult, the new and ultimate arbitrator of political power in Pakistan? Recent events suggest that there still might just be a few twists in this tale. Months after memo-gate, a new political scandal broke on to the scene, but this time it involved the judiciary and the Chief himself. Rumors began surfacing on Pakistani news channels and social media in the early summer of 2012 that the Chief Justice's son was involved in some questionable financial transactions. Then a video of a Pakistani journalist based in Washington, DC was posted on YouTube, which elaborated on the rumors explaining that there was evidence that Arsalan Iftikhar, Iftikhar Chaudhry's son, was extorting and accepting bribes from one Malik Riaz, a Pakistani real-estate baron and owner of Bahria Town, Pakistan's largest real-estate developer.[32] The accusations were especially powerful because the Chief Justice had adjudicated several court cases involving this particular real-estate developer. While many journalists quickly stood to the defense of the Chief Justice, for the first time news reports on the channels began casting doubt on the credibility of Iftikhar Chaudhry.

There were only speculative media reports, but in reality, the precedent had been long set. For too long, the judge had followed up on exactly such badly sourced media reports of corruption and exposed wrong doers of people in public office. If the Chief did not act this time, it would reek of double standards. So two days after the YouTube video surfaced, the Chief Justice Iftikhar Chaudhry took official notice of the news reports and ordered a hearing to which he summoned the businessman Malik Riaz and his business associates as well as his own son Arsalan Iftikhar. Initially, he even sat on the bench to hear the case but then recused himself from the case. While it was clear to legal experts that the Chief Justice could not possibly hear a case for reasons of conflict of interest,[33] his decision to sit in the first hearing almost seemed like a calculated statement. It was as if the top judge was proving a point that, unlike the politicians who enjoy amnesty from charges of corruption and appoint their children as top office bearers in their own parties, even the judge's own son was not safe from his sharp eye for justice. Still, for the first time since he became a hero fighting Musharraf, the Chief's name came under a gloomy cloud of suspicion, thanks to the media's unending coverage of the scandal.

It was during these hours of coverage on television that the scandal also quickly engulfed the news channels themselves. Once again, the rumbling of trouble began online when a list of 19 prominent journalists was leaked online in a document that suggested that they had received bribes and kickbacks from the same real-estate developer, Malik Riaz, who was accused of being involved in corrupt exchanges with the Chief Justice's son. Many from the list were journalists from the private TV news channels. The list sent shock waves through Pakistani TV journalism and the named journalists scrambled to clear their names. They began pointing fingers at each other, accusing one another for being unethical. The news media itself had become embroiled in a political scandal and in the process nearly everyone's credibility was damaged.

The authenticity of the list was still in question when another YouTube video emerged online that caste an even graver shadow on the credibility of private TV journalists as upholders of ethical values. The clip showed two popular political talk show hosts speaking candidly with Riaz, the real-estate developer, during a commercial break during a live talk show about the scandal. Though nothing definitively incriminating was said, it suggested an uncomfortably cozy relationship between the anchors and the guest, who was under investigation by the Supreme Court. At one point in the video, one of the journalists even received a call on his personal phone during a commercial break from a person who appeared to be the son of the former Prime Minister, intervening in the interview. It was an ugly revelation for many. The video suggested that the TV journalists, far from being impartial observers on the side of the public, were knee deep in the political scandals they were supposed to be covering impartially and fairly. They were turning into the corrupt power players they had once stood against, on the side of the public.

Conclusion

It is too early to tell how the continuing flurry of political scandals and violent conflict being covered by the private television channels will play out for the democratic institutions and larger issue of social justice in Pakistan. After more than eight years, Iftikhar Chaudhry finally retired as Chief Justice in December 2013. While it is unclear whether the new Chief Justice will continue in his predecessor's confrontational tradition, it is undeniable that the long partnership between the judiciary and the private TV channels has forever changed the dynamics of power in Pakistan. For all the chaos that has engulfed the country since the military ruler Musharraf first attempted to fire a sitting Chief Justice, there are also many lessons to be learned by all the players in the Pakistani state structure.

Firstly, the episode involving the Chief Justice's son and the journalists accused of getting kickbacks will serve as a reminder that the

Pakistani TV news channels, no matter how sympathetic to the judiciary or apparently driven by ideology, are after all businesses chasing the bottom line. In their infancy and without any strong guiding principles the channels have shown a propensity to run with apparently 'juicy' stories based on flimsiest of evidence, and they have learned the hard way that they are not immune from scandal if they fail to define their ethical boundaries clearly. The lack of boundaries has made the channels highly vulnerable to manipulation, equally by the executive and legislature, the judiciary and the military, who can all offer up juicy 'leaks' of their own to meet their own narrowly defined ends.

But this is not all bad news. The episodes also show that the private business of television news in Pakistan still operates as a marketplace of ideas. The severe competition between channels ensures that the free flow of information, however faulty and tainted, will continue. This, in the end analysis, is a better place than facing a closed information environment of the years before the media boom. Eventually, the news channels, and the news media at large, will need to define for themselves a role in democratic society. The TV news media have a long way to go in this regard. Being a tool for one institution of the state or the other to the detriment of the other is not a sustainable plan, and one that Pakistani journalists will likely not settle for. As Pakistan's institutional setup will resettle after tumultuous years that have seen the rise of the judiciary, the TV news channels will need to define for themselves how they will use their newfound power and influence to add to a healthy environment for an open and just society. For this reason they will need to create their own safeguards that ensure that journalists remain shielded from conflict of interest and the lure of political influence. This is especially important because of the high stakes involved in their coverage of political events in Pakistan.

A code of conduct for TV news media remains elusive despite many attempts, but it will be vital for self-regulation. If TV news media continue along their present trajectory without any internal checks, enforced regulation will appear more and more justified, and this would risk a step back toward old times of blatant censorship by the state and the military. In the end, nobody but the journalists themselves should feel the need to define the news medium's power, and ensure its maturity and sustainable growth. As is apparent from the events of the past decade, an undefined, unwieldy, unpredictable, and erratic electronic media is easily manipulated. Clearly, such a news media suits everyone, except perhaps the institution of journalism itself.

Notes

1. The photo can be viewed on the Flickr page of the photographer Sajjad Ali Qureshi at: http://www.flickr.com/photos/pkjournalist/3361088716/
2. For a comprehensive discussion on the history of press censorship and the response by journalist, see Niazi, Zamir (1994). *The Web of Censorship.* Karachi: Oxford University Press.
3. For a detailed discussion of the historical weaknesses of the Pakistani judiciary, see International Crisis Group. *Building Judicial Independence in Pakistan.* Asia Report No. 86. November 10, 2004. It can be accessed at: http://www.crisisgroup.org/en/regions/asia/south-asia/pakistan/086-building-judicial-independence-in-pakistan.aspx
4. For a detailed discussion of the historical weaknesses of the Pakistani judiciary, see International Crisis Group. *Building Judicial Independence in Pakistan.* Asia Report No. 86. November 10, 2004. It can be accessed at: http://www.crisisgroup.org/en/regions/asia/south-asia/pakistan/086-building-judicial-independence-in-pakistan.aspx
5. For statistics on the growth of the Pakistani economy, see World Bank Country Partnership Strategy for the Islamic Republic of Pakistan for the Period FY 2010–2013, July 30, 2010. Available at: http://siteresources.worldbank.org/PAKISTANEXTN/Resources/293051-1264873659180/6750579-127990135 0261/PakistanCPSJuly2010.pdf

   Also, Letter of Intent, Memorandum of Economic and Financial Policies, and Technical Memorandum of Understanding by the International Monetary Fund. Available at: www.imf.org/external/np/loi/2008/pak/112008 .pdf
6. Musharraf, Pervez. 'A Plea for Enlightened Moderation', *The Washington Post,* Tuesday, June 1, 2004, p. A23. Available at: http://www.washingtonpost. com/wp-dyn/articles/A5081-2004May31.html
7. For American response to Musharraf's program, see *The 9/11 Commission Report.* p. 369. Available at: http://www.9-11commission.gov/report/index .htm

   For reaction from the Muslim world, see *Final Communiqué of the Tenth Session of the Islamic Summit Conference.* Available at: http://unispal.un.org/UNISPAL.NSF/0/78F5DF4ED4C1652185256DE800547C44

   For domestic response, see Sethi, Najam. 'Fate of "Enlightened Moderation" ', *The Friday Times.* June 18, 2004. p. 1. Available at: http://www .najamsethi.com/fate-of-%E2%80%98enlightened-moderation/
8. The original court order and case docket can be found online at the Supreme Court of Pakistan website: http://www.supremecourt.gov.pk/web/page.asp ?id=281
9. Gall, Carlotta. 'Picture of Secret Detentions Emerges in Pakistan'. *The New York Times,* December 19, 2007. Available at: http://www.nytimes.com/2007/12/19/world/asia/19disappeared.html?_r=0
10. Gall, Carlotta. 'In Remote Pakistan Province, a Civil War Festers'. *The New York Times,* April 2, 2006. Available at: http://www.nytimes.com/2006/04/02/world/asia/02pakistan.html?pagewanted=all
11. Khan, M. Ilyas. 'Judge Row Prompts Pakistan Democracy Questions', *BBC News.* Available at: http://news.bbc.co.uk/2/hi/south_asia/6442829.stm

12. Iqbal, Nasir. 'CJ Suspended, Escorted Home: Justice Iftikhar Summoned by SJC on 13th for Reference Hearing Ex-judges Call It a Blow to Judiciary's Independence; Minister Defends Decision Whither Judicial Activism?' *DAWN*, March 10, 2007. http://archives.dawn.com/2007/03/10/top1.htm

13. Khan, Kamran. 'Army Seizes Control in Pakistan', *Washington Post*, October 13, 1999 Page A1. Available at: http://www.washingtonpost.com/wp-srv/inatl/longterm/southasia/stories/pakistan101399.htm

14. PTV website: http://www.ptv.com.pk/introduction.asp

15. For a comprehensive explanation of the development of Pakistan Television, see 'Television in Pakistan: An Overview', by Seemi Naghmana Tahir in *Contemporary Television: Eastern Perspectives* ed. David French and Michael Richards. Sage Publications: New Delhi.

16. For a detailed account of American involvement in the Kargil conflict, see Riedel, Bruce. 'American Diplomacy and the 1999 Kargil Summit at Blair House', Center for Advanced Study of India. University of Pennsylvania. Available at: http://media.sas.upenn.edu/casi/docs/research/papers/Riedel _2002.pdf

17. Mufti, Shahan, 2007. 'Musharraf's Monster', *Columbia Journalism Review*, November/December 2007. Available at: http://www.cjr.org/feature/musharrafs_monster.php, p. 48.

18. Ibid., p. 49.

19. McCarthy, Rebecca. 'Atlantans Help Create Pakistani News Network', *The Atlanta Journal-Constitution*, Wednesday May 1, 2002.

20. For a discussion of the social effects of electronic TV media in Pakistan, see Naqvi, Tahir H. (2010). 'Private Satellite Media and the Geo-politics of Moderation in Pakistan', in *South Asian Media Cultures*, ed. Shakuntala Banaji. London: Anthem.

21. 'Media Embroiled in Pakistan's Judicial Crisis', *BBC Monitoring World Media*, March 16, 2007.
    Aziz, Faisal. 'Pakistani Media Finds Anti-government Partner in Judiciary', *Reuters*, October 23, 2010. Available at: http://www.reuters.com/article/2010/10/23/us-pakistan-media-idUSTRE69M11Q20101023

22. Mufti, Shahan, 2007. 'Musharraf's Monster', *Columbia Journalism Review*, November/December 2007. p. 47. Available at: http://www.cjr.org/feature/musharrafs_monster.php

23. Ibid.

24. Haqqani, Hussain. 'How Pakistan Lets Terrorism Fester', *The New York Times*, May 10, 2012. Available at: http://www.nytimes.com/2012/05/11/opinion/how-pakistan-lets-terrorism-fester.html

25. Ijaz, Mansoor. 'Time to Take on Pakistan's Jihadist Spies', *Financial Times*, October 10, 2011.

26. In a typical exchange during that time, Hussain Haqqani responded on a political talk show to questions of treason by saying: 'If anyone claims that a Pakistani citizen has said such things that a foreign country should be involved in the affairs of Pakistan, while this is not treason, it is an objectionable point of view.'
    Video can be seen: http://www.youtube.com/watch?v=Kc7PuvRdFqw

27. Fazl-ur-Rahman. 'Memogate: All Except President Submit Statements COAS, DG ISI Submit Statements Through AG', December 16, 2011 http://www.thefrontierpost.com/article/145459/

28. 'Newborn Baby Recovered After Suo Moto Notice', *GEO News*, October 15, 2011. http://www.geo.tv/10-15-2011/87639.htm

29. 'CJP Takes Suo Motoi Notice of Missing NATO Containers', *Daily Times*, July 1, 2010. Available at: http://www.dailytimes.com.pk/default.asp?page=2010\07\01\story_1-7-2010_pg7_13

30. As one recent illustration of this popular perception, a 2013 Pew Research Center survey found that while 25% of people were satisfied with the direction of the country when the newest democratic government took over power from the military in 2008, this number had dropped to 8% by 2013. The number of people dissatisfied grew from 73% to 91% in that same period. The same poll found that the military was perceived to be the most positive of all institutions and leaders listed in the survey, with 79% saying it was a good influence on Pakistan. The Pakistani president was listed as a good influence by 15%. The full survey can be seen at: http://www.pewglobal.org/files/2013/05/Pew-Global-Attitudes-Pakistan-Report-FINAL-May-7-20131.pdf

31. Declan Walsh. 'Pakistan Court Widens Role, Stirring Fears for Stability', *The New York Times*, January 22, 2012. Available at: http://www.nytimes.com/2012/01/23/world/asia/pakistan-high-court-widens-role-and-stirs-fears.html?pagewanted=all

32. 'Scam to Trap Chief Justice Iftikhar Muhammad Chaudhry?' The full video can be viewed at: http://www.youtube.com/watch?v=v0hNxhiknLc

33. 'Conflict of Interest' Editorial. *Express Tribune*, August 30, 2012. Available at: http://tribune.com.pk/story/428502/conflict-of-interest/

11
The Changing Structure of Media and Ethics in India

Bharat Bhushan

In discussing the changing structure of media and ethics in India, my emphasis in this chapter will be not so much on ownership patterns but on the internal structure of the media and its impact on media practitioners and journalists.

Ownership patterns of media houses in India are changing fairly rapidly of late. Closely held family-owned newspapers have set up new cross-media companies that have gone public. Some privately owned television companies have also listed themselves on the stock exchange (e.g. New Delhi Television and TV Today). The government has allowed 26% foreign direct investment (FDI) in print media in news[1] – although substantial control over the editorial processes, production, and distribution remains in the hands of Indian owners (e.g. *Mail Today* is a joint venture of Associated Newspapers of the UK and the India Today Group and *CNN-IBN* has CNN investment in Network18 which runs the channel). Private corporations have also started to invest in media; for example, the Oswal group has invested in New Delhi Television; Blackstone PE has invested in Jagran Media, which in turn has bought *Mid Day* multimedia; and Malaysia's Astro All Asia Networks has acquired stakes in NDTV Lifestyle, Turmeric Vision, and Sun Direct TV.[2] India's largest private sector company Reliance Industries Limited (RIL) has acquired the country's largest news broadcaster Network18 Group, which through its subsidiary TV18 Broadcast Ltd runs a number of TV channels, including *CNN-IBN*, *IBN7*, *CNBC-TV18*, and *CNBC Awaaz*. The group also runs nearly a dozen regional-language TV channels through another subsidiary ETV News Network.[3]

While media ownership has become more public through stock market listings of their shares and FDI in print media has helped infuse new capital into the media market, a process of consolidation is taking place in the media sector. The foray of newspapers and news magazines into television and radio broadcasting (e.g. the *Times of India* has its own TV channel called Times Now and FM radio channel Radio Mirchi; Living Media India Ltd – the publishers of *India Today* – has acquired interests in television and radio, as well as the newspaper business) and television media entering the newspaper market (Zee TV, e.g., owns the *DNA* newspaper) have led to the emergence of integrated media enterprises. The inflow of corporate investment in the media – along with a vertical integration between television broadcasters and cable distributors – will also contribute to consolidation in the media sector, reducing competition and choices for TV viewers and newspaper readers.

Of these, the Reliance–TV18 deal is the most significant. The TV 18 deal gives preferential content access to RIL from all its platforms – TV channels as well as websites. RIL has followed this with the signing of another deal between Mukesh Ambani's Reliance Infotel, which has an all-India 4G telecom license, and his younger brother Anil Ambani's Reliance Infratel for the use of the latter's 50,000-strong fiber-optic tower network – most other mobile phone companies use microwave towers which are less suited for reliable high-speed data transfer. Once RIL launches its 4G services, bundled with free devices capable of news and entertainment delivery, the media content sourced from TV 18 can be distributed through smart phones and tablets – bundled with free 4G subscription – by Reliance Infotel.

The consequences of the huge inflows of corporate investment in the media are predictable: One, as vertical integration takes place between TV broadcasters and distributors – whether cable distributors or mobile service providers – a consolidation will take place in the media sector, reducing competition and choice for the users of news. Two, pluralism and diversity in the media will suffer as the bigger players will tend to set the news agenda. Three, news will increasingly be seen as one more product to be delivered in easily consumable and palatable forms to consumers. And, four, the already shaky boundary fence between the Church and the state in news organizations is likely to be obliterated as boardroom influence on the newsroom will increase. Corporate business and political interests will increasingly determine the color and flavor of news products.[4]

However, in my mind, the most significant changes that have impacted the media have taken place in the internal structures of the media, that is, the journalistic labor process which governs the production of news and views. It is these changes that have impacted the ethics of media in India, making it almost monochromatic and less irreverent. At a time when media ought to have played the role of a constant critic of Indian democracy, it is in danger of reducing itself to the role of a cheerleader of the series of corrupt governments that have ruled India of late. When the media swings the other way, it can once again end up attempting to sway public opinion in a partisan manner as it did during the 2014 general election in favor of the main challenger, Narendra Modi, and his party – the Bharatiya Janata Party.[5] A TV news head almost rationalized his channel's coverage of Modi by claiming that viewership of the channel shot up whenever it showed Modi; the anchors of another news channel were accused of becoming cheerleaders for Modi by trashing his adversaries during the election, and in yet another TV channel they were apparently advised not to tweet critically about Modi.[6] It is not at all clear whether this was being done for increasing viewership, for ideological reasons, or other considerations; or whether the media had been co-opted by politicians to further their agenda. But the partisanship of the media was noticeable, especially by those adversely affected by it.[7,8] It was not only the private media which came in for criticism for partisanship. The public TV broadcaster *Doordarshan* also came in for criticism for censoring comments made by Modi about the Congress party's lead campaigner Priyanka Gandhi and about her relationship with Congress leader Ahmed Patel.[9] Indeed, the impression one gets is that the media itself seems to have become corrupt – by supporting the dominant elites and as its ranks swell with self-seekers. This is the direct result of changes in the internal structures of the media.

In this chapter, I will discuss the following: (a) the economic factors which drive the media – both print and television – in India; (b) the contradictory tendencies that exist in most newsrooms – of supporting the value structure of the dominant political and business elite and of going against it – and the usefulness of these two tendencies, essentially what one might call the 'internal value structure of the media'; and (c) the restructuring that is taking place in the media to generate new revenue streams and its impact on the practice of ethical journalism.

Factors that drive the media

In the Indian context, three factors have impinged on media content:

1. media expansion which implies a rapidly expanding market for newspaper readership and television viewing;

2. the changing role of the editor; and
3. a growing ideological consensus between the state, the corporate world, and the media.

Market expansion

The deliberate marketing strategy of low pricing by English-language dailies to one Indian rupee (about US 1.8 cents), compared to prices of newspapers in other languages which were more than double in 1992, resulted in a tremendous market expansion. The market for English-language newspapers expanded in two ways – many urban households started buying two newspapers for the price of one, and in addition, a large number of households which had previously only subscribed to regional-language newspapers started buying English newspapers as well for a marginal extra cost.

Since then the 'one-rupee-per-copy' pricing strategy has given way to other innovative pricing strategies – cheaper newspapers on weekdays compared to weekends, paired pricing of English newspapers with pink (business) papers or other regional-language newspapers owned by the same media house, and/or free gifts (sports shoes, branded shirts, linens, blankets, travel bags, watches, cameras, etc.) with annual subscriptions which make the subscriber copy virtually free. In effect, Indian newspapers and magazines 'buy' their large readerships through various incentive schemes associated with long-term subscription. This is how the expanded market is retained or expanded further.

Relatively inexpensive web offset printing presses had started becoming available, and by the early 1990s, India was exporting web offset printing presses rather than importing them. Earlier, these printing presses had to be imported, were custom-made, and took 3–5 years from placing an order to delivery. The Indian presses could be delivered in six months to a year. Market expansion was, therefore, also helped by the availability of new and cost-effective technologies of printing and communication. As the cost of expansion declined, new markets opened up – most provincial capitals and market towns had their own edition of the major newspapers. The *Dainik Bhaskar*, a Hindi daily, for example, had only one edition in 1958, but today along with its flagship Hindi daily, it also has a Gujarati daily *Divya Bhaskar*, a Marathi daily *Divya Marathi*, and stake in an English daily – *DNA*. It covers 14 states with 58 editions. In addition, it also publishes *Business Bhaskar*, *DB Star*, and magazines such as *Aha! Zindagi, Balbhaskar, Young Bhaskar*, and *Lakshay*.[10]

The story of television in India is similar. Cheap television receivers, the availability of transponders for up-linking through international satellites, cheap satellite receivers, and the sudden mushrooming of decentralized cable distribution networks and Direct-to-Home (DTH) telecasts have meant that over 600 TV channels are now available to Indian viewers. There are dozens of 24-hour news channels in some states. The market, through growing advertising revenues, supported this media expansion. The manufacturers of soap, shampoos, fast food, skin lightening creams, and undergarments came out in hordes to advertise their products and, in the process, helped the media expand. The point is that the media expansion in India was not an editorial phenomenon fuelled by armies of investigative reporters or editors with penetrating insight. It was the result of aggressive and innovative marketing as well as the availability of technology.

The market extracted a price – media content went on a discount. It was no longer important to even sell newspapers to people who would read them or to broadcast television programs which would be interesting and informative. In the case of newspapers, what mattered was whether the readers 'recalled' seeing one newspaper more than the others in random readership surveys. This was paralleled by the TRP (Television Rating Point) and TAM (Television Audience Monitor) ratings being developed for television programs. Those who covered hard news got hardly any viewership and those who ran so-called news and entertainment news segments like *Meri Bibi Dayan Hai* (My wife is a witch), *Bhooton ki Shaadi* (The marriage of ghosts), or showing someone eating lizards or snakes during prime-time viewing got high TRP ratings. As a result, the most popular programs on news channels are cheap crime shows like *Sansani* (Sensational), *Wardat* (Crime), *Jurm* (Guilt), and *ACP Arjun*. The afternoon television hours focuses exclusively on entertainment – soap operas, Bollywood gossip, or shows about astrology and religion – catering to the stay-at-home women viewers. The ratings of these shows are then used to impress advertisers and more often than not used as justification for hiking advertising rates or seeking future ads.

This stupendous expansion of the media has also had several positive effects. As dependence on state-controlled TV channels declined, the choice available to the newspaper readers and television viewers increased. The response time to news events was shortened. Newspapers became visually more pleasing as they were forced to redesign themselves and reconfigure their content to remain interesting in the face of competition from television. And the mobility and salaries of journalists saw a quantum jump.

However, the most negative fallout of this market expansion was that the frontier of control between journalists and marketing managers shifted decisively in favor of the managers. It was not the editor who strode through the newsroom directing his colleagues what to do but the marketing directors.

In keeping with international media trends, newspapers and television channels wanted news to focus on readers in the 18–35 age group and among households who had higher disposable incomes. The several facelifts that the newspaper *Hindustan Times* has undergone to look more youthful, the deliberate editorial strategy to make the newspaper *Times of India* a youth brand,[11] and the successful launch of a youthful tabloid *Mail Today* by the India Today Group are evidence of this strategy.[12] Advertisers of consumer goods wanted to target these groups and, therefore, the editorial content also had to be designed to attract them. In turn, the marketing and sales departments sold the lifestyle of their readers, their socio-economic profile, and their purchasing power to the advertisers. In the process, an overall de-skilling of journalists has taken place. Editors either fell in line with the new editorial content requirements or made way for those who fitted the new job requirements better. The new editors were not required to have the ability to direct the paper; such directing now came from the marketing department. The importance of marketing department vis-à-vis the editorial department has been all too visible, for example, in the two largest newspapers in the country – the *Times of India* and the *Hindustan Times* – where advertising sales and marketing personnel have a far greater say in the editorial direction of the newspaper than the editors themselves.

Political and diplomatic correspondents, who were essentially the interpreters of how the state related to its people and to the outside world, lost their importance as political reporting became virtually undesirable. The space for foreign news actually shrank during this period of expansion of the media. Whatever space was given to international news was weighed in favor of Hollywood news, fashion, or health fads. Commentary about domestic as well as international news within newspapers was also in decline. If needed, such comments were outsourced to retired bureaucrats, retired military generals, and policemen, as well as IFS (Indian Foreign Service) officers, all of whom had precious little insight to add as alternative interpretations. The Indian foreign secretaries and several senior diplomats who retired in the last one decade, for example, unless they were re-employed by the government, have all become newspaper columnists and television commentators. It is the same with several retired cabinet secretaries and secretaries to the government, retired Intelligence chiefs, and several senior armed forces personnel. These are the people who write and edit page articles on foreign policy, internal security matters, terrorism, and even politics.

An easier way out of promoting a culture of investigative journalism in media houses has been to simply buy content from the international syndication services. Today, the commentators of the *New York Times* are better known in India than Indians writing on world affairs, because a number of newspapers subscribe to the Times Syndication Service.

Changing role of the editor

What became of the editor in this process? Those so inclined to be editors became brand ambassadors for their newspapers. They were expected to rub shoulders with the powers that be in the world of politics and business and essentially show that they were not at variance with their own worldview to those of the owners and advertisers. From being daily reporters and interpreters of history, the editors became part of the ruling elite and were expected to highlight the elitist value systems.

Those who lacked the social skills to be a part of the cocktail-set ensured their survival by becoming liaison persons. They facilitated mutually beneficial relationships between the media barons and the ruling government. This became even more significant as media houses diversified into cross-media and non-media activities, including real estate, running malls, power generation and education. Every expansion – from publishing a new title to getting a license for a television channel, acquiring government contracts, getting public land allotted for private purposes – requires intensive interaction with the government. And it is in this kind of world that editors came in handy.

Liaison work with the government requires reciprocal responsibilities – a quid pro quo between the media owners and the state. And scores of editors have connived and continue to connive in this process for their own survival. One can understand the impact both these activities – of the editors who became brand ambassadors and those who became facilitators for their newspaper organizations – have had on the value structure of the media.

This process of intimate interaction with the state and corporates became so valued and important that it had three direct implications for newspapers. First, the tendency for media owners to declare themselves as editors increased. This process started first in the Hindi media and later even took place in the English-language media.[13] The owners who become editors probably asked themselves: Why should my employee, a mere journalist, be rubbing shoulders with the prime minister and the cabinet ministers when I can do it myself and more effectively? One only has to see how many such owner-editors queue up to board the prime minister's official aircraft whenever he travels abroad and then seek private meetings with him on the aircraft. Second, editors and journalists saw self-affirmation not in running good newspapers or news channels but in the recognition of their worth by the state. So they lobby for state honors – from seeking national awards such as Padma Shri and Padma Bhushan, being on government-nominated committees and commissions, to dreaming of a nominated seat in the Rajya Sabha, the Upper House of Indian Parliament. Rajya Sabha has five eminent persons nominated by the president on the recommendations of the government of the day, and each time a seat becomes vacant, editors fall over each other lobbying to get nominated as an MP (Member of Parliament). Senior journalists and editors who support certain political parties then either seek or are rewarded by them with state honors and government recognition when these parties come to power. There are a number of such fellow-traveler editors who have not only become nominated MPs, but have accepted state honors without demur. Some have even been appointed ambassadors abroad. There are also instances of senior journalists serving as members of statutory commissions with the rank of ministers and still continuing with their newspaper columns or reportage. There is hardly any notion of conflict of interest either among the journalists seeking such honors or the media owners who themselves crave such recognition.

Third, a journalist–corporate nexus emerged which saw powerful journalists trying to influence the government and their readers in connivance with corporate lobbyists. The revelations of the Nira Radia Tapes in December 2010 underline the nexus between corporate houses, corrupt politicians, and equally corrupt journalists – at least half a dozen top editors were exposed in those surreptitiously recorded audio tapes. The Radia tapes contained conversations of a corporate lobbyist Nira Radia, who was very close to the then telecom minister of India, with senior journalists and corporate honchos, taped by the Indian Income Tax Department in 2008–2009. They were leaked in the press and the conversations revealed that several top Indian journalists were involved in planting stories, trying to influence policymakers by coating purely partisan interests as being of public interest and even trying to influence the appointment of cabinet ministers.[14] More importantly, the Radia tapes also showed how the media initially tried to suppress the publication of the transcripts even though they were widely available. And it is the same media which does not think twice before quoting

Lord Northcliffe grandly that 'News is something which someone wants suppressed. Everything else is just advertising.'

Neo-liberal consensus between the state, corporate sector, and media

The high-income, high-spending group among the media readers and viewers represents a consensus around the neo-liberal ideas of free market, free movement of capital, of state controls being essentially bad as they hinder investment and growth, but also the idea of the state itself as being evil – unless, of course, it can be used to further these very ideas. Since ownership patterns in Indian media are still protected through government legislation – the maximum foreign equity allowed in the news media (print) business is only 26% – the state helps in restricting the market in the interests of the local owners and, thus, it has enormous clout over them.

How much space does all this leave for the practice of fair and just reporting, of raising social issues, or of holding a mirror to the state? Not much. The media has, by and large, adopted the state's agenda which in turn has adopted the agenda of big business unquestioningly. Except in some marginal and non-mainstream publications one would not find this consensus being seriously questioned. Indeed, what one finds is support for violence by the state to implement this agenda.[15] The media has been excessively critical of civil-society-led movements against public corruption[16] and of not-for-profit organizations or non-governmental organizations (NGOs).[17] Sometimes, the media have gone to the extent of criticizing the state for not facilitating big business in the extractive and mining industry, citing environmental reasons, social activists, and the judiciary;[18] and at others, it has criticized attempts at improving laws governing compensation and rehabilitations of those affected by forcible land acquisition for industrialization by the state.[19]

What we are witnessing then is a relentless homogenization of the media. The market helps the media expand but it also ends up shaping it. The media has become part of an intensely market-driven process of prioritizing lifestyles, promoting uniform identities, and market-driven ways of thinking about the world.[20]

Internal value structure of the media

There are two contradictory tendencies within the editorial departments of Indian media. Having been editor-in-chief of a large newspaper,

I can specifically address practices which dominate India's newspaper industry.

There is the tendency to support the dominant consensus – the views shared by the owners, the ruling political and corporate elite, and the marketable readership and viewership. For example, on the issue of economic liberalization which is seen to marginalize those who do not have the purchasing power to actively participate in the market or the construction of big dams, giving mining leases in traditional tribal lands, and the setting up of special economic zones by the government acquiring agricultural land for private industry, the voice of those affected – the poor, tribal groups, and farmers – hardly ever gets heard in normal circumstances. These activities are blindly supported by the media as necessary for development. Only when agitation of the affected population, such as the Maoist insurgency in northeast and south India, takes a violent turn does it get reported, forcing the government to re-examine its policies.

Similarly, the dominant internal security paradigm of the state is reflected in reporting on Jammu and Kashmir or the dozens of sub-nationalist insurgencies which thrive in India's northeastern states. There is no attempt to see why the Kashmiris seem dissatisfied with the Indian government or why people in India's northeast feel alienated or demand greater autonomy to manage their affairs. For editors in the mainstream media, the openness in addressing these subjects seems to be limited by the perspective of the ministry of home affairs or the foreign office, particularly when it involves understanding or addressing Pakistan's position on the Kashmir issue.[21]

The second tendency, within the editorial departments of newspapers, is toward integrity and honesty, of trying to report facts and trying to practice journalism as politics by other means. A number of young journalists still come to journalism out of a sense of idealism. However, this tendency is more likely to be found at the lower rungs of the editorial and reporting hierarchy. There is, therefore, a sizeable number of journalists in India who have been reporting boldly on civil rights violations in conflict situations, about caste and inter-community violence; about famines; about farmers' suicides; about conflicts over land and big industrial projects, forest, and water; and about other environmental conflicts – in short, holding a mirror to the society and the state. This second tendency within newsrooms serves two functions. One, it provides legitimacy to newspapers in terms of good and accurate reporting. Two, it also provides an alternative channel of information to those in power so that they can take appropriate corrective action to protect their interests. Both these functions serve what one might call the democratic role of the press.

However, the impact and presence of the adversarial reporting can be very easily undermined through actions such as punitive comments at editorial and news meetings as well as through consciously directed actions in terms of not assigning certain kinds of stories, assigning them but not using them properly, using them but not displaying them properly, or even holding them back till they are overtaken by parallel developments. Thus, for example, the Indian media have not followed up with any seriousness the land deals of Congress party president Sonia Gandhi's son-in-law Robert Vadra which prima facie seem questionable, and nor has the media investigated the allegation that some of the top Indian corporate houses were involved in money laundering by main- taining illegal accounts in Swiss banks – both charges were made by social activists agitating against corruption in public life. Some pro- Congress newspapers have also tended to play down the allegations of corruption against the government or have reproduced the govern- ment's version without raising serious questions about the truthfulness of such accounts.

However, even the most junior reporters quickly realize that unless they are reporting on issues on which the nation's attention is focused – that is, the agreed agenda of the opinion-making elites – their chances of moving up the editorial hierarchy are limited. So every couple of years you get a new crop of youngsters doing radical, adversarial, and investigative reporting while others get busy climbing the greasy pole to the top. Both sets of journalists have their uses for the editors and the newspapers.

Restructuring to generate new revenue streams and its impact on media ethics

Advertising continues to be the principal source of revenue for media houses. Subscription or news-stand sale or circulation-based sale pro- vides a significant chunk of revenue only in the magazine business and not for newspapers. For newspapers and television, the main source of revenue is advertising. What happens with advertising is that the dom- inant player (largest newspapers and biggest television houses) takes most of the advertising in a particular market and the rest is divided among smaller media players. The market is so competitive that the media houses have to do a lot of running to even attract advertisers to stay soluble.[22]

Media companies, therefore, have been trying to build revenue streams from different sources with varying degrees of success. To give an idea of what these revenue streams can be, I briefly list some of the innovative revenue streams being pursued:

1. Content re-selling: The main customers are dotcoms. The content is usually not exclusively generated for the customer, but it is shared. Portals like MSN.com, Yahoo.com, and others have tie-ups with newspapers for carrying their exclusive content on their portals.
2. Customized content generation: Here, exclusive content is generated for customers who could either be other media houses, principally print and online, or non-media customers like banks, insurance firms, and investment firms.
3. Custom publishing: Here the entire job of content creation, production, and marketing is outsourced to a media house. These could be airlines' on-board travel magazines, magazines for specific car manufacturers, and so on.
4. Paid news: Here content is simply carried against payment. The *Times of India* has set up a separate company Medianet which sells editorial space in supplements like *Mumbai Times* and *Delhi Times* for cash. This is a paid public relations exercise and contributes about 4% of the total revenue of the company and is apparently expected to double within a few years.[23] The selling of news 'packages' to political parties during polls by prominent newspapers is another example of paid news.
5. Private treaties: This is another innovation of the *Times of India*, where the newspaper accepts ads from small companies in exchange for equity.
6. Conferences, awards, and seminars: This is a rapidly growing area, where media houses use their ability to pull in participants and provide editorial expertise to run both their own and franchised conferences, seminars, and awards of interest to sponsors.
7. Books and collector's issues: This is a relatively small revenue source for media houses. This is not to be confused with publishing houses which also happen to be owned by media houses (Penguin, HarperCollins) which are really stand-alone businesses.
8. Archives: This monetizes old content.
9. New media: Customized content delivered to mobiles, iPads, and iPhones. Small earner so far, but holds maximum potential, as the market grows in size and content.

10. Brand extensions: This can range from publications (food, entertainment, or travel guides) to watches, CDs, and other gift items.

The important point to note, however, is that the focus on some of these so-called alternative revenue streams has had a negative impact on content and the practice of journalism. In their search for new revenue streams, newspapers often enter into deals with advertisers and corporate houses in return for assured coverage. Sadly, the reader is unaware if the news report in such newspapers is genuine or not, especially if it appears in a credible newspaper with a long and illustrious history such as the *Times of India*. Unfortunately, in India it is the hitherto credible and immensely profitable newspapers which have been at the forefront of erasing the thick black line that is used to separate news from advertising. This line disappears when newspapers sell news space to advertisers and keep their readers in the dark about where news columns end and advertisements begin.

When media houses erase the distinction between advertising and news, they cheat their consumers who can no longer distinguish between the two. The practice of 'paid news' has largely come into focus during elections where political parties and their candidates pay newspapers and news channels to project them in a favorable light to the voters. The candidates are assured coverage in terms of column centimeters every day during their campaign for a pre-negotiated rate. The readers are the losers because while they expect that objective reporting will help them make up their mind, what they are served is public relations material masquerading as news. The Election Commission of India and the Press Council of India are trying to fight this menace, but the battle is still on. Only recently has a Member of the Legislative Assembly, Ms. Umlesh Yadav, been disqualified for using paid news in two Hindi newspapers – *Amar Ujala* and *Dainik Jagaran* – during her election campaign.[24] The unethical practice of paid news not only undermines democracy by distorting the electoral process but shows how unethical newspapers and television media conspire with political actors to breach the rules that govern elections in this country (see Vipul Mudgal's chapter in this book for a greater discussion on paid news).

However, 'paid news' is not limited to times of elections alone. We have seen the pernicious practice of newspapers getting equity in corporate entities in return for advertisements – the 'private treaties' I mentioned above. The question then is whether this also goes with unspoken guarantees of publishing only favorable information about the corporate entities and censoring anything unfavorable? One can well imagine what this can potentially do to the role of the editor and what one understands of the journalistic goal of providing objective, fair, and neutral reportage. As the line between advertising and news gets blurred, so does the distinction between editors and advertising sales managers. What used to be shifting frontier of control between editors and marketing and sales department has become an open and porous border.

Conclusion

I have tried to draw linkages between these changes that are taking place within the media to show how difficult the practice of journalism has become in India. I would, however, like to end this chapter by pointing to a specificity of Indian politics and how the lack of journalistic ethics and morality can be disastrous for Indian democracy. Over the years in India, as the dominance of a single party – the Congress party – declined and the polity got fractured, the role of providing the alternative voice in our democracy was thrust upon the non-government or independent media. Earlier, the vibrant alternative voice of the press – such as the glorious role played by newspapers like *Indian Express* and magazines like *Seminar* during the 19-month state of emergency declared by the then Prime Minister Indira Gandhi in 1975 – used to keep the government on its toes. In the era of coalition politics where parties often change sides, and in completely unpredictable ways, that role has become diffused. The irreverent, if not oppositional, role – the role of whistle-blowers and those who hold a mirror to the government of the day – was thrust upon the news media. The entire media was never irreverent in its approach in India. However, if a large section of the media is compromised as it is today, its ability to be irreverent is to that extent subdued and attenuated. If everyone supports the dominant consensus, the space for independent journalism shrinks and that cannot be good for any democracy.

Notes

1. 'Government Allows 26% FDI in Print', *The Times of India*, June 25, 2002.
2. Guha Thakurta, Paranjoy and Subi Chaurvedi, 'Corporatisation of the Media Implications of the RIL-Network18-Eenadu Deal', *Economic and Political Weekly*, February 18, 2012, Volume XLVII, Number 7.
3. Shukla, Archana, 'It's Official: Reliance Now Controls News Broadcaster TV18', *The Indian Express*, May 30, 2014, http://indianexpress.com/article/business/companies/ril-to-acquire-control-of-network-18-to-spend-rs-4000-crore/

4. Guha Thakurta, Paranjoy, 'Media Ownership Trends in India', *The Hoot*, July 3, 2012, http://thehoot.org/web/MediaownershiptrendsinIndia/6053-1 -1-16-true.html

5. Rukmini, S., 'Modi Got Most Prime Time Coverage: Study', *The Hindu*, May 8, 2014, http://www.thehindu.com/elections/loksabha2014/modi-got -most-primetime-coverage-study/article5986740.ece

6. Bhushan, Sandeep, 'How the Television News Industry Scripted the Indian Elections', *Caravan*, May 5, 2014, http://caravanmagazine.in/vantage/ television-scripted

7. Sood, Pramod, 'Media Favouring Narendra Modi', Sibal, MSN Election 2014, http://news.in.msn.com/elections-2014/media-favouring-narendra-modi -sibal

8. 'Media Working in Favour of Modi, Accuses Maya', *The Asian Age*, April 26, 2014, http://www.asianage.com/india/media-working-modi-favour-accuses -maya-792

9. Ramachandran, Smriti Kak, and Joshua, Anita, 'Doordarshan Denies Editing Modi Interview', *The Hindu*, May 1, 2014, http://www.thehindu.com/news/ national/doordarshan-denies-editing-modi-interview/article5966627.ece

10. Dainik Bhaskar Group. http://www.dainikbhaskargroup.com/dainik-bhaskar .php

11. Auletta, Ken, 'Annals of Communication – Citizens Jain. Why India's Newspaper Industry Is Thriving', *The New Yorker*, October 8, 2012.

12. Bhushan, Bharat, 'A Tabloid for "Middle India"', *The Hoot*, May 26, 2012. http://thehoot.org/web/A-tabloid-for-Middle-India/5978-1-1-4-true.html

13. Pande, Mrinal, 'Hindi Media and the Unreal Discourse', *The Hindu*, November 19, 2009, http://www.thehindu.com/opinion/lead/hindi-media-and-an -unreal-discourse/article50449.ece

14. 'The Raja-Radia Tapes', *Outlook*, November 18, 2010, http://www. outlookindia .com/article.aspx?268064. See also among others, Some telephone conversations – Inside the networks of lobbyists and power brokers that dictate how this country is run, Open, November 20, 2010, http://www .openthemagazine.com/article/nation/some-telephone-conversations, and 2G SCAM: Hot Tapes Expose Mediamen as Power Players, *Mail Today*, November 19, 2010, http://indiatoday.intoday.in/story/2g-scam-hot-tapes -expose-mediamen-as-power-players-/1/120436.html

15. No velvet glove, editorial recommending use of state violence against Singur land acquisition agitation in *The Telegraph*, Calcutta, http:// www.telegraphindia.com/1061205/asp/opinion/story_7092106.asp. See also another editorial in the same newspaper, Disturbed Area, *The Telegraph*, Calcutta, http://www.telegraphindia.com/1070504/asp/opinion/story_7730 081.asp

16. 'They, the People', *Indian Express*, April 7, 2011, http://indianexpress.com/ article/news-archive/web/they-the-people/; Mihir S. Sharma, 'Not a very Civil Coup', *The Indian Express*, April 11, 2011, http://indianexpress.com/ tag/not-a-very-civil-coup/

17. Tavleen Singh, Our Sainted NGOs, *The Indian Express*, April 17, 2011, http:// indianexpress.com/article/opinion/columns/our-sainted-ngos/99/.

18. Gupta, Shekhar, National Interest: Current Accountability Deficit, *The Indian Express*, October 30, 2013, http://archive.indianexpress.com/news/national -interest-current-accountability-deficit/1159250/0

19. Aiyer, Swaminathan A., 'Land Acquisition Bill Is a Luddite Throwback to 19th Century', *The Times of India*, August 25, 2013, http://blogs.timesofindia .indiatimes.com/Swaminomics/land-acquisition-bill-is-a-luddite-throwback -to-19th-century/

20. Bhushan, Bharat, 'News in Monochrome: Journalism in India', Index on Censorship, July 25, 2013, http://www.indexoncensorship.org/2013/07/ news-in-monochrome-journalism-in-india/

21. Donthi, Praveen, 'The Known Unknowns – India's Compromised National Security Beat', *Caravan*, December 1, 2013, http://caravanmagazine.in/ reportage/known-unknowns

22. Bhushan, Bharat, 'Money Matters', *The Hoot*, March 18, 2012, http://thehoot .org/web/Money-matters/5808-1-1-4-true.html

23. Auletta, Ken, Op.cit.

24. Balaji, J., ' "Paid News" Claims First Political Scalp as EC Disqualifies MLA', *The Hindu*, October 21, 2011, http://www.thehindu.com/news/national/ article2556366.ece

Index

Note: The letter 'n' following locators refers to notes.

Qur'anic standards, 143–6
social and religious meanings, 145
textual sources, human reasoning,
146
value of *adl*, 145
Jyllands Posten (Danish newspaper), 1

Karan, K., 103
Kaviraj, Sudipta, 52
Kellner, D., 118n.20
Kelly, Erin, 141
Khadduri, Majid, 144, 145
Khan, General Ayub, 179
Khan, Kamran, 192n.13
Khan, M. Ilyas, 191n.11
Khilnani, Sunil, 52
Kiss, Elizabeth, 56n.4
Knaus, Gerald, 41n.4
Koda, Madhu (Chief Minister of
Jharkhand), 112
Kony 2012' campaign, 1
Kotb, Sayed, 143, 144
Krishnan, S., 100
Kumwenda, O., 65
Kunelius, Risto, 47
Kuper, A., 63, 65, 68
Kuper, J., 63, 65, 68

Law of Peoples The (Rawl's essay), 46
Laxman, Bangaru, 110
Lebacqz, Karen, 45
Life and letters of Raja Rammohun Roy,
The (Collett), 169
Livingstone, Sonia, 47
localism
ethical system *vs.*, 29–30, 33, 37–8
globalism *vs.*, 24, 35, 41
news media, 38
universalism *vs.*, 18, 31
Locke, John, 44
Louw, E., 103, 117n.5
Love and Saint Augustine (Jasper), 50
Lunga, C., 67, 68, 74

Maclean, Charles, 161
Mail Today, 194, 199
Majumdar, R. C., 169, 171
Malema, Julius, 63, 71
Malloch-Brown, Mark, 35

Mangcu, Xolela, 64
Manoff, R. K., 104
Marquess of Hastings, *see* Hastings,
Warren (Governor General)
Marshall, P. J., 159, 160
Martin, R. M., 170
Mason, Andrew, 36
Mattelart, Armand, 121
Matthew, Samuel, 110
Mazdoor Kishan Shakti Sangathan
(MKSS), 113
McCarthy, Rebecca, 192n.19
McChesney, Robert W., 3, 98
McQuail, Denis, 65
'Media Appeals Tribunal' (South
Africa), 62
Media Certification and Monitoring
Committees, 112
media diversity, 60, 109, 111, 114
Media Diversity and Development
Agency, 60
media globalization, 1–4, 15, 121
media institutions, 9, 55, 142, 146,
148–51
media organizations, 1, 5, 18, 81, 104,
109, 116–17, 149
media outlets, 4, 65, 104, 114,
149–50
media-tization, 105–6, 109
Mehta, Vinod, 107, 108, 117n.8
Mgibisa, M., 63
Mill, John Stuart, 141
Miller, David, 28, 31, 32, 36
Mills, J. S., 159
minority rights, 130–1, 133
Mirat-ul-Akhbar, 164–5, 168, 170
Modi, Narendra, 103, 196
Moeller, S. D., 74
Moorthy, S., 59
Moralbewusstsein und Kommunikatives
Handeln (Habermas), 45
Mowlana, Hamid, 147
MSNBC (TV channel), 127
Mudgal, V., 19, 100
Mufti, Shahan, 19, 173, 192n.17,
192n.22–3
'Muhammad Cartoons', 1
Muhlmann, Geraldine, 121
Mukherjee, Asha, 53

Printed and bound by CPI Group (UK) Ltd, Croydon, CR0 4YY